Six Masters of the Spanish Sonnet

FRANCISCO DE QUEVEDO

SOR JUANA INÉS DE LA CRUZ

ANTONIO MACHADO

FEDERICO GARCÍA LORCA

JORGE LUIS BORGES

MIGUEL HERNÁNDEZ

Essays and Translations
Willis Barnstone

SOUTHERN ILLINOIS UNIVERSITY PRESS
CARBONDALE AND EDWARDSVILLE

Publication of this work was made possible in part through a grant from The Program for Cultural Cooperation Between Spain's Ministry of Culture and United States Universities.

Ink portraits of the poets by Willis Barnstone

Library of Congress Cataloging-in-Publication Data

Barnstone, Willis, 1927–
    Six masters of the Spanish sonnet : Francisco de Quevedo, Sor
Juana Inés de la Cruz, Antonio Machado, Federico García Lorca, Jorge
Luis Borges, Miguel Hernández : essays and translations / Willis
Barnstone.
        p.   cm.
    Includes bibliographical references.
    1. Sonnets, Spanish. 2. Sonnets, Spanish—Translations into
English. I. Title. II. Title: 6 masters of the Spanish sonnet.
PQ6176.B338   1993
861'.04208—dc20   92-12099
ISBN 0-8093-1772-9   CIP

For Edwin Honig and Alan Trueblood,
friends of a lifetime,
of the poem in Spanish and its English version

and Luis Beltrán, seventh master
of the Spanish sonnet

Contents

Contents

Contents

Contents

Contents

Contents

Contents

xiii

Preface

Time plays tricks on each book one writes. There is increasingly a sense that, however slowly or quickly the book seems to have been written, it has been dependent on every earlier attempt to put pages together. Everything was a preparation. In this instance there were specific events that led me to an obsession with a persistent anachronism, the sonnet, that like democracy, Walt Whitman, surrealism, and spring doesn't know it is dead and keeps resurrecting in our century among experimental modernists and later figures—in César Vallejo, Rafael Alberti, Paul Celan, Rainer Maria Rilke, Anna Akhmatova, W. H. Auden, Dylan Thomas, Robert Lowell, and Marilyn Hacker.

My lucky events were that my daughter Aliki and I, working on a book together, had to translate the complete sonnets of the sixteenth-century French poet Louise Labé; that while I was in Buenos Aires in 1975 and 1976, I collaborated with Jorge Luis Borges on rewording his sonnets into English; that fifteen years earlier I finished a dissertation on the poetry of Antonio Machado, whose last powerful, moving poems during the Spanish Civil War were in a form he had written against with disdaining humor—the sonnet. Finally, instructed by the experience of translation, one night in November 1977, the sonnet bullied its way preponderantly into my own work. After so much surrender to its tyrannical form, in this book I have turned my experience with the sonnet back to the Spanish masters—used what I have learned to translate them. As a final twist I remember an incident at Columbia University in the one course I took in creative writing with Louise Bogan. One day Ms. Bogan commanded us to write a sonnet. I did so, the first, clearly imitating a sonnet by Miguel Hernández, beginning "No, I will not conform" (No me conformo).

The other events that were preparation for this book are personal and relate to the four poets who have written in our century: Machado, Lorca, Borges, and Hernández. I am lucky to be old enough (a fearful paradox) to have known close friends and relatives of the poets and in the case of Borges, to have a shared a friendship with him for nearly two decades. In the biographical segments, I include documented information in conventional format, yet there is some information which is personal memoir and I am obliged to state or imply it as such. For example, there were long conversations with the Spanish linguist Tomás Navarro Tomás in New York and the philosopher Juan Roura-Parella in Middletown, Connecticut, both companions of Antonio Machado in the military ambulance that took them out of Spain in January 1939 and across the Spanish border to safety in France; and talks with Louis MacNeice about the days he knew Antonio Machado in Barcelona, just before the flight to France.

My first acquaintance with Antonio Machado was through Middlebury College's summer language and literature program. In 1947 I had just come from Mexico (my Mexican stepmother Matilde Franco lives there still) where I had spent a year working with the American Friends Service Committee in a small Indian village and later studying at the University of Mexico. Even in Mexico I had become close to the aftermath of the Spanish Civil War: while in the capital I lived in an orphanage (run by the Spanish Republican government in exile) for Spanish orphans of the war who were then enrolled in Mexican universities. From Mexico then, and the bean-and-potato tortilla meals of our Spanish orphanage, I went to the pastoral hills and lawns of Middlebury and the eloquent, expansive princes of contemporary Spanish poetry. That summer in Vermont the American diaspora of Spanish literature had congregated. Pedro Salinas and Navarro Tomás were on the faculty. One evening after a poetry reading there was a small gathering at which Luis Cernuda and Jorge Guillén showed up. Francisco García Lorca was the summer school director for many years. These were my years of first acquaintance and immersion in that extraordinary rebirth of poetry in Spain in our century—and in its oral history by the Spanish poets of exile.

As a result of Middlebury, I spent a week that autumn visiting Jaime Salinas in Baltimore. Each evening Jaime's father, Pedro Salinas, remembered, as he did in his books, the poets of his generation. At Columbia, Navarro Tomás spoke to me in great detail about his last days with Machado in Spain, at the border, and in France. I recorded his memories in a notebook. In Greece in 1951, where I was then teaching, Louis MacNeice talked about Machado in Barcelona—a tired, disheartened, glorious man chain-smoking, the ashes falling much of the time on his black suit. In 1952 in Madrid I had the first of many conversations that would take place over the next three decades with Vicente Aleixandre about Federico and Miguel—Lorca and Hernández—his two closest friends who had died directly as a result of the war. I went to Soria in 1962 and was still able to speak to a gentleman who had attended Machado's wedding there in 1911; and in Baeza I was given a now often-reproduced picture of Antonio Machado sitting with his fellow teachers at the *instituto*, where he is grave and distinguished in part by the dust, rather than shine, on his shoes. In 1961 I drove from Madrid to Segovia with the poet Francisco Brines, and we spent a fine morning and afternoon with Machado's former landlady at the house where he had lived from 1919 to 1931. Machado's rooming house, on the Street of Abandoned Children, overlooks a little church where much of the dismembered body of Saint John of the Cross lies buried. The landlady told us of Machado's habit of writing through the night, sitting at a small table with a charcoal brazier under it, the warmth held in by a blanket drooping down from the table over his knees and down to the floor. There he would sit, writing draft after draft of new poems, filling the wastepaper basket, and blackening the wood floor with his cigarette ashes. Later in the morning after he was up or gone to school, his housekeeper, cook, and landlady would dutifully empty the basket and throw out all the tossed-away poems. Although his protector could not read or write, she spoke Spanish, as Brines remarked, with the dignity of an empress. She regretted not only throwing out the poems but even rubbing the burn marks off the floor, which she said she did for years and would not have done had she known that her house was to become a national museum. Machado's handsome, hump-backed landlady had her own wit and profundity that came out in a torrent of anecdotes.

The following year, 1962, I spent many hours in Madrid with Luis Rosales in whose house Lorca was hiding when the paramilitary thugs came in and took him away. His recollections have been essential in piecing together those last awful days in Granada. In the part on Lorca, I note the few differences of memory that distinguish what I then recorded and what Ian Gibson did some years later. In Orihuela I went to find Miguel Hernández's widow, Josefina. She was in another town that Sunday, but I did spend some hours with Miguel's brother-in-law. He had been imprisoned with Miguel in Alicante, smuggled his last writings (recorded on toilet paper) out of the prison, and carried the poet's tubercular corpse out of the hospital section to its burial.

As for Jorge Luis Borges, the friendship was long and at least for me, crucial in my life. We met in New York in 1967 where I had been asked by Juan Marichal to arrange a bilingual poetry reading at the Kaufman Auditorium of the Poetry Center. Then it was on other continents. I was in Argentina between 1975 and 1976, lived a few blocks away from Borges, and saw the poet two or three times

Preface

a week. He came to Indiana University in 1976 and in 1980 spent a month in Bloomington. We traveled together in Argentina and America. My last conversation with Borges, the year before he died, was in Beijing. I had arranged for him to visit China (I was there for a year teaching), but at the last moment his doctor would not let him make the trip. Our telephone words between Beijing and Buenos Aires were like any other wonderful conversation with Borges, except that in this last one, he talked about Lao-tzu, the Tao, and *The Dream of the Red Chamber.* Of course he knew the Chinese classics and wanted to come to China. How could he not want to come to China? he asked. Did I think he was mad?

I was a lucky person to have known Borges. He often talked about his *habit,* by which he meant his persistence in living his literary habits, and his *destiny,* which was to follow his obsession with the word. He granted me both.

Almost half the poems in the last two decades of Borges's life were sonnets, in part because once blindness took over, he could compose and keep them in his head until he found a scribe to dictate them to. Returning now from the poets to their work, I wish to say a few words more on the sonnet form.

Not only people, events, and the reading and study of Spanish poetry have been the preparation for this book, but the sonnet itself has been preparing its own way. It keeps waking up in the work of Borges and Dylan Thomas, in Lorca and Richard Wilbur, in Neruda and David Wojohn, when many might have thought that Baudelaire and Wordsworth, or possibly Yeats, had written the last ones we would read as vibrant, original poetry.

The older sonnets, lost or neglected, also have a way—like dead writers—of resurfacing. So we have John Donne's seventeenth-century "Holy Sonnets" coming up to help form what Sonia Raiziss has called "the metaphysical passion" in contemporary American poetry; there are Gerard Manley Hopkins's unpublished nineteenth-century "Terrible Sonnets," which (like Melville's forgotten *Billy Budd* manuscript) entered the canon in our time.

This collection of sonnets, with its informational remarks and meditations on the poets and their poetry, is offered with the hope of making six poets who wrote in Spanish over the past four centuries a part of our reading experience in English today.

Willis Barnstone
Bloomington, 1992

Acknowledgments

I wish to thank Sharon Sieber, who helped me creatively and meticulously in the preparation of the book manuscript. I also wish to thank Luis Beltrán, who helped me decipher many difficult lines, especially in Quevedo's and Lorca's poetry.

The persons and institutions listed below kindly granted permission to reprint the following:

The poems of Jorge Luis Borges, by permission of Smith/Skolnik: JLB. Copyright 1993 by María Kodama.

The poems of Federico García Lorca, by permission of Mercedes Casanovas. Copyright 1993 by the heirs of Federico García Lorca.

The poems of Miguel Hernández, by permission of Lucía Izquierdo. Copyright 1993 by the heirs of Miguel Hernández.

Portions of the essay on Jorge Luis Borges were adapted from my forthcoming *With Borges on An Ordinary Evening in Buenos Aires*, University of Illinois Press.

Six Masters of the

Spanish Sonnet

Introduction

SPANISH POETRY TO QUEVEDO

The sonnet vagabonding into Spain

The sonnet began in Sicily with Giacomo da Lentino (fl. 1215–33), although it is not unlikely that some earlier Provençal poet put together an octave and a sestet in a manner which later was to be called the Italian or Petrarchan sonnet. After working its way through the Sicilian court, the sonnet became a favored form of Dante and Petrarch. It entered Spain almost secretly through the work of El Marqués de Santillana (1398–1458), who wrote the first sonnets in the Spanish language. But his forty-two invisible sonnets *fechos al itálico modo*, modeled after Petrarch, were unpublished and unknown in the early Spanish Renaissance when, quite separately, two Spanish gentleman writers, Juan Boscán and Garcilaso de la Vega, discovered the poetry and prosody of Italy.

The popular advent of the sonnet in Spain coincided with a revolution in Spanish poetry in the early sixteenth century. In the ferment of traditions, poetry in Spain changed from its medieval cast of Castilian *romances* (ballads) and lyrics, its sometime imitation of French or Provençal verse forms (Catalan poetry was often inseparable in mode and tongue from Provençal) to an acceptance of Italian models as the foundation of Renaissance poetry in Spain. Thereafter, the Renaissance in Western Europe was coincidental with the flourishing sonnet. Spain, like France, Portugal, and later Germany, the Netherlands, and England, became sonnetized.

In England the sonnet was transformed. Introduced in its Italian form, Edmund Spenser—who thought himself of an earlier century—altered the Petrarchan rhyme pattern of *abba abba cdecde* to *abab bcbc cdcd ee*, and William Shakespeare—who *was* the age—wrote 154 sonnets in *abab cdcd efef gg*. These changes in the rhyme pattern were not imitated outside of English until Jorge Luis Borges, one-quarter English through his maternal grandmother from Northumberland, wrote at least a quarter of all his poems as Shake-

1

spearean sonnets. So the Spanish sonnet, a literary vagabond in courtly dress, began in the court of the Sicilian Frederic II, went up to Rome and Florence, wandered west to Spain, north again to England, and finally, seven centuries after its Italian birth, with its picaresque wits and form intact, dropped down just above the Antarctic Circle to appear in the poems of the Argentine Anglophile, Borges.

Spanish poetry of the Renaissance and baroque age

The Renaissance began in Spain during the period of the Catholic Kings. In 1474, Isabela I ascended the throne of Castile. Five years later her husband Fernando inherited the crown of Aragón, and thus for the first time in eight centuries, Spain was united politically, religiously, and linguistically. Castilian became the national language. Poetry in Galician-Portuguese and Catalan disappeared and was not heard again until the nineteenth century when it emerged as the reborn voice of regional nationalism. Castilian became, moreover, a relatively standardized literary vehicle during this period as a result of two important events: the introduction of printing in Spain in 1473 and the publication in 1492, by humanist Antonio de Nebrija, of the *Arte de la lengua castellana*, the first Spanish grammar and the first systematic grammar of any modern European language. In the same year, 1492, the Spanish Jews who had not converted to Christianity (those Jews who had converted were called *conversos*) were driven from their ancient homes into exile, the last Islamic kingdom of Granada fell before the armies of the Catholic Kings, and Columbus set sail for a new empire. (The Spanish Inquisition and its flames had been established in 1478 to check on the sincerity of the *conversos*.)

While through conquest and national and cultural unification Spain was increasing hegemony and wealth, its very "purification" of religion and people within the country led to an ultimate poverty of cultural isolation and economic backwardness. The expulsion in 1492 of those Jews from Granada who did not immediately become New Christians and in 1610 of the large Moorish population (the *moriscos* or forced Islamic converts to Christianity, whose last rebellion took place in the Alpujarras mountains south of Granada) turned the large, cosmopolitan city of Granada for the next four hundred years into a small, provincial city, a shabby relic of itself. Federico García Lorca, whose last book of poems, *Diván del Tamarit*, was about Granada and modeled after the Arabic verse forms of the *casida* and *gacela*, knew what the conquest meant: "It was a disastrous event, even though they may say the opposite in the schools. An admirable civilization, and a poetry, astronomy, archi-

2

tecture and sensitivity unique in the world—all were lost, to give way to an impoverished, cowed city, a 'misers' paradise' " (1085).

Yet in the dynamics of history the currents never all flow one way and by the time of Carlos V, Holy Roman Emperor (1516–56), Spain had become the dominant power in the world and was at the height of its own political and cultural renaissance. It was the age of El Greco, Velázquez, San Juan de la Cruz (Saint John of the Cross), Santa Teresa (Saint Teresa), Lope, Cervantes. In the arts it had entered the *Siglo de oro*, which means "golden age" or, literally and symptomatically, the "century of gold."

The major influences on Spanish intellectual life came from Italy and Flanders: the new poetics and classical orientation of the Italians; the humanism of Erasmus and other German and Flemish thinkers. In very general terms we may associate the poetry of Garcilaso de la Vega with the Italians and that of the Spanish mystics with the philosophical seriousness of the north. But this is at best a simplification, for certain philosophical tendencies, such as Neoplatonism, were rooted in both Italy and Flanders and affected Garcilaso as well as Juan de la Cruz. While San Juan and his teacher and fellow mystical poet Fray Luis de León were both imbued with biblical and kabbalistic literature (surely reflecting their common *converso* background), they had little interest in the courtly manners and concerns of Castiglione's *Cortegiano*. Nevertheless, they turned to Italy for their prosody and wrote their major poems in the *lira*, an Italian poetic form borrowed from Bernardo Tasso.

The revolution in Spanish poetry that gave Spain the sonnet can be traced to a particular event in 1526, which has the quality of a fairy tale. Unquestionably a comparable change would have taken place without this stimulus, but the incident did occur, is documented, and deserves special attention. It begins with a conversation between Juan Boscán (1493–1542), a young aristocratic Catalonian poet, and the Venetian ambassador to Spain, Andrea Navagero. Boscán had translated Castiglione's *Cortegiano*, which prescribes the comportment of a Renaissance courtier. The Venetian was himself a fine example of a Renaissance gentleman: statesman, scholar, historian, poet, and humanist steeped in Latin and Greek classics and the Italian poetry of his time. He met Boscán on the banks of the Darro River in Granada, while accompanying young Carlos V on a state visit to the Alhambra and strongly urged the poet to write sonnets and other forms used by good Italian authors. A few days later while riding home alone, records Boscán, he tried composing in the new forms, in his head. He found them "of a very capable disposition to receive whatever material, whether grave or subtle or difficult or easy, and in itself good for joining with any style that we find among the approved ancient authors"

3

(Barnstone, *Spanish Poetry* 9). Accordingly, he composed *canzoni,*
ottava rima, and *sonetos* (sonnets).

Boscán was a competent poet but had no evident genius. How-
ever, his intimate friend, Garcilaso de la Vega (1501–36), who had
a marvelous talent for words, tried the new forms and achieved a
perfect harmony of form and idea. He was not published in his
lifetime. In 1536, at only age thirty-five, the courtier and knight of
the Order of Santiago died heroically in the presence of his king as
a result of leading an assault, unhelmeted, up a ladder on a tower
near Fréjus in France. After his death his loyal friend Boscán pre-
pared a joint edition of their poetry, but he died in 1542 without
seeing it through publication. His widow took over, and a year
later, the volume was published—*Obras de Boscán y algunas de*
Garcilaso de la Vega (Works of Boscán and some by Garcilaso de la
Vega). In that volume appeared the first printed sonnets written in
the Spanish language. By 1560 sixteen more editions had appeared.
Although Garcilaso composed relatively few poems—thirty-eight
sonnets, five *canciones,* three *églogas,* and an epistle in verse—they
established the new poetry of his age and made him one of the most
influential poets in the Spanish language.

Garcilaso's poetry was the foundation of the Italian Renais-
sance in Spain. His sonnets and his eclogues gave Spanish poetry
the ideals of Petrarchan love and Virgilian pastoral imagery. Few
poets in any language have mastered a poetic diction so serenely
musical and natural. Pervading his poems is a painfully pure sensi-
tivity to beauty and to love. His world is pastoral, often mythologi-
cal, but such artifice does not diminish the real grief and passions
beneath the surface. In contrast to the Middle Ages when few echoes
of pagan antiquity are heard, Garcilaso raised an angelic voice in a
forest cathedral peopled only by mythical figures.

Primarily concerned with love, he imitated, modeled, emu-
lated, and disguised his work on immediate Italian precursors. The
tradition, however, begins with Provençal courtly love poetry (and
perhaps earlier with the Goliard Latin poets and the mystico-erotic
poets of Arabic Spain), and the theme of the distant lady of the
troubadours culminates in Beatrice of the *Vita Nuova* and Petrarch's
Laura. Garcilaso's Laura was called Elisa, and in the manner of
Petrarch, the poet placed her in the classical setting of Virgilian
eclogue. He also has an affinity with Theokritos, the first of the
Greco-Roman pastoral poets, and his nature imagery recalls scenes
from the *Idylls.* Both nature and love are imbued with beauty and
melancholy, which, as in a dream, are perfect—but one awakes to
find the rose withered in the cold wind. The *carpe diem* theme is
universal, and no less tragic for its artifice. The same note found in
the anonymous Greek epigram

Introduction

> The rose blooms for a brief season. It fades,
> and when one looks again—the rose is briar.
>
> (*Sappho and the Greek Lyric Poets* 191)

is heard in Garcilaso's famous sonnet 23:

> While there is still the color of the rose
> and lily in your face, and your bright gaze
> in its sincerity can set ablaze
> a heart, and yet control the flame it shows;
> and while the vivid flying wind still blows
> and tangles up and knots the golden maze
> of your soft hair—hanging in a white haze
> about your slender white neck and dark clothes,
> consume the sweet fruits of your happy spring
> before the sullen blast of time can chill
> the lovely hilltop in a glaze of ice.
> The rose will wither in the snowy wind
> and cunning age will alter all at will,
> for time can be controlled by no device.[1]

Garcilaso's lines express an elegant despair. His world is pure, yet the emotion, however distilled and dictated by convention, is genuine. He is a young man, apparently endowed with all good things—handsome appearance, position, love, poetry; but his poems speak constantly of the frustration of all things, the cruelty of time, the slow poison that is life itself. In Garcilaso the beauty of grief was transformed into the perfection of art.

The new poetry was not accepted immediately by everyone, and there was an angry split and rivalry between Italianists and traditionalists. The traditionalists satirized the Garcilaso school for their self-pitying sorrows and utter lack of humor, their foreign origin, their distance from the common people and popular anonymous song and verse. Several centuries later Lorca, sympathetic to Garcilaso, defending him as a national poet of foreign myths, nevertheless puts his finger on Garcilaso's preciosity in those sonnet lines brought to Spain from Italy, referring to the "endecasyllable which he carried to us with his perfumed gloves" ("La imagen poética de Góngora" 64).

By the end of the sixteenth century, however, the conflict between traditionalists and Italianists, between those who wrote

---

1. All translations carry a book reference except for unpublished versions done by myself for the Introduction; sonnets or parts of sonnets that appear later in the translation sections also do not have a book reference.

Introduction

poetry *de tipo tradicional* (of a traditional type) in popular Castilian forms and those who used imported *culto* stanzas, had disappeared. The agon was gone because both sides triumphed. We find a splendid use of both the formal and popular modes in the same authors, a phenomenon unique to literature in Spanish. We see the learned and popular in the baroque masters, Lope de Vega, Luis de Góngora, Francisco de Quevedo, Sor Juana Inés de la Cruz, and all the way to Antonio Machado and Federico García Lorca in the twentieth century. So Machado and Lorca wrote popular songs and ballads as well as sonnets, and Borges wrote his sonnets as well as his lyrics for the *milonga*, a fast version of the tango, in his case, documenting the lives of lowlife heroes and outlaws.

An interlude of mystical elsewhereness

The second half of the sixteenth century saw the end of imperial growth in Europe and the discovery of new lands in the Americas. *Conquistadores* and colonists went to the New World and sent back tomatoes, maize, chocolate, tobacco, and gold—a meager and unhealthy compensation for the economic work force of Jews and Arabs that had been expelled. The diverse intellectual currents from northern and southern Europe, which had nourished Spain under Carlos V in the first half of the century, were now less vigorous. With all his military ventures against the Turks, French, and Protestants, Carlos emptied the Spanish treasury and filled it with debit notes to German and Genovese bankers. Spain was bankrupt by the time Carlos retired to a small palace by the monastery of Yuste in Extremadura. He chose an almost magically wooded part of Spain, and the buildings today remain austerely elegant, but as the name Extremadura suggests, the emperor retired to a region at furthest remove from his Flemish origins. Under Felipe II (1556–98), although the foreign debts grew, Spain drew into herself, into the new national isolation that was to deepen during the next three centuries. The withdrawal is reflected in the brief interlude of mystical otherness by its meditative poets.

Fray Luis de León (1527–91) and San Juan de la Cruz (1542–91) renounced the apparent world of things and events and escaped into the interior world of the soul—a luminous garden within their minds, with its own extraordinary, allegorized beauty, love, and heavens. But outside the monastery and its writer-saints, by the seventeeth century the nation was well into political and economic decline. The once-invincible Armada had been destroyed; and a pessimism in intellectual life reflected the uncertainties of a tired empire, evident in the moral allegories and gentlemanly concepts of the unhappy Jesuit Baltasar Gracián (1601–58), whom Borges

Introduction

called a Spanish "superstition,"[2] and the ingenious vigor of Quevedo's black humor and bleak vision of nation and existence.

Yet national power and the arts need not obey the same clock. While the nation faltered in corruption and debt and its European empire withered under three Felipes, the arts in Spain prospered. The classically calm, credible, simple agonies of Garcilaso the lover gave way to the metaphysical complexities of the baroque antagonists Góngora and Quevedo and to the philosophical burlesque of Cervantes—the impoverished artist and giant of European fiction. And with Zurbarán, El Greco, and Velázquez—to name a few of the painters—the arts under Felipe IV (1621–65) prospered as never before or since. Lope, Góngora, Quevedo, Calderón, and Sor Juana gave Hispanic poetry a century of unsurpassed poetic excellence and diversity. It was the baroque age, that turbulent period in Spain of violent contrasts and cultural warfare.

There was, however, that interlude between Renaissance belief and the brilliance, energy, and cynicism of baroque decadence: the mystics. Theirs was a spiritual escape into meditation, the night of aridity, illuminative vision, ecstatic flights, and transcendental union. The three best-known mystics, Santa Teresa for her prose and Fray Luis de León and San Juan de la Cruz for their poetry, were of the Church and also from families of *conversos*. Santa Teresa's parents, from Toledo, actually converted back to Judaism before 1492 because the slaughter and drowning of *conversos* in the Tagus River made it less dangerous to be a Jew than a *converso*.

In the instance of Luis de León and Juan de la Cruz, their Jewish background infused their lexicon. San Juan used the mystical vocabulary of León Hebreo, a Jew in exile in Naples, whose imagery was the Song of Songs, and as Mario Szatz has fully documented, the Kabbalah with "the world inscribed in the word" went through his writing. Fray Luis de León was an Augustinian monk and professor of Latin, Greek, and Hebrew at the University of Salamanca. He translated three versions of the biblical Song of Songs (*shir hashirim*) into Spanish directly from Hebrew, as well as Proverbs and Job, and also wrote elaborate commentaries on the Hebrew text. He was jailed by the Inquisition for nearly five years in Valladolid, accused of "Judaizing." His grave offense was the act of having translated Song of Songs into the vernacular—vernacular translations were prohibited by the Inquisition—and worse, he had used as his source

---

2. After a conversation between Borges and myself on Whitman and Poe (included as part ten of *Borges at Eighty: Conversations*), in the question-and-answer period, a member of the audience asked Borges what he thought of Gracián. Borges replied, "Gracián is a superstition."

"the corrupt original," meaning the Hebrew text, as opposed to the authoritative Latin *Vulgata*. The opposition to translating the Bible into a popularly comprehensible vernacular is particularly ironic since the approved *Vulgata* is Latin for "vernacular," referring to the quality of everyday vernacular Latin in Jerome's Latin Bible. León's response was to charge his Dominican professor accusers with hypocrisy, idiocy, perjury, and never speaking the truth except by mistake. When the Holy Inquisition released him, he wrote the moving *décima* (a ten-line poem), "Al salir de la cárcel" (On leaving prison):

> Here their envy and lies
> locked me behind the gate,
> yet glad the humble state
> of him withdrawn and wise,
> far from the evil world,
> in this delightful field,
> spending his life alone,
> with modest room and board,
> with God his sole reward
> and jealousies unknown.
>
> (León 43)

Many of Luis de León's best poems were written in his cell at Valladolid. Though San Juan was imprisoned for only nine months in a monastery cell in Toledo, and by a competing order of the Carmelites over the serious matter of worldly wealth or poverty, of shoes versus bare feet (ultimately resolved by the adoption of sandals), he probably wrote the most important poem of his life, if not of Spanish literature, "La noche oscura del alma" (The dark night of the soul), while in his prison cell. The poem, written in the voice of a woman, traces an escape from the cell to a rendezvous with the lover with whom she sleeps, an allegory for the soul's escape from the prison of worldly senses to mystical immersion in God. In the mystical process, he says in his *Commentaries*, in order to obtain spiritual union with God one must pass through three stages: the *vía purgativa*, the *vía iluminativa*, and the *vía unitiva*. His "simile," to use his word, for the union of soul with God is the climax of human sexual love. In this he follows the mysticism of Hebrew and Arabic poets before him. The mystical experience is ineffable, like the experience of gazing directly at the sun, as Plato explains in the Allegory of the Cave. San Juan's poem works on the surface level of erotic narration—whether or not one wishes to read into his Song of Songs lexicon the mystical dimension that has been traditionally imposed on the biblical sequence of songs:

On a dark secret night,
starving for love and deep in flame,
   O happy gambling flight!
   unseen I slipped away,
my house at last was calm and safe.

   Blackly free from light,
disguised and down a secret way,
   O happy gambling flight!
   in darkness I escaped,
my house at last was calm and safe.

   On that happy night—in
secret; no one saw me through the dark—
   and I saw nothing then,
   no other light to mark
the way but fire pounding my heart.

   That flaming guided me
more firmly than the noonday sun,
   and waiting there was he
   I knew so well, who shone
where nobody appeared to come.

   O night that was my guide!
O night more friendly than the dawn!
   O tender night that tied
   love and the loved one,
loved one in the lover fused as one!

   On my flowering breasts
which I had saved for him alone,
   he slept and I caressed
   and fondled him with love,
and cedars fanned the air above.

   Wind from the castle wall
while my fingers played in his hair:
   its hand serenely fell
   wounding my neck, and there
my senses vanished in the air.

   I stayed, forgot my being,
and on my love I leaned my face.
   All ceased. I left my being,
   leaving my cares to fade
among the lilies far away.

                (John of the Cross 39)

    The two Spanish mystical poets wrote no sonnets—or none that
have come down to us. (We do have two sonnets dubiously attributed

Introduction

to Luis de León, which are imitations in Spanish of two well-known sonnets by Petrarch.) Fray Luis's Neoplatonism was directed toward a celestial God, not toward a remote lady; and imbued as he was with both Greco-Latin and Hebraic-Christian traditions, he managed to reconcile the formal perfection and concision of Horace and Virgil with a soaring personal mysticism. Like the English meditative poets, he moved tranquilly through an inner universe. Music was his way—of Pythagoras, mathematician-philosopher, and Francisco Salinas, his blind organist friend in Salamanca:

> The air becomes serene
> and robed in beauty and an unknown light,
>   Salinas, when the unseen
>   deep music soars in flight,
> governed by your hand that is wise and right.

(León 45)

Luis de León was the poet of "the unknown light" and the evening spheres' "unheard music" or to use San Juan de la Cruz's phrase in the *Cántico espiritual* (Spiritual canticle), *la música callada* (the music of a silence). As San Juan chose the allegory of human love, Fray Luis moved into the geometry of the night heavens to seek God in the sounding harmony of its celestial bodies. Francisco de Quevedo felt a kinship with Luis de León, and after León's death it was Quevedo who gathered and published the mystical nature poet's poetry.

Góngora and his gang against Quevedo and his mob

One reason for Quevedo's publication of the works of Fray Luis was to reinforce his side of the literary battle between two camps of the baroque poets: the *cultistas* (the more aesthetically oriented poets) whose main exponent was Góngora and the *conceptistas* (who valued meaning over form) whose main exponent was Quevedo. The categories were of course not that clear and each poet strays into the other camp, but there is validity to the general distinctions.

While in the early Renaissance the ideals of clarity and equilibrium prevailed in poetry as in the visual arts, in the baroque period geometrically simple planes were broken up into intricate, embellished masses. Imitation of nature was replaced by artifice. Góngora and the *cultistas* who followed his lead invented new words based on Greek and Latin roots (neologisms), distorted the normal syntax of language (hyperbaton), and used audacious metaphors and indeed all possible rhetorical tropes of classical poetry—including ellipsis, hyperbole, anaphora, metonymy—to enrich their text and dazzle

10

Introduction

the reader. In addition they peppered their verse with exotic geographies and mythological allusions. Many of their poems are metric word games that can be deciphered only by a prose paraphrase. The masterpiece among these aesthetic-linguistic tours de force is Góngora's *Las soledades* (The solitudes). The late hybrid child of *The Solitudes* is Sor Juana Inés de la Cruz's "Primero sueño" (First dream), hybrid because in addition to its imitation of Góngora's verbal trickeries, it also has an intellectual core of ontological speculation worthy of Quevedo's *conceptismo*.

Yet if Góngora's meaning is obscure, it is not necessarily profound. More often than not the prose paraphrase is of little circumstance. As in the case of many of Pound's *Cantos*, the inscrutable meaning is not of great import (and in Pound's political and economic diatribes only of negative import). To use the now-worn phrase, in Góngora's amazing *Soledades* the medium is the message, or said more traditionally, form overrides content. In fiction the same holds true of the least-read masterpiece of our century, *Finnegan's Wake*. The message is the beauty of the language, the extravagant images, the colorful and audacious diction, which in its time extended both the musical and linguistic possibilities of the Spanish language. Góngora created his own Byzantium, imposing Greek and Latin syntax on Spanish and images that exist only in dream—or in poetry. It is poetry of a beauty related only to art and to literature and its mythologies; it is occasionally poetry of the grotesque. There are no verses that will get the author into prison. Góngora's birds sing on a golden tree for lords and ladies, and unpleasant feeling or ugly fabric seldom intrudes. But likewise there is never a hint of sentimental slop or sop, which is one of the reasons, along with the use of the surreal-fantastic, that Góngora became—as the English Metaphysicals did for early twentieth-century poetry—the preeminent model for the Spanish Generation of 1927. His cold metals and liquids and colors come through in his well-known sonnet beginning "O bright honor of the liquid element." The "liquid element" in the first line, which simply refers to "water," displays the *cultista* games of verbal substitutions:

O bright honor of the liquid element,
fresh tiny brook of luminescent silver,
across the fields of grass your sloping water
slowly and gracefully makes its descent!
When Eros looks at you, painting a tableau
of her for whom I freeze or turn to flame,
he shows the snow and scarlet of her face
in the suave peaceful gesture of your flow.
Examine how you move and do not lose

11

the crystal bridle's wavy rein with which
you hold in tow the arrant moving current:
it would be wrong for so much beauty to
be caught, jumbled and sunken in that ditch,
seized by the Master of the dripping trident.

Three hundred years after Góngora wrote his sonnets, his *Soledades* and his *Polifemo y Galatea*, Spain rediscovered and celebrated Góngora, named a whole generation of major poets after him, the poets of 1927 (in reference to three-hundredth anniversary of Góngora's death in 1627). Federico García Lorca, Rafael Alberti, Pedro Salinas, Jorge Guillén, and Vicente Aleixandre found in the "rehabilitated" Góngora a modernity and antidote to the sentimental late *fin-de-siècle* poetry they were vehemently rejecting. Góngora's "brilliant obscurity" in the *Soledades*, unblemished by moral or philosphical concern, his artifice, flare, and his flashing surfaces revolutionized Spanish letters.

Although the Generation of '27 produced the most important poetry in Spanish literature in three centuries, I have always regretted that Quevedo, equally brilliant on the surface but immensely more moving and more metaphysically interesting than Góngora, had so little effect on that wondrous generation of modern Spanish poets. Of all the poets of '27, Jorge Guillén, relentlessly metaphysical, had a natural affinity with Quevedo. But Guillén, despite the darkness of *Clamor*, is truly the poet of *Cántico: fe de vida*'s buoyant happiness, and he is alien to Quevedo's brooding, sometimes nihilistic, obsessions with time, the transitory, and the permanent work of death's worms. Besides the traditional reasons for marginalizing Quevedo as a poet—his satires were too violent, his conceptual darknesses too dark, his inventive, neologistic tongue and shrewd ear unappreciated by limited critics—Emilia Navarro de Kelley has suggested another fascinating reason for Quevedo's lower status earlier in the century:

In the case of Quevedo, the advance [of his reputation] has been slower and more thorny, which is easy to understand for several reasons. In the first place, Quevedo, the Quevedo of the *Buscón* and of the *Sueños* already enjoyed a respectable and definitive place in Spanish letters. It was the love and metaphysical poet, the religious and tormented one, who remained almost completely ignored or, at least, relegated to a secondary place. (Kelley 9)

In other words his very reputation as a stylist and author of two prose masterpieces detracted critics from his originality as a poet. Perhaps even more significant is that the Generation of '27 was

Introduction

not ready for him—in contrast to the development in English and
American contemporary poetry in our century that began by eulo-
gizing the metaphysical passion of our seventeenth-century poets.
Quevedo was too powerful and grave for that youthful renaissance
in Spanish literature.

Now, ironically, Quevedo has usurped the place of Góngora as
the major figure in his period, and his reputation has never been so
solid and high as it is today among readers and the first generation
of scholars who caused the revaluation, including Dámaso Alonso,
A. A. Parker, Arthur Terry, Jorge Luis Borges, James O. Crosby,
Raimundo Lida, and Manuel Durán. We can hope that literary
theory will permit us to remember the text and Quevedo in the
future—a safe bet—and he, like Hopkins, Góngora, Greco, and other
discovered obscurities, will remain bright—even in his darkest eve-
nings and "in the cloisters" where the wounded "soul lies silenced."

In the days when Góngora and Quevedo were slugging it out,
the *cultistas*, Góngora, and *gongorismo* did not go unchallenged.
The center of the violent opposition was the *conceptista* Francisco
de Quevedo. And there was a fundamental philosophical difference
in the ways in which Góngora and Quevedo depart from the ideals
of Renaissance harmony. Luis de Góngora—Jorge Guillén speaks of
him as *ruiseñor, facilísimo del pío* (a nightingale, extreme ease in
trilling)—transforms the visible world into a heavenly garden of
absolute beauty, pagan, amoral, existing only in artifice of poetry.
He was the Parnassian and symbolist Verlaine of his time, with
much greater range, strength, and fantasy, utterly devoid of poesy
and self-pitying sentimentality. But the analogy of the art for art's
sake "ivory tower" holds. No untidy passions or painful metaphysi-
cal inquiry (until his own last letters of physical suffering and
despair, which Dámaso Alonso has analyzed with compassion).
Objects are depicted not directly but by complex analogy, created
in perfection, as arabesque forms. Hence a bird is "a flying zither."
At the same time he does share with Quevedo the classical regret
about fleeting time and certain death as revealed in the title of the
sonnet "De la brevedad engañosa de la vida" (Concerning the decep-
tive brevity of life) and like Andrew Marvell in his "To His Coy Mis-
tress," reminds Licio, his classical speaker in the poem, not to pursue
and embrace deceptive shadows. The characteristic tone of Góngora
is displayed in a sonnet beginning "To compete with your hair the
sun's gold shines in vain" and in which, as in the "Coy Mistress," he
catalogues his lady's physical virtues and warns her that dust awaits
her. Marvell's gallows humor is relentless:

    then worms shall try
  That long preserved virginity:

13

And your quaint [cunt] honor turn to dust;
and into ashes all my lust.

Góngora's final line is without humor but implacably dark:

but you and I together will end
in earth, in smoke, in dust, shadow, in nothing.

Yet Góngora's poem is a conventional praise and enticement lyric, with dire warnings, in contrast to his follower Sor Juana Inés de la Cruz (she was also the heir of Quevedo), who at the end of the century, in colonial Mexico, borrows and slightly transforms the line to show in her most powerful, uncompromising poem, in true Quevedesque manner, how all life, and specifically a flattering portrait of her, is a lie, concealing doom:

it is a foolish labor that can only fail:
it is a wasting zeal and, well observed,
is corpse, is dust, is shadow, and is nothing.

Quevedo's answer to the colorful exuberance and linguistic acrobatics of the *cultistas* and its leader Góngora was pitiless. Of course when he mocked Góngora in his poems, he too indulged in the exuberant word games that marked the baroque style. And time and time again, there is a crossover of means and tone. But the main lines of difference and combat remain clear. In one poem called simply "Góngora," the model is the classical Greek lampoon from the *Palatine Anthology*. Quevedo fulminates against his rival, whom he mocks as a Jew (he wasn't), just as in other insult and burlesque poems he cruelly and brutally ridicules lying priests, fornicating monks, murderous doctors, and torturer dentists or shits on the emblem of the royal king and mocks his aids. In "Desengaño de las mujeres" (Disillusionment with women), he even scorns great ladies who are whores and confesses that he, Quevedo, is himself a whore:

A whore is any man who trusts a whore.
A whore is one who hungers juicily
for whores. Whorish the cash he pays to score
and guarantee their whorish company.
Whorish the taste, whorish the happiness
of moments with a whore. And as for shady
illusions, whores are those who won't confess
that you are also a grand whore, my lady.
But call me also just a whore in love

14

Introduction

if I don't leave you as a whore one day,
and like a whore I'll perish burning hot
if, I brag about the whores who've come my way;
for serious-minded whores now cost a lot
and little cheap ones curse and kick and shove.

Francisco de Quevedo

(1580–1645)

Spain

Francisco de Quevedo

A metaphysical monster of nature

Francisco de Quevedo was, like his Golden Age contemporaries Lope de Vega and Miguel de Cervantes, a *monstruo de la naturaleza* (monster of nature). The term was originally coined to describe the playwright and lyric and epic poet Lope de Vega because of Lope's extravagantly enormous production. Quevedo was also immensely prolific and versatile but with the major difference of uniform quality. In the modes in which he wrote, the picaresque novel, the fantastic, the lyric poem, he has a quality of perfection and extraordinarily original imagination, so that his novel *El Buscón* (The swindler), 1626, is the seminal work of Spanish picaresque realism, and *Los sueños* (The visions), 1627, a Dantean journey through the grotesque, a nightmarish vision of hell, and in the end a brutal moral satire. Borrowing, alluding, inventing—as the most original of authors have done—Quevedo construes his own literary genre. As a poet Quevedo is a giant figure of the European seventeenth century. Movingly stoic, profoundly metaphysical, exquisitely amorous or obscenely erotic, his work is at times morosely and harshly nihilistic, and no sooner said, it is hilariously and cruelly burlesque. Like Swift, Dostoyevski, and Kafka, he is one of the tormented spirits and visionaries of world literature and also one of the funniest writers ever to pick up a sharp, merciless pen. Jorge Luis Borges, calling him "the first artificer of Spanish letters," wrote that "like Joyce, like Goethe, like Shakespeare, like Dante, Francisco de Quevedo is like no other writer and is more than a man; he is an extensive and complex literature" ("Quevedo" 64).

Francisco de Quevedo

I am a man well born in the provinces . . . I am lord of my house in the Montaña; the son of parents who honor me with their memory, as I mortify them with mine.

Abundance and years I always deal with in such a way that afterwards the abundance is greater, the years less.

Francisco de Quevedo

> Those who care for me call me lame, and being so I seem
> that way because of personal neglect, and I am, between lame-
> ness and reverence, an elegant lame, whether I choose so or
> not. [This is a pun on "es cojo o no escojo." *Es cojo* means "he
> is lame"; *escojo* means "I choose"; when spoken, *es cojo* and
> *escojo* are the same.]
> My personality is neither abhorrent nor given to anger; and
> since I don't seek praises, I don't remember the curses and
> laughter of those who see me.
> I have been bad, along many roads, and now having left off
> being bad I am not good, since I have given up the badness of
> the tired man, and not of the repentant.
> —Quevedo, in a letter to the countess of Olivares

Don Francisco de Quevedo y Villegas was born in Madrid on
September 17, 1580, on the old Calle del Niño, which now bears
his name. Today, around the corner are the houses of Miguel de
Cervantes and Lope de Vega. Of an aristocratic family, his father,
Pedro Gómez de Quevedo, was private secretary to Princess María,
the daughter of Carlos V, and his mother was María de Santibáñez,
who was lady-in-waiting for Queen Ana. Francisco was brought up
at court, and all his life he had a clear vision of the palace's brilliance,
gaiety, conspiracy, and corruption. Historians are in accord that by
the time of his king, Felipe III, who came to the throne at the age
of twenty in 1598, there was spectacular poverty throughout the
land while moneys at the top went to the monarch's high-pensioned
favorites and to luxurious embellishment for palace ceremonies. At
least his later king, Felipe IV (who reigned 1621–61), was a patron
of the arts and even wrote plays, but actual rule was, for twenty-
two years, in the hands of Gaspar de Guzmán, the count-duke
of Olivares. Despite Olivares's attempts to make reforms, Spain
declined, the European empire fell apart, the treasury was a record
of debts, and the good offices of the government and Church were
a catalogue of greed and abuse. The national plight was not absent
from Quevedo's writing.

Little is recorded of Quevedo's childhood. We do know that his
legs were deformed, and he was very myopic as a result of which in
later life he wore pince-nez eyeglasses (in Spanish *quevedos*). In
portraits the poet was painted with metal-rimmed glasses set on
his nose. As a young man he was also an expert swordsman and in
confusing paradox, something of a gallant. Orphaned at an early
age—he was just six when his father died—he was entrusted to the
Jesuits in Madrid at the Colegio Imperial de la Compañía de Jesús
for his early education. Later he went to Alacalá de Henares to study
humanities, and in 1600 he received his *Bachiller en Artes* from
there. Then he went to Valladolid for theology. A bookish, broadly

Francisco de Quevedo

educated man of his age, he acquired a knowledge of Greek, Latin, Hebrew, Arabic, and French, as well as Italian perfected after long residence in Italy. Presumably as a bit of proud modesty about his own mistreatment of the more difficult tongues, he is said to have commented, "If the languages weren't dead one would have to kill them." He also studied human letters, civil and canonical law, mathematics, astronomy, politics, medicine, and philosophy. By 1600 his satiric poems were bringing a precocious and prolific poet early fame.

His own wild student life is reflected in his masterpiece, *El Buscón* (written between 1603 and 1604 though not published until 1626), which begins as a savage treatment of the student milieu in Salamanca. His early reputation as a poet, including "Poderoso caballero es Don Dinero" (A powerful gentleman is Don Money), was enhanced when eighteen of his poems were included in Pedro de Espinosa's anthology, *Flores de poetas ilustres* (1605).

In this same year part one of *Don Quijote* was published. Cervantes's magnanimous epic of world literature, with its Whitmanian vastness, changed Spanish and world letters. The insolently stubborn knight of the imagination was pure creative lunacy. Quevedo's rogue-hero Pablos, in the tradition of Lazarillo de Tormes, is the obverse mirror of Quijote's nobility. Yet because of Quevedo's mastery, this scoundrel *buscón* is a perfectly realized figure, and the novel, despite its episodic plot, has the perfection of an immaculate sonnet (in marked contrast to the diffusion of Mateo Alemán's *Guzmán de Alfarache* and other rambling picaresque works). As with Federico García Lorca, the innate sense of balance, form, and lexical purity is there—whether the subjects be adventure, deception, the wild excremental vision of enema buffoonery, or simply general low-life roguery.

Poet and diplomat, glory and troubles

When a year later in 1606 Felipe III moved his court from its brief stay in Valladolid back to Madrid, Quevedo followed. The author was already amazingly productive. In addition to poetry, in these years he had written his picaresque novel, *El Buscón*, in Valladolid; in Madrid, he did the first part of *Sueños* (Visions) and translated from Greek, Latin, and Hebrew. And in the literary capital he became the friend of writers and attended their *tertulias*. He knew Cervantes, was praised by Lope, and met Góngora, his later rival. Already from Valladolid, Quevedo had corresponded in Greek and Latin with the Belgian humanist Justus Lipsius, who in turn praised his erudition. He was also on good terms with important people at the court.

Francisco de Quevedo

Since Quevedo lived in the world of the court and diplomacy, many stories have been told, none of them verifiable, about cloak-and-dagger intrigues and even a novelesque duel outside the Church of San Martín in Madrid to safeguard an unknown woman from abuse. He may or may not have been involved in a quarrel with a well-known fencing champion, Luis Pacheco de Narváez, whom Quevedo, after objecting to a maneuver, is said to have defeated by knocking off the champion's fencing hat. There was said to be a feud between the two gentleman that lasted for years, carried out by mutual lampoons about each other. After 1609 Francisco de Quevedo was also entangled for two decades in disputes concerning the estate at Torre de Juan Abad (near Villanueva de los Infantes), which he had inherited, along with village property, from his mother. The legal battles obliged him to keep up his ties with this pastoral setting by way of extended residences there. It became a refuge, reflected in the poems, as it was later to be the site of his first imprisonment when his patron and friend, the duke of Osuna, fell from power and was thrown into prison to die there.

Quevedo's diplomatic career began in earnest when Osuna invited him to Italy to be his aid. Pedro Téllez Girón, third duke of Osuna, was also viceroy of Sicily (1611–16). Quevedo became the duke's advisor, confidant, and agent. In addition to diplomatic tasks, the poet had countless amorous adventures. Dangerous ones, his biographers say. The poet of being, time, and love, whose poetry carried the myths and lines of classical antiquity, who breathed the language of his baroque age, was also a man thoroughly *engagé* in the world of state and church powers, knew those precincts intimately, and his social poetry of admonition, satire, and burlesque is based on the reality of his experience. Quevedo was not separated from his worlds. He loved his books, carried them with him in his pockets like modern paperbacks, and spent his spare hours punishing his already myopic eyes with voluminously wide reading. But just as he was a bookworm, he was both streetwise and a lover of his refuge in nature. In a period where rhetoric, convention, and linguistic complexity might replace the warm and cold visible terrains, he was there. In his most famous sonnet beginning "Miré los muros de la patria mía," he says "salíme al campo" (I went into the fields). In all ways, all places, he went to the fields.

He went to Nice, Genoa, and Milan on secret assignments. One major mission occurred in the autumn of 1615. The duke sent his poet-friend to Madrid to deliver 300,000 ducats of Sicilian tax funds to the king. He also had the sensitive mission of convincing the king's advisors to make Osuna the viceroy of Naples. In his letters to the duke, Quevedo described the corrupt ministers of the court and how he distributed bribes shrewdly to gain the appointment.

Francisco de Quevedo

His second major commission was to carry a biennial contribution of 1,800,000 ducats from the Naples parliament to the Spanish king. On the way he had an audience with Pope Paul V in Rome. It has been assumed that his mission before the pope was to seek the papal assistance for Osuna's plan to destroy the power of the city-state of Venice and bring it under Spanish hegemony. When the poet reached Madrid he was himself treated like a viceroy. Felipe III received him in the Escorial, perhaps about Osuna's plans to bring Venice under the Spanish flag. For all his activities for the crown, the king presented him with the cloak of the Order of Santiago, making him a member and providing him with a regular yearly stipend.

As for what happened next, there are several versions of a legend that has been repeated in many ordinary histories and biographies. The most colorful one of all is that Quevedo himself went to Venice disguised as a beggar in order to carry messages to the participants. One day in 1616, there was a dramatic spectacle of many foreigners displayed hanging in the Plaza of San Marco. Osuna's plot failed. Someone had talked. Some constables found Quevedo and wanted to kill him, but he talked them out of it, confusing them by speaking in perfect Venetian dialect. And the next day the city burned Quevedo in effigy. All these constantly repeated tales are false. Quevedo was in Spain, not Italy, when the failed revolt took place. Had he been there, however remarkable his language talents, the poet could not have picked up the Venetian dialect without a very long stay in the city.

The king was not pleased with Osuna's failure, embarrassing as it was and hard to explain to his Italian subjects. Although Quevedo tried to defend him in Madrid—and the poet too had lost eminence—he was not able to do so. Osuna lost his viceroyalty and was thrown into prison where he died in 1624. Quevedo shared his disgrace and was placed in a prison at Uclés in 1620 for his connections with the duke of Osuna. After six months he was banished to his estate at Torre de Juan Abad, on an extended leave of absence from the city and public life, very beneficial to his literary pen. He wrote voluminously. With the death of Felipe III and the ascension of his son Felipe IV, the count-duke of Olivares took the reins of power and freed Quevedo in March of 1623. The poet then returned to Madrid where, for most of twelve years, he was on good terms with Olivares to whom he dedicated his important poem, "Epístola satírica y censoria" (Satiric letter of censure), which begins:

I won't keep quiet though you move your finger,
now touching your mouth or now your forehead;
you counsel silence or you threaten fear.

Francisco de Quevedo

Will there never be a spirit of courage?
Will one always regret what one says?
Or will no one ever say what one feels?

The next years were filled with writing and publication. He had also returned to favor and participated in 1623 in the festivities when Prince Charles of England came to Madrid to seek the hand of Princess María, the sister of Felipe IV. Not only did he accompany the king on a tour of Andalusia, but Quevedo hosted the king at his estate at Torre de Juan Abad. In 1626 he became secretary to the king, an honorary office. Also, Quevedo continued to have excellent relations with Olivares, and when he edited and wrote a prologue to the poems of the mystical poet Fray Luis de León, he dedicated the edition to the count-duke. Meanwhile his picaresque novel, *El Buscón*, became increasingly popular and began to be known in translation throughout Europe. The extraordinary *Sueños* came out in multiple editions in Spain and also appeared in French.

One of the controversies of the day was whether Santa Teresa, canonized in 1622, should share the patronage of Spain with Santiago. Santiago, one of the twelve Apostles and perhaps brother of Jesus, supposedly lay buried in a tomb in a monastery in Santiago de Compostela. During the battle of Clavijo in the ninth century against the Moors, Santiago is said to have come out of the tomb on a white horse to lead the troops against the heathens; his shout "Santiago Matamoros!" (Santiago the Moor slayer!) became the cry of the victorious Christian armies. As a knight of the Order of Santiago, Quevedo was passionately in favor of retaining Santiago as the sole patron saint of Spain. His enemies induced Olivares to require him again to withdraw to Torre de Juan Abad where he wrote his *Memorial for the Patronage of Santiago*. But Olivares and the king also favored Santiago, and Quevedo's writings were evidently very helpful to them. Santiago backers won, and Pope Urban VIII made it official. As a reward for his efforts, Olivares offered the poet an ambassadorship in Genoa, but after his Naples-Sicily adventures with Osuna, he had had enough of political life in Italy and declined the offer.

The misogynist marries

As for his relations with women, they were as ambiguous as most aspects of his life. Was he a misogynist, a cynic, or a hopelessly intoxicated lover? In his poems he is certainly all three, and I would say those attitudes reflect more than literary poses; and given his diverse character and the extreme diversity of his writings, I see consistency in his contradictions. As he vituperated against Góngora, he railed against all and everything—the court, the monarchy, religions, people—in life and art; yet there is in other poems a deep pathos and humanity and, yes, a generosity. There is never a hint of sentimentality and romantic bathos. Even in his love poems, Quevedo, while passionately candid, is made of crystal and iron. And so there is always an arcade of strong self-contradiction in his many voices. As for women, he both idealized and assailed them and had his share of affairs, ranging from a sonneteer's courtly love idealization in poems to Lisi, to a worldly attachment to Señora Ledesma, his lady for many years, with whom he had children. Finally, however, his friends the duke of Medinaceli and the countess of Olivares persuaded him to marry, and apparently they joined in some matchmaking. In 1634, at age fifty-four, Quevedo blundered into legal marriage with Doña Esperanza de Mendoza, a well-born widow, but they were separated after about three months. The separation was definitive. Thereafter, as a sign of her disappointment, Doña Esperanza signed all her official documents as the widow of her first husband.

Quevedo's political fortunes were peaceful during most of these years, despite the Santiago episode out of which he came through vindicated and rewarded. But in 1639 everything fell apart. We still do not know the true reasons why Quevedo was arrested. A persistent story explains that one morning King Felipe sat down to eat breakfast and under his breakfast setting was a satiric poem, criticizing the realm and urging him to change his policies. Quevedo was accused of being the poem's author, which is extremely unlikely, even though there is no question that his satire extended to the monarchy itself. A line from a famous poem, probably from his youth, reads: "Cágome en el blasón de la monarquía" (I shit on the blazon of the monarchy). Although we do not know who denounced Quevedo—and he had many literary and political enemies—it is probable that Olivares himself had lost confidence in him, as recently discovered correspondence between Olivares and the king suggests. In any case the poet was arrested at the house of the duke of Medinaceli and taken away half-dressed to prison. Under mixed conditions of care and abandonment, he languished at the Monastery of San Marcos in León.

Futile, pitiful letters that Quevedo wrote to friends in power, pleading for release or amelioration of his cell conditions, reveal horrendous suffering and a crushed spirit. To the count-duke of Olivares, the probable author of his imprisonment, he wrote a weary and desperate letter—to no avail:

1642

Excelentísimo señor Except for my hope in your excellency, I lack all else: health, sustenance, reputation. Blind in my left eye, half paralyzed, and cancerous, mine is no longer a life but a proximity to death. . . . I do not ask your excellency for my freedom, but a change of place and prison. The hunger and barrenness here cannot be accepted in the times of your excellency. I would be better off in regard to the generosity of food in the basement of a public jail than to be here . . . let your excellency take pity on me so that I might live at your feet or I might finish with it and die. I ask for a change of place. In the Gospels it says that Christ conceded a great many demons what they asked him for. When my ways imitate that, I hope that the religion and mercy of your excellency will imitiate it in regard to me. (*Obras en verso* 975)

Despite the conditions, even in confinement he went on with his writing. There is a history of writing in prison conditions in the Spanish world, from San Juan de la Cruz and Fray Luis de León to César Vallejo and Miguel Hernández. Even during the last year, his worst, somehow Quevedo composed a book on the life of Saint Paul. After four years, when Olivares himself fell from grace, Quevedo was released. By then, there seems to have been uncertainty as to why Quevedo was imprisoned to begin with. There had been no formal charges. On his return to freedom, he continued to add to his translations—he rendered *Marcus Brutus* from Plutarch and wrote a commentary on it, wrote poems and stoical and religious tracts, and looked over editions of his books. Half-blind, his health broken, he died two years later.

The perilous siren of many voices and varied melodies

Quevedo is a master of the Spanish language, in poetry and prose, handling intricacies with ease, and inventing language, usually the tongue of invective, with Joycean pleasure and gusto. An example of Quevedo at his malicious best (or worst if you are Góngora, his target) is a sonnet entitled "Contra el mismo" (Against the same one). It begins by attacking "that stupid writer of songs who aspires to herons and comes up with reptiles." Although I have annotated the poem in Spanish, deciphering known words and acknowledging the unknowable creations (at least by me and Spanish friends), I have not attempted to turn this marvel of calumny into an imitation in English—anything less than imitation would fail poetically. Here are the last six lines in Spanish, which a little Latin and Greek will help to understand:

> Tu forasteridad es tan eximia,
> que te ha de detractar el que te rumia,
> pues ructas viscerable cacoquimia,

Francisco de Quevedo

farmacofolorando como numia,
si estomacabanuania das tan nimia,
metamorfoseando el arcadumia.

(Barnstone, *Spanish Poetry* 362)

Quevedo has "many voices and varied melodies," to paraphrase
the Bishop Theobaldus's Latin bestiary description in the "Sirens":
political, burlesque, confessional, philosophical, amorous. And he
excels in each domain. There are sonnets that combine his preoccu-
pations, and one of the most compelling is "Amor constante más
allá de la muerte" (Love constant beyond death). The uncynical
poem concerns love and death, and for all the darkness of the final
shadow of judgment day (that becomes the last white day of resur-
rection), his soul "will be dust but will be dust in love." For all the
attempts of critics to sentimentalize the conclusion of "dust in
love" into a satisfying state of eternal love, the image of love-and-
death's impossible resolution persists as love reduced to dust, and
in heaven or the grave that condition of total decay, expressed
in beautiful words, is not humanly beautiful. Rather, once again
destroying time prevails over symbolism and wishful conventions,
and the poem ends with cruel and exquisite irony. Yet while the
lies and flattery of death are gone, the soul does persist and remem-
ber, and for what it's worth, the belief in the soul's survival, with
memory intact, is the poem's affirmation. That last affirmation is,
distinct from authorial intention, the reader's decision to treat as
irony or faith. The sonnet is one of the most completely accom-
plished and important poems in Spanish or any language.

> The final shadow that will close my eyes
> will in its darkness take me from white day
> and instantly untie the soul from lies
> and flattery of death, and find its way,
> and yet my soul won't leave its memory
> of love there on the shore where it has burned:
> my flame can swim cold water and has learned
> to lose respect for law's severity.
> My soul, whom a God made his prison of,
> my veins, which liquid humor fed to fire,
> my marrows, which have gloriously flamed,
> will leave their body, never their desire;
> they will be ash but ash in feeling framed;
> they will be dust but will be dust in love.

Quevedo's personal confessional mode recalls the Chinese
Tang poets Wang Wei and Du Fu or our own century's existential
poets—Mandelstam, Roethke, and Robert Lowell, who translated

Francisco de Quevedo

Quevedo's sonnets. In many important poems Quevedo has the disarming colloquial simplicity we associate with the landscapes and speaker in a poem by Antonio Machado. Nature and confession are Quevedo's way in "Enseña cómo todas las cosas avisan de la muerte" (He shows how all things warn of death):

> I went into the fields. I saw the sun
> drinking the springs just melted from the ice,
> and cattle moaning as the forests climb
> against the thinning day, now overrun
> with shade. I went into my house. I saw
> my old room yellowed with the sickening breath
> of age, my cane flimsier than before.

But when he is a poet of inventive invective, Quevedo is wholly classical. Beginning with the outrageous candor of Archilochos in the eighth century B.C. and the acidity of Hipponax, a century later, the lampoon has been a traditional instrument for personal and public attack. The Latin satirists, whom Quevedo knew and translated, carried the tradition of comedy and anger to the West. Quevedo's attack on the pop-up figures of the human comedy have their predecessors in the *Greek Anthology*, in Martial (translated by Quevedo), Juvenal, and Perseus. In Spanish literature Quevedo's satires are not unique, but they went further than all others in lexical range and in realistic anatomical detail.

The language itself is a web of ingenious puns, and what can we do but gasp when he connects a fart with a nightingale (to the ears of gay male whores), as he does in a sociocomic poem in which he also "shits on the royal emblem of the kings"?

> La voz del ojo, que llamamos pedo
> (ruiseñor de los putos) . . .

> The voice from the red eye we call a fart
> (a nightingale to the male whores) . . .

As a poet with a scatalogical vision, he is—with Swift, Sade, Burroughs, and their explicator Norman Brown—one who explored with relentless sincerity the grotesque and hidden realms of the human psyche. Unfortunately, Spanish letters in the past have been so puritanical that critics and anthologies have excluded this vital, fantastic side of Quevedo, usually with a few words of apologetic commentary. Spanish criticism has yet to explore the dark Quevedo.

For lack of a better word, Francisco de Quevedo is a poet of the soul. *Soul, alma* in Spanish, is a word Quevedo used and would

have been comfortable with to describe that area in which this
diverse poet wrote his major poems. These are the metaphysical
poems of time, existence, consciousness. They are the poems of the
interior world as they are also speculations and observations of the
nation that he treats as a national soul in trouble. His concern
with the decadence of political Spain and of the monarchy—"and
everything I looked at bore / a warning of the wasted gaze of
death"—with the brevity of beauty, a woman's love, of life itself,
led to his darkest themes: his obsession with time and death, and
a virtual philosophy of nihilism. This is evident in "Représentase
la brevedad de lo que vive" (Described is the brevity of what is being
lived):

> I am a was, a will be, and a weary am.
> To now, tomorrow, and the past I tie
> diapers and winding sheet. I am a bed
> of torturing successions of the dead.

And when he attacks purple tyranny—and one of the purple-shining
Felipes cannot be far from his gaze—he has no soft words for all
"tyrants living by their vain illusions," whom, as in traditional
medieval "La danza de la muerte" (The dance of death), death levels
equally, and causes king and pauper alike to sleep in the same
eternal bed:

> Do you see this fat giant of a man
> strolling along with haughty gravity?
> Well, inside he's a mess of rags, a pan
> of trash, a young brat keeps from anarchy.
> He moves about, parading his live soul,
> and aims his greatness anywhere he wants;
> yet gaze astutely at this emerald mole,
> you'll laugh at all the ornaments he flaunts.
> Such are the grandiose and pretentious ways
> of tyrants living by their vain illusions,
> those eminent, fantastic bags of germs.
> They burn in purple as their fingers blaze
> with diamonds and hard gems in white profusion,
> while inside they are nausea, earth, and worms.
>
> > (Desengaño de la exterior apariencia
> > [Disillusionment with external appearances])

Quevedo's despair is absolute—which did not prevent him from
laughing his way into death. He saw everywhere the misery and
vanity of all things, and he assailed himself as mercilously as he
did others. And even more so. His poems are verbal perfections of

time's complexities, love's idiocies, and gloom's victories. Those full and lively verbal objects contain words of enduring salvation in an existence of exuberance and disaster. In the course of our lives of disaster, time, through which life breathes, gets around to killing us all. The poem endures in its disturbing wisdom and pathos, providing us interludes of hope.

Enseña cómo todas las cosas avisan de la muerte

Miré los muros de la patria mía,
si un tiempo fuertes, ya desmoronados,
de la carrera de la edad cansados,
por quien caduca ya su valentía.
Salíme al campo, vi que el sol bebía
los arroyos del hielo desatados;
y del monte, quejosos, los ganados,
que con sombras hurtó su luz al día.
Entré en mi casa, vi que amancillada
de anciana habitación era despojos;
mi báculo más corvo y menos fuerte,
vencida de la edad sentí mi espada,
y no hallé cosa en que poner los ojos
que no fuese recuerdo de la muerte.

A Roma, sepultada en sus ruinas

Buscas en Roma a Roma, ¡oh peregrino!
y en Roma misma a Roma no la hallas:
cadáver son las que ostentó murallas,
y tumba de sí propio el Aventino.
Yace, donde reinaba, el Palatino;
y limadas del tiempo las medallas,
más se muestran destrozo a las batallas
de las edades que blasón latino.
Sólo el Tibre quedó, cuya corriente,
si ciudad la regó, ya sepultura
la llora con funesto son doliente.
¡Oh Roma! En tu grandeza, en tu hermosura,
huyó lo que era firme, y solamente
lo fugitivo permanece y dura.

He Shows How All Things Warn of Death

I gazed upon my country's tottering walls,
one day grandiose, now rubble on the ground,
worn out by vicious time; only renowned
for weakness in a land where courage fails.
I went into the fields. I saw the sun
drinking the springs just melted from the ice,
and cattle moaning as the forests climb
against the thinning day, now overrun
with shade. I went into my house. I saw
my old room yellowed with the sickening breath
of age, my cane flimsier than before.
I felt my sword coffined in rust, and walked
about, and everything I looked at bore
a warning of the wasted gaze of death.

To Rome, Buried in Its Ruins

You look in Rome for Rome, O peregrine!
You cannot find the site of Rome in Rome.
What glowed as walls is now a corpse's home,
a tomb for its own being, the Aventine.
The Palatine lies ruined, a mere cage,
and its medallions are filed down by time;
destruction from the battle wounds of age
command great Latin emblems now in slime.
Only the Tiber flows, yet its current
watering the city now is watering a tomb
for which it mourns in painful funeral song.
O Rome! of your magnificence a tent
remains; gone is your beauty, depth. A room
of darting lights endures to make us long.

Pronuncia con sus nombres
los trastos y miserias de la vida

La vida empieza con lágrimas y caca,
luego viene la mu, con mama y coco,
síguense las viruelas, baba y moco,
y luego llega el trompo y la matraca.
En creciendo, la amiga y la sonsaca,
con ella embiste el apetito loco;
en subiendo a mancebo, todo es poco,
y después la intención peca en bellaca.
Llega a ser hombre y todo lo trabuca;
soltero, sigue toda perendeca;
casada, se convierte en mala cuca.
Viejo, encanece, arrúgase y se seca;
llega la muerte y todo lo bazuca,
y lo que deja paga, y lo que peca.

Significa la propia brevedad de la vida, sin pensar
y con padecer, salteada de la muerte

¡Fue sueño ayer, mañana será tierra;
poco antes nada, y poco después humo,
y destino ambiciones, y presumo
apenas punto al cerco que me cierra!
Breve combate de importuna guerra,
en mi defensa soy peligro sumo,
y mientras con mis armas me consumo,
menos me hospeda el cuerpo que me entierra.
Ya no es ayer, mañana no ha llegado,
hoy pasa, y es, y fue con movimiento,
que a la muerte me lleva despeñado.
Azadas son la hora y el momento,
que, a jornal de mi pena y mi cuidado,
cavan en mi vivir mi monumento.

He Enumerates, with Proper Terms,
the Mishaps and Miseries of Life

A life begins with tears and turds. Then come
the gurgles, mamas, and the bogeyman,
followed by smallpox, drivel, snot and scum,
then rattles, spinning tops, a noisy can.
Grown up he finds a girlfriend to seduce
with whom he gluts his crazy appetite.
As a young man he feels his words are trite
and every declaration a mere ruse.
As a real man he is a hopeless pest,
a bachelor chasing every hooker in
the street. Married he's cuckold in his nest.
As an old man he wrinkles, dries up, grays.
And when death comes, upturning all, he pays
for gurgles, girlfriends, and each groaning sin.

He Points Out the Brevity of Life, Unthinking
and Suffering, Surprised by Death

My yesterday was dream, tomorrow earth:
nothing a while ago, and later smoke;
ambitions and pretensions I invoke,
blind to the walls that wall me in from birth.
In the brief combat of a futile war
I am the peril of my strategy,
and while cut down by my own scimitar
my body doesn't house but buries me.
Gone now is yesterday, tomorrow has
not come; today speeds by, it is, it was,
a motion flinging me toward death. The hour,
even the moment, is a sharpened spade
which for the wages in my painful tower
digs out a monument from my brief day.

La vida fugitiva

Todo tras sí lo lleva el año breve
de la vida mortal, burlando el brío,
al acero valiente, al mármol frío,
que contra el tiempo su dureza atreve.
Antes que sepa andar, el pie se mueve
camino de la muerte, donde envío
mi vida oscura; pobre y turbio río,
que negro mar con altas ondas bebe.
Todo corto momento es paso largo,
que doy a mi pesar en tal jornada,
pues parado y durmiendo siempre aguijo;
breve suspiro, y último, y amargo,
es la muerte forzosa y heredada;
mas si es ley, y no pena, ¿qué me aflijo?

Represéntase la brevedad de lo que vive
y cuán nada parece lo que se vivió

¡Ah de la vida! ¡Nadie me responde?
Aquí de los antaños que he vivido;
la fortuna mis tiempos han mordido;
las horas mi locura las esconde.
¡Que sin poder saber cómo ni adónde,
la salud y la edad se hayan huído!
Falta la vida, asiste lo vivido
y no hay calamidad que no me ronde.
Ayer se fue, mañana no ha llegado,
hoy se está yendo sin parar un punto;
soy un fue, y un seré y un es cansado.
En el hoy, y mañana, y ayer, junto
pañales y mortaja, y he quedado
presentes sucesiones de difunto.

Fleeting Life

The brief year of a human life carts all
away, turning bravado on the wheel
of folly as it pits a hardened wall
of frozen marble and courageous steel
against the teeth of time. Before the foot
learns how to walk, it takes the road of death.
On it I loose my obscure life, a rut
for my dark river swallowed in a breath
of black sea and high waves. Brief moments are
long steps, reluctant, on this road I take,
and standing, even sleeping, I spur on.
Inherited, forced death is quick, is far,
an ultimate brief bitter sigh, last dawn.
Since it is law, not punishment, why ache?

Described Is the Brevity of What Is Being Lived and How What Has Been Lived Seems to Be Nothing

Where are you, life! Can no one answer me?
My early days I simply wasted here;
Fate has comsumed my temples, robbed each year,
the hours have hid my madness thoroughly.
How helpless not to have a clue of how
and where my health and age have fled my gaze!
My life is void, I'm haunted by old ways,
and every cataclysm plagues me now.
The past is gone; tomorrow hasn't come;
unceasingly the now is racing by.
I am a was, a will be, and a weary am.
To now, tomorrow, and the past I tie
diapers and winding sheet. I am a bed
of torturing successions of the dead.

Conoce las fuerzas del tiempo
y el ejecutivo cobrador de la muerte

¡Cómo de entre mis manos te resbalas!
¡Oh, cómo te deslizas, edad mía!
¡Qué mudos pasos traes, oh muerte fría!
¡Pues con callado pie todo lo igualas!
Feroz de tierra, el débil muro escalas,
en quien lozana juventud se fía;
mas ya mi corazón del postrer día
atiende el vuelo, sin mirar las alas.
¡Oh condición mortal! ¡Oh dura suerte,
que no puedo querer vivir mañana
sin la pensión de procurar mi muerte!
Cualquier instante de la vida humana
es nueva ejecución, con que me advierte
cuán frágil es, cuán mísera, cuán vana.

Repite la fragilidad de la vida y señala
sus engaños y sus enemigos

¿Qué otra cosa es verdad, sino pobreza,
en esta vida frágil y liviana?
Los dos embustes de la vida humana
desde la cuna son honra y riqueza.
El tiempo, que ni vuelve ni tropieza,
en horas fugitivas la devana;
y en errado anhelar, siempre tirana,
la fortuna fatiga su flaqueza.
Vive muerte callada y divertida
la vida misma; la salud es guerra
de su propio alimento combatida.
¡Oh, cuánto inadvertido el hombre yerra
que en tierra teme que caerá la vida,
y no ve que, en viviendo, cayó en tierra!

He Is Familiar with the Forces of Time
and the Fact That Death Is an Insistent Collector

O how you slide away out of my hands!
O how my age slithers into the earth!
What muted steps you take, O frozen death,
cutting down silently until all stands
the same! Voracious for the earth, you spring
over the flimsy wall where green youth lay.
My heart already waits for that last day,
heeding the flight, not looking at its wing.
O mortal situation! O coarse fate!
I cannot live tomorrow without weight
of my death leaning on me now! And each
quick second of this human life is plain-
ly a decree—warning me in plain speech:
how all is fragile, miserable, and vain.

He Cites the Fragility of Life and Points Out
Its Tricks and Its Enemies

What other thing is true but poverty
in a life frail and fed by trivial strife?
From cradle on, the ruins of human life
are traps of honor and prosperity,
and time that never stumbles or comes back
spools out its hours, renders them fugitive;
in errant craving, always punitive,
our fortune wastes us weary on the wrack.
Silent death lives, and life itself becomes
a joke, a game; our health turns into war,
assaulted by its very nourishment.
Oh how a man blunders through unseen scum!
On earth I fear I'll fall and disappear,
yet fail to see by living I ferment.

En vano busca la tranquilidad

A fugitivas sombras doy abrazos,
en los sueños se cansa el alma mía,
paso luchando a solas noche y día
con un trasgo que traigo entre mis brazos.
Cuando le quiero más ceñir con lazos,
y viendo mi sudor se me desvía,
vuelvo con nueva fuerza a mi porfía
y temas con amor me hacen pedazos.
Voyme a vengar en una imagen vana
que no se aparta de los ojos míos;
búrlame, y de burlarme corre ufana.
Empiézola a seguir, fáltanme bríos,
y como de alcanzarla tengo gana,
hago correr tras ella el llanto en ríos.

Amor constante más allá de la muerte

Cerrar podrá mis ojos la postrera
sombra, que me llevare el blanco día;
y podrá desatar esta alma mía
hora a su afán ansioso lisonjera;
mas no de esotra parte en la ribera
dejará la memoria en donde ardía;
nadar sabe mi llama la agua fría.
y perder el respeto a ley severa;
alma a quien todo un Dios prisión ha
   sido,
venas que humor a tanto fuego han dado,
medulas que han gloriosamente ardido.
su cuerpo dejarán, no su cuidado;
serán ceniza, mas tendrá sentido;
polvo serán, mas polvo enamorado.

Futilely He Looks for Peace

I hug the shadows as they slip away,
only in dreams my soul stumbles on peace.
Alone I go on battling night and day,
a phantom in my arms I won't release,
and when I want to lash it tighter in
these ropes, watching the sweat fall off of me,
I'm back, lost in my own obstinacy,
with an obsessive love that makes me spin.
I'm out for vengeance. Her false image will
not leave my eyes. She mocks me; in the fact
of making me a fool, I have the shivers.
I start to follow her. I have no will,
yet since I feel like drowning her, my act
is for my dirge to follow her in rivers.

Love Constant Beyond Death

The final shadow that will close my eyes
will in its darkness take me from white day
and instantly untie the soul from lies
and flattery of death, and find its way,
and yet my soul won't leave its memory
of love there on the shore where it has burned:
my flame can swim cold water and has learned
to lose respect for laws' severity.
My soul, whom a God made his prison of,
my veins, which a liquid humor fed to fire,
my marrows, which have gloriously flamed,
will leave their body, never their desire;
they will be ash but ash in feeling framed;
they will be dust but will be dust in love.

Persevera en la exageración de su afecto amoroso y en el exceso de su padecer

En los claustros de l'alma la herida
yace callada; mas consume hambrienta
la vida, que en mis venas alimenta
llama por las medulas extendida.
Bebe el ardor hidrópica mi vida,
que ya ceniza amante y macilenta,
cadáver del incendio hermoso, ostenta
su luz en humo y noche fallecida.
La gente esquivo, y me es horror el día;
dilato en largas voces negro llanto,
que a sordo mar mi ardiente pena envía.
A los suspiros di la voz del canto,
la confusión inunda l'alma mía,
mi corazón es reino del espanto.

Dice que su amor no tiene parte alguna terrestre

Por ser mayor el cerco de oro ardiente
del sor, que el globo opaco de la tierra,
y menos que éste el que a la luna cierra
las tres caras que muestra diferente,
ya la vemos menguante, ya creciente,
ya en la sombra el eclipse nos la entierra.
Mas a los seis planetas no hace guerra,
ni estrella fija sus injurias siente.
La llama de amor que está clavada
en el alto cenit del firmamento,
ni mengua en sombras ni se ve eclipsada.
Las manchas de la tierra nos las siento.
Que no alcanza su noche a la sagrada
región, donde mi fe tiene su asiento.

He Persists in the Exaggeration of His Amorous
Affection and in the Excess of His Suffering

The wound found in the cloisters of the soul
lies silenced but insatiably consumes
my life that through my veins is feeding fumes
and flames into bone marrow, spreading whole.
Drinking up fervor my hydropic life
(which is a lump of amorous coal unfed,
a corpse made out of handsome fire) is rife
with light in smoke, in dark, and dead.
People I shun, and day to me is horror;
in endless voices I dilate black tears
which my hot pain sent off to a deaf sea.
I gave my voice of song to sighs, while fears
and chaos inundate my soul. I see
my heart become a nightly realm of terror.

He Says That His Love Has No Terrestrial Place

Because the border of the burning gold
of sun is vaster than our opaque globe
of earth, and less than earth's enclosing robe
holding the moon's three faces in her fold,
we see her waning or about to grow;
eclipse drops us in shadow on the floor
although across six planets there's no war,
nor does a fixed star feel each hurting blow.
My lover's flame—bare in the airless strip
in the high zenith of the firmament—
never grows weak in shade, nor is eclipsed.
I don't feel stains of earth; I'm ignorant
of how her night lies on her holy face,
that region where my faith has found its place.

Muestra lo que es una mujer despreciada

Disparado esmeril, toro herido,
fuego que libremente se ha soltado,
osa que los hijuelos le han robado,
rayo de pardas nubes escupido.
Serpiente o áspid, con el pie oprimido;
león que las prisiones ha quebrado;
caballo volador desenfrenado;
águila que le tocan a su nido.
Espada que la rige loca mano;
pedernal sacudido del acero;
pólvora a quien llegó encendida mecha.
Villano rico con poder tirano,
víbora, cocodrilo, caimán fiero,
es la mujer, si el hombre la desecha.

Desengaño de las mujeres

Puto es el hombre que de putas, fía,
y puto el que sus gustos apetece,
puto es el estipendo que se ofrece
en pago de su puta compañía.
Puto es el gusto, y puta el alegría
que el rato putaril nos encarece;
y yo diré que es puto a quien parece
que no sois puta vos, señora mía.
Mas llámenme a mí puto enamorado,
si al cabo para puta no os dejare,
y como puto muera yo quemado
si de otras tales putas me pagare:
porque las putas graves son costosas,
y las putillas viles afrentosas.

44

He Depicts What a Slighted Woman Is

A small exploding gun, a wounded bull,
a fire extravagantly on the loose,
claiming her offspring is the vile abuse
of thieves, a lightning bolt spitting clouds full
of murk. A snake or asp, a squashed-down foot,
a lion who has escaped her prison cell;
a flying horse—no reins to keep her put
in place, a nested eagle wild to yell,
a sword gyrated by a maddened hand
and flint compounded out of solid steel;
gunpowder waiting for the burning wick.
Rich peasant with a terrible command,
viper, caiman, ferocious crocodile
is woman—if the man withholds his prick.

Disillusionment with Women

A whore is any man who trusts a whore.
A whore is one who hungers juicily
for whores. Whorish the cash he pays to score
and guarantee their whorish company.
Whorish the taste, whorish the happiness
of moments with a whore. And as for shady
illusions, whores are those who won't confess
that you are also a grand whore, my lady.
But call me also just a whore in love
if I don't leave you as a whore one day,
and like a whore I'll perish burning hot
if I brag about the whores who've come my
    way;
for serious-minded whores now cost a lot
and little cheap ones curse and kick and shove.

La mayor puta de las dos Castillas

La mayor puta de las dos Castillas
yace en este sepulcro, y, bien mirado,
es justo que en capilla esté enterrado
cuerpo que fue sepulcro de capillas.
Sus penitencias no sabré decillas,
pues de correas sin número contado
tan bien con el cordel se ha meneado,
que vino a los gusanos hecha astillas.
Diéronla crecimiento de priores,
después de un pujamiento de donados
que en el siglo vivieron de pernailes.
Aborreció seglares pecadores,
buscó instrumentos vivos y pintados,
porque tienen capillas como frailes.

La voz del ojo, que llamamos pedo

La voz del ojo, que llamamos pedo
(ruiseñor de los putos), detenida,
da muerte a la salud más presumida,
y el propio Preste Juan le tiene miedo.
Mas pronunciada con el labio acedo
y con pujo sonoro despedida,
con pullas y con risa de la vida,
y con puf y con asco siendo quedo.
Cágome en el blasón de los monarcas
que se precian, cercados de tudescos,
de dar la vida y dispensar las Parcas.
Pues en el tribunal de sus gregüescos,
con aflojar y comprimir las arcas,
cualquier culo lo hace con dos cuescos.

The Greatest Whore from All the Two Castiles

The greatest whore from all the two Castiles
lies in this sepulcher, and well observed,
it's right that in a chapel she's interred:
her body was the tomb of friars' drills.
I can't describe her holy penitence
since to an endless chain of belted monks
her shaking ass became a sacred bunk;
their snakes they used to counter abstinence.
They showered her with priestly deep reward,
after each pumping feat, from each good brother
who in our century lives for his thighs.
But all those laymen sinners she abhorred;
she worshiped eager rods that dance and rise
inside her chapel from each prelate lover.

The Voice from the Red Eye We Call a Fart

The voice from the red eye we call a fart
(a nightingale to the male whores) has smell
to kill the health of proud men out of hell,
and even Mongol kings shake in their heart.
It's most distinct when with its sour lip
and sonorous squeeze it lets a big one fly,
giving a life to laughter, filthy drip,
and nauseating puffs that linger by.
I shit on the royal emblem of the kings
who boast, ringed in by Germans and
    buffoons,
how they bequeath us life and shape our
    Fate.
Well, in the court of their broad pantaloons,
by loosening and straining one tight ring,
any fat ass easily farts out his weight.

Que tiene ojo de culo es evidente

Que tiene ojo de culo es evidente,
y manojo de llaves, tu sol rojo,
y que tiene por niña en aquel ojo
atestado mojón duro y caliente.
Tendrá legañas necesariamente
la pestaña erizada como abrojo,
y guiñará con lo amarillo y flojo
todas las veces que a pujar se siente.
¿Tendrá mejor metal de voz su pedo
que el de la mal vestida mallorquina?
Ni lo quiero probar ni lo concedo.
La mierda es mierda, y su orina, orina;
sólo que ésta es verdad y esotra enredo,
y estánme encareciendo la letrina.

Góngora

Yo te untaré mis versos con tocino,
porque no me los muerdas, Gongorilla,
perro de los ingenios de Castilla,
docto en pullas, cual mozo de camino.
Apenas hombre, sacerdote indino,
que aprendiste sin *christus* la cartilla,
hecho carnero en Córdoba y Sevilla
y bufón en la corte, a lo divino.
¿Por qué censuras tú la lengua griega,
siendo sólo rabí de la judía,
cosa que tu nariz aun no lo niega?
No escribas versos más, por vida mía;
que aun aquesto de escribas se te pega,
pues tienes de sayón la rebeldía.

That Your Ass Has a Nether Eye Is Clear

That your ass has a nether eye is clear,
and your red sun a handful of wet keys;
the pupil of that winking eye looks blear,
squeezing back hot and blackened soggy cheese.
Of course its lashes stiffened like a thorn
have the moist duty to conceal the eye,
and every time it feels like pushing corn
it blinks against the yellow lumps of pie.
Will your fart have a better roar than ones
by the disheveled poor Mallorca whore?
I'm not about to try it, I admit.
Your piss is piss and yes, your shit is shit.
That is the only truth, the rest a bore,
and now I feel an urge to purge my buns.

Góngora

I will annoint my works with bacon juice
so you won't try to bite them, Gongorilla,
dog of the men of genius of Castilla,
learned in farts, a streetboy on the loose.
Hardly a man, not worthy as a priest,
learning creed like a Christless imbecile,
a cuckold in Córdoba and Seville,
and in the Court a clowning preachy beast.
Why do you look for faults in the Greek tongue
when you are just a rabbi of the Jews,
a matter which your nose cannot deny?
Don't scrawl more poems—save us, God in the sky!—
though being a scribe is right for one among
those executioners and vengeful crews.

A una nariz

Érase un hombre a una nariz pegado,
érase una nariz superlativa,
érase una nariz sayón y escriba,
érase un peje espada muy barbado.
Era un reloj de sol más encarado,
érase una alquitara pensativa,
érase un elefante boca arriba,
era Ovidio Nasón más narizado
Érase un espolón de una galera,
érase una pirámide de Egito,
las doce tribus de narices era.
Érase un naricísimo infinito,
Frisón archinariz, caratulera,
Sabañón garrafal morado y frito.

Sacamuelas que quería concluir con la herramienta de una boca

¡Oh tú, que comes con ajenas muelas,
mascando con los dientes que nos mascas,
y con los dedos gomias y tarascas
las encías pellizcas y repelas;
tú, que los mordiscones desconsuelas,
pues en las mismas sopas los atascas,
cuando en el migajón corren borrascas
las quijadas que dejas bisabuelas;
por ti reta las bocas la corteza,
revienta la avellana de valiente,
y su cáscara ostenta fortaleza!
Quitarnos el dolor quitando el diente
es quitar el dolor de la cabeza,
quitando la cabeza que le siente.

To a Nose

There was a man appended to a nose,
a nose imposing like a towering hill,
a beaker from a half-dead dripping still,
a bent-beard swordfish never in repose.
It was a sundial crooked as a crime,
an elephant, its snout on high, a blur
of nostrils on a scribe and executioner
and Ovid Naso in his nosy prime.
It was a galley's pointed battering ram;
it spread like an Egyptian pyramid
and was twelve tribes of noses of a nation.
It was a noseness grown ad nauseam,
a mask, a Frisian archnose ugly as a squid,
a fried and purple swollen ulceration.

The Toothpuller Who Wanted to Turn a Mouth into a Grinding Machine

O you who eat with someone else's teeth,
chewing with molars, mumbling groans to us,
your gluttonous dragon fingers bite beneath
the gums, and pinch and nibble flesh and pus.
You who dissuade us from indulgent forms
of eating dive into a soup like stones
down wells; for a few crumbs, in rampant storms
you plunge in with your grandmother's jawbones.
Because of you, a peeling blames a mouth,
a hazelnut explodes in brave defeat,
its shell still boasting it a fortress bed.
Relieving hurt by pulling out a tooth
is getting rid of pain from head to feet,
and feels the same as pulling off your head.

Médico que, para un mal que no quita,
receta muchos

La losa en sortijón pronosticada,
y por boca una sala de viuda,
la habla entre ventosas y entre ayuda,
con el *denle a cenar poquito o nada.*
La mula en el zaguán tumba enfrenada,
y por julio, un *arrópenle si suda;*
no beba vino, menos agua cruda;
la hembra, ni por sueños ni pintada.
Haz la cuenta conmigo, dotorcillo,
para quitarme un mal, ¿me das mil males?
¿Estudias medicina o Peralvillo?
Desta cura me pides ocho reales;
yo quiero hembra, y vino, y tabardillo,
y gasten tu salud los hospitales.

Significa la interesable correspondencia
de la vida humana

El ciego lleva a cuestas al tullido;
dígola maña y caridad la niego;
pues en ojos los pies le paga al ciego
el cojo, sólo para sí impedido.
El mundo en estos dos está entendido,
si a discurrir en sus astucias llego;
pues yo te asisto a ti por tu talego;
tú, en lo que sé, cobrar de mí has querido.
Si tú me das los pies, te doy los ojos;
todo este mundo es trueco interesado,
y despojos se cambian por despojos.
Ciegos, con todos hablo escarmentado;
pues unos somos ciegos y otros cojos,
ande el pie con el ojo remendado.

A Doctor Who for an Ill He Doesn't Cure
Prescribes Many Others

Prognosticated is the grave's round clay,
and from his mouth a widow's sunny room.
He speaks and for his farts she has to pay,
for his "Just feed him tidbits for the tomb."
His waiting room? A bridled mule drops dead;
July? He orders: "Bundle him to sweat;
no wine, no unboiled water in his bed,
no females, not in dreams nor painted wet."
Add up my bill, you pompous doctor squirt.
To cure me once, you sicken me for good.
Did you learn medicine or how to kill?
For your sage cures you kill me with your bill.
I want my wine, my females, want to flirt,
and *you* to rot in bed like stinking cod.

Signifying the Interesting Correspondence
of Things in Human Life

The blind man lugs a cripple on his shoulders;
such charity is but a cunning feat:
with eyes he pays the blindman for his feet;
the cripple by himself cannot hurl boulders.
If I begin to blab about sly ways,
in these two can the world be understood:
well, I took care of you for money's blaze
and you soaked me for everything you could.
If you give me your feet, my eyes you'll find;
in this world all is bartered selfishness
and plunder is exchanged for plunder shared.
I learn from talking with the blind, and yes,
since some of us are cripples, others blind,
the foot is walking with the eye repaired.

Desengaño de la exterior apariencia con
el examen interior y verdadero

¿Miras este gigante corpulento
que con soberbia y gravedad camina?
Pues por de dentro es trapos y fagina,
y un ganapán le sirve de cimiento.
Con su alma vive, y tiene movimiento,
y a donde quiere su grandeza inclina,
mas quien su aspecto rígido examina,
desprecia du figura y ornamento.
Tales son las grandezas aparentes
de la vana ilusión de los tiranos,
fantásticas escorias eminentes.
¿Veslos arder en púrpura, y sus manos
en diamantes y piedras diferentes?
Pues asco dentro son, tierra y gusanos.

Conveniencia de no usar de los ojos,
de los oídos y de la lengua

Oír, ver y callar, remedio fuera
en tiempo que la vista y el oído
y la lengua pudiera ser sentido,
y no delito que ofender pudiera.
Hoy, sordos los remeros con la cera,
golfo navegaré, que (encanecido
de huesos, no de espumas) con bramido
sepulta a quien oyó voz lisonjera.
Sin ser oído y sin oír, ociosos
ojos y orejas, viviré olvidado
del ceño de los hombres poderosos.
Si es delito saber quién ha pecado,
los vicios escudriñen los curiosos,
y viva yo ignorante y ignorado.

Disillusionment with External Appearances, and So an Inner and True Examination

Do you see this fat giant of a man
strolling along with haughty gravity?
Well, inside he's a mess of rags, a pan
of trash, a young brat keeps from anarchy.
He moves about, parading his live soul,
and aims his greatness anywhere he wants;
yet gaze astutely at this emerald mole,
you'll laugh at all the ornaments he flaunts.
Such are the grandiose and pretentious ways
of tyrants living by their vain illusions,
those eminent, fantastic bags of germs.
They burn in purple as their fingers blaze
with diamonds and hard gems in white profusion,
while inside they are nausea, earth, and worms.

Advantages of Not Using Eyes, Ears, and Tongue

To hear, to see, and to say nothing might
heal us in time; let sight and hearing and
the tongue be felt as something fully right
and not transgression ready to offend.
With rowers deaf, wax in their ears, my choice
has been to sail the gulf (which has turned white
from bones and not from foam) whose siren site
entombs those who have heard its flattering voice.
Being unheard, my ears unhearing, my eyes
lazy, I live forgotten to the frown
of forceful men who always rule the world.
If it's a crime to know who's sinned—and spies
and snoopers love to see a vice unfurled—
please let me live unknowing and unknown.

Sor Juana Inés de la Cruz

(1648/51–1695)

Mexico

Sor Juana Inés de la Cruz

A Mexican nun is the last great voice of the Spanish Golden Age

Sor Juana Inés de la Cruz (1648/51–1695) extended the life of the *Siglo de oro*, the Golden Age, until the end of the seventeenth century. In reality the gold had turned to brass by the time Juana Inés was born, some three years afer Quevedo's death. Garcilaso, the mystics, and Cervantes were long dead. Gone also were Góngora and Lope. Tirso de Molina, author of *El burlador de Sevilla*, the first formal Don Juan play, died in 1648, the probable year of Sor Juana's birth. Among the giants only Calderón de la Barca (1600–1681), the great baroque playwright, was still active, along with the painters Zurbarán and Velázquez who lived on into the sixth decade of the century while Sor Juana was an adolescent in colonial Mexico. Not only did her works become popular in her lifetime in Mexico (and in Spain where they were principally published) but until 1725, they went through many editions. Harder to explain is the shift of taste away from the baroque, meaning that only after two centuries of indifference to Sor Juana did the Spanish world do a modern edition of her work, in 1940, when Emilio Abreu Gómez brought out her *Poesías completas* in Mexico City.

After its virtual demise in Spain, the brilliance and complexity of the baroque survived some years in the unique (and last) great voice in the New World—in the poems of Juana Inés. Presumably, the literature from Spain, passed around readily among literary friends in Spain, took a while to reach the Americas. Among her mentors, Sor Juana was a child of the baroque poets Góngora and Quevedo. They were her masters and her model, and to use a musical term, her own poetry has significant literal "quotations" from their work. Taking from both poets—the rhetoric and elusive symbolism of Góngora and the metaphysical profundity of Quevedo—she combined these qualities in the unsurpassed, single long poem of the Golden Age, "Primero sueño" (First dream).

"Primero sueño"—her own title for it was simply "El sueño" (The dream)—is an extended meditation worthy of her contemporary John Donne's "Anniversaries," yet in imagination and intrinsic poetic value, it goes beyond any single, long metaphysical work in English of the time. Only Thomas Traherne's "felicity" poems and his "Centuries of Meditations," so odd and wildly imagistic, have a *parenté d'esprit*. In Traherne's poems as in "First Dream," the body sleeps and the winged soul comes awake and voyages, seeking revelation, and wanders high over the moon. But oddly, Sor Juana's real companion for the rest of her work was her sister poet Anne Bradstreet (1612?–72) who with clear feminist voice was the first great colonial author of English America and its first published poet. Both women came to be called (along with Louise Labé in France), "the tenth Muse," a term applied to Sappho from a couplet in the *Greek Anthology*, falsely attributed to Plato:

> Some say nine Muses—yet count again.
> Gaze on the tenth: Sappho of Lesbos.

> (*Sappho* 180)

It is difficult to know quite why this epithet of pagan divinity, "tenth Muse," feels silly and patronizing, but perhaps it is because it suggests an element of surprise and unreality that a woman could be both a mortal and a major poet. To be so, she must not be mortal but an unreal goddess. The women themselves, Labé, Sor Juana, and Anne Bradstreet, were no silly Muses. Sor Juana's *Response to Sor Filotea* is the first compelling feminist prose document in the West. It is a defense of a woman's right to write and have a room of her own—in her case, a convent cell. A few decades earlier Anne Bradstreet's verses revealed the dramatic plight of the woman poet:

> I am obnoxious to each carping tongue
> Who says my hand a needle better fits,
> A poet's pen all scorn I should thus wrong,
> For such despite they cast on female wits:
> If what I do prove well, it won't advance,
> They'll say it's stol'n, or else it was by chance.

> ("The Prologue")

Sor Juana Inés de la Cruz: A daughter of the Church and her books

Juana Ramírez de Asbaje was born on a hacienda in a village southeast of Mexico City called San Miguel de Nepantla. Nepantla in Nahuatl signifies "land in the middle," and her village lay between the great volcanoes of Popocatépetl and Ixtacihuatl. Her mother, Isabel Ramírez de Santillana, was a small landowner of the larger hacienda in this high, fertile region on the route Cortez took when he marched with invading troops from the coast toward the Aztec capital of Tenochtitlán (now Mexico City). Isabel was a *criolla*, meaning a Spaniard born in New Spain: the viceroyalty of Mexico, Central America, the Indies, and Philippines from 1535–1821. Her father, Pedro Manuel de Asbaje, came from the Basque province of Guipúzcoa. Juana was a "daughter of the Church"—a euphemism of the day to say that she was illegitimate.

The young Juana scarcely knew her father, whom she did not see after childhood, and there is even uncertainty as to whether his name was Asbaje or Asvaje or Azuaje. His indeterminate name reflects the traditional social question of ascertaining fatherhood in contrast to the normal certitude of the true mother and recalls the similar dilemma over the father's name in the case of her poetic ancestor, the first "tenth Muse," Sappho: "Her father's name was given by Herodotos as Skamandronymos; but it also appears as Skamandros, Skamon, Eunoninos, Eurygyos, Euarchos, Ekrytos, Semos, and Simon. Her mother's name was Kleis" (*Sappho* 271). We have further information on Juana's mother from her will, which declares that she, Doña Isabel Ramírez de Santillana, is the mother of six children, five female and one male, all illegitimate, the first three conceived with Pedro Manuel de Asbaje and three more with Captain Diego Ruiz Lozano.

We may ask how Juana Ramírez, "a daughter of the Church," was able to become the foremost literary figure in the New World. Octavio Paz, in his superb study of Sor Juana's life, work, and thought, to which we are all indebted, informs us that Isabel Ramírez was a woman of very strong character who managed a hacienda with skill and authority and obviously cared for and helped her children. Further, Paz gives us a general picture of the mores in seventeenth-century Mexico, which explains, if not Juana's genius, the possibility that her time afforded her to develop and reveal it:

Landholders, clerics, captains, nuns: how did these people reconcile their strong beliefs with Isabel Ramírez's love affairs? How were the sisters of Juana Inés able to marry and how did she herself succeed in being accepted into the palace to become a lady-in-waiting to the Vicereine? How can the harmony among sisters and mother be explained? We must modify our ideas about seventeenth-century morality. Sexual orthodoxy was much less rigorous than religious orthodoxy. The Ramírezes were a typical criollo family, as were their relatives. . . . Contemporary documents reveal that the behavior of Isabel Ramírez was far from being a scandalous exception. Everyone accepted without reserve the existence of natural children, and José Miguel de Torres, secretary of the university and father of several clerics and nuns, found nothing particularly censurable in the bastardy of his wife or that of many of his nieces and nephews. (Paz 67–68)

So while political and religious orthodoxies were dangerous to offend, the passions of the senses were safer terrain, and "free behavior" by women, Paz contends, would not seem to have any great effect on the reputation of a woman or on her ability to marry well and place her children in the Church, university, and military. We have the confluence of extreme religiosity and extreme sensuality: the equivalent of John Donne writing libertine poems and devout sermons. Paz, who has often provoked his Mexican people, "the children of the mire," into confronting their history and traditions, offers his own offbeat homily: "The lax sexual morality of the Mexican people is surely a legacy of New Spain. It is unwise to condemn it: if machismo is a tyranny that darkens relations between man and woman, erotic freedom illumines them" (71).

Despite this picture of sexual tolerance, even illumination, and the fact that Isabel Ramírez was able to marry her other children off to people of modest distinction, Juana, as Paz and others have commented, was later disadvantaged at the court in regard to marriage because she was essentially an orphan without a real dowry. These facts probably entered into her decision not to seek marriage but a life in the convent. There at least she could write and did so. But Juana was also to suffer criticism from the Church for the erotic implications and religious impropriety of her profane poems as well as for the very activity of her writings, their publication, and her intellectual investigations. Her famous *Response* to the bishop's accusations was articulate in its prose but disastrous for her life. In response to tormenting criticism, she chose a way leading directly to literary silence.

A young reader

As a young girl Juana was precocious in reading, writing, and literary composition. In her autobiographical observations she describes herself as imaginative and mischievous in her childhood. We gather some idea of her extraordinary notions of the physical and spiritual universe, which she was to elaborate in her "First dream" in the *Response to Sor Filotea* ("Filotea" was a pseudonym for the bishop of Puebla who had chastised her): "Once in my presence two young girls were spinning a top, and scarcely had I seen the motion and the figure described when I began, out of this madness of mine, to meditate on the effortless *motus* of the spherical form, and how the impulse persisted even when free and independent of its cause" (*Sor Juana Anthology* 225).

Sor Juana Inés de la Cruz

Juana learned to read at the age of three by tagging along with an older sister who was being tutored by a teacher, perhaps her grandmother. The source for information on her childhood comes from her *Response* and reveals a young child singularly obsessed with words, writing, Latin, philosophy, theology. After a short time she could read better than her mother, but she kept this a secret, fearing she would hurt her mother's feelings or possibly earn herself a whipping for having acted without her permission. As part of her self-discipline to keep up her reading, she refrained from eating cheese because she heard that it made people stupid, and her desire for learning was stronger than her desire for eating. She also engaged in other forms of mild self-castigation, which recall notions of another great writer of solitude, Franz Kafka. In his journal Kafka tells in meticulous detail how he put nails under the desk top so that if he leaned back to sleep when reading or writing, his knees would come up against the nails and alert him back to his literary duties. Juana used scissors or a knife:

> I began to study Latin in which I believe I took less than twenty lessons, and my concern was so intense that although the natural adornment of hair is so important among women—and especially so in the flower of their youth, I would cut off two or three inches, after first measuring its length. And I made a rule that when it began to grow back to that length without my knowing it, I would cut it again as a punishment for my ignorance. It turned out that it grew back and I hadn't learned what I was supposed to, because the hair grew quickly and I learned slowly. And so I cut it again as a punishment for my ignorance, for it did not seem right to me that my head should be adorned with hair that was so naked in knowledge, which is a more desireable adornment. (*Response* 776)

Her few Latin lessons were enough for her to go on learning by herself. They set her on a course where eventually she would compose poems in Latin. The experience of learning Latin by herself was characteristic, then and later in the convent, of her autodidactic means of accumulating knowledge. She would direct her entire life to adding to the books of her memory. After demonstrating by logic and geometric similes how all important branches of knowledge are related and essential to each other, Sor Juana affirmed her need therefore to study many subjects. And then, after a brief rhetorical flourish of false modesty and self-abasement in which she declares that "not having benefited from all this is due to my own ineptitude and weakness in my understanding, not the fault of diversity" (*Response* 781), she declares that one reason she elected to be a nun was to insure that she might live alone and have no other obligations to intrude in her freedom of study nor community noises to impede the calm silence of her books. Her teacher was her silent books as her classmate was her insentient inkwell.

As proof of the need for knowing the natural world in order to know the divine mysteries, she writes in the *Response* that as a child of a Saint Jerome and a Saint Paul, she herself could not be the idiot daughter (779). She lists the accomplishments of great figures. Without knowledge they would not have been plausible. Could Daniel, she asks, have computed the mysterious meanings of the years and days without arithmetic; how without geometry could the holy arches and holy city of Jerusalem have been constructed; and how without architecture could the great temple of Solomon have been designed by God or could Solomon, his supervisor, have executed those plans? Her reasoning tells us that since the patriarchs had to be fluent in arithmetic and geometry and God himself had to possess architectural knowledge, we too should aspire to that condition of gnosis.

At six or seven Juana heard of the university in Mexico City, and she writes, "I began killing my mother with insistent and annoying requests to be sent there so I could study there" (*Response* 775). She asked that she be dressed as a man so they would let her in. When her mother rejected her strategy, she consoled herself by immersing herself in her grandfather's library. Like Borges, Sor Juana found paradise in the small labyrinth of the family book collection. When she did go on a visit to the capital, she confessed that she had read so many books from that family library that she recited sections at length, at a time when she was hardly old enough, people thought, to know how to speak.

About the time Juana Inés was five or six years old, her father Pedro Manuel de Asbaje left her mother definitively. It is not certain whether he had actually lived in the house, but since Sor Juana scarcely mentions her father, it is probable that after his departure she did not see him or had little or nothing to do with him. But was he really dead in her mind? Octavio Paz thinks not. In fact he hypothesizes that he may be the fantasized lover of her poems and she, the widow of that relationship. She may have taken her mother's place:

> The absent father, if not dead, had disappeared. His absence provoked nostalgia and idealization: in our fantasy the absent loom large as either heroes or monsters. Maybe her feelings were not those of pride but those of grief and shame: how could she have known whether he was adventurer or wretch, dissolute hidalgo or unworthy priest? In any case, the image she had of her father, as I have said, was a mixture of resentment,

nostalgia, and—why not?—secret admiration. If, as her attitude suggests, she killed him in her imagination and buried him in silence, her poetry exhumed him, transfiguring them both: she was his widow and he her dead husband. (Paz 75)

A confusion of lovers

If her biological father was now a haunting ghost, her mother's new lover, Captain Diego Ruiz Lozano, was a physical presence and usurper of her father in the household, a role Juana herself held in part by the very nature of her studies and prestige ensuing therefrom. But it seems that her stepfather, Ruiz Lozano, treated the children well, as he did his own children he was to have with Juana's mother Isabel; and he provided for her education in the convent of San Jerónimo and legally pledged a dowry if the need arose. The very presence of the new lover provided the possibility for the child and adult Sor Juana to idealize and transform her real father into that very real lover/spouse who figures in her love poems.

The lover in her poems is not without psychological foundation (whatever the source of inspiration), not without passion, and certainly not merely a *convention* of Petrarchan or Neoplatonic idealization, as some critics who read her poems lightly have supposed. Along with her original voice there are, of course, Petrarchan or Neoplatonic echoes—as there were throughout European literatures in those centuries. Echo, influence, and emulation are inevitable if we dare assume the existence of canon and tradition. Terminological notions should not, however, lead the reader away from her expression of love—whether it was actual (from secret or unreported friendships at court or convent) or imagined; whether conscious or deeply transposed from the unconscious. Through Sor Juana's cunning art and passion, the voice in each poem is fully realized.

Having speculated on the background of the love poems, I also wish to argue for letting them stand alone. They need no explanatory justification. The love poems are powerful and should not be overread contextually to the point of their losing autonomous, artistic being. And it is certainly absurd to refute the love element by asserting that Sor Juana was merely a nun. Insofar as my awareness of Sor Juana as a nun colors my reading—and surely it must—I confess that, given her complete dedication as a woman of letters, her being a nun intensifies and dramatizes the love situation. And beyond who Sor Juana was or was not, beyond biography and psychological conjecture, it is only fair to look first at the poem. Who reads Lope or Tirso and colors each love passage, reducing it to the notion that it was composed by a priest or a monk?

The question of the relation between the life of the poet and the poems is always, and particularly today, a critical focus of argument in literary theory. The balance between a reader's external knowledge of the poet's life and work, on the one hand, and the autonomy of the poem, on the other, is always debatable. There were causes for her inventive and imaginative love poems, but to read Juana Inés as a primarily confessional poet (which she was not) is to deprive a seventeenth-century baroque artist of her imagination and to encode her work into nineteenth-century strategies of romantic allusion and evasion. In the astonishing instance of Sor Juana, these questions of voice appear to loom larger. I prefer to believe, however, that a fair reading of the poems will overwhelm the reader and that questions of speaker will be muted, allowing the poems to live in their own space. In her relentlessly metaphysical poems, Sor Juana acknowledges illusion and the images of her invention. We should accept her assertion of fantasy as put forward in "Que contiene una fantasía contenta" (In which her fantasy is contented):

> Don't leave me, shadow of my love, elusive
> and obsessed image which I care for most,
> handsome deceit for whom I'd be a ghost,
> sweet fiction for which pain is not abusive.
> If my own body of obedient steel
> serves as a magnet fated to your grace,
> why flatter me with lover's commonplace,
> only to drop me, run, while I congeal?
> And yet you cannot brag of anything,
> of any triumph through your tyranny.
> If you elude the narrow noose I've set
> to capture your fantastic form, and spring
> out of my arms, who cares? You flee, and yet
> I've got you locked up in my fantasy.

As for her mother, the real, earthly, sexual, active companion of men, Juana was ambivalent. She rejected her mother insofar as she, Sor Juana Inés, turned to a spiritual sublimation of the world, and conversely, she identified with her mother insofar as she, the daughter, transformed her father-ghost into the lover in the sonnets and elsewhere. Let us remember that Sor Juana Inés de la Cruz assumed the female name corresponding to San Juan de la Cruz, the mystical poet-saint of erotic love in the text and of mystico-erotic love in its interpretation. (I exclude San Juan's own books of interpretive commentary, whose theological discourse is radically intentional but irrelevant to the poems.) Like Juan de la Cruz, Juana Inés de la Cruz was not unwilling to assume the voice, for whatever reasons and implications, of the passionate lover.

The poet San Juan de la Cruz appears throughout Sor Juana's

own verse as a literary model for her *liras* (the *lira* is a five-line stanza, sometimes six-line, in endecasyllables and octosyllables, borrowed by Spanish Renaissance poets from the Italian). Her play *El divino Narciso* (The divine Narcissus) draws its imagery and pastoral eros from San Juan's discursive *liras* in "The Spiritual Canticle" based on the biblical Song of Songs. More important, San Juan's own erotic mysticism, in which fully sensual physical love is the simile for mystical union with God, is expressed in the voice of a woman in his three major mystical poems: "The Dark Night of the Soul," "O Living Flame of Love," and "The Spiritual Canticle." It would have been inappropriate for San Juan to have spoken through a male speaker while making love with the male godhead. So we read in the opening lines of "Dark Night": "En una noche oscura / con ansias en amores inflamada" (On a dark and obscure night, inflamed with hunger for love) and the key word is *inflamada*, "inflamed," with the feminine ending. Juan spoke in the voice of a Juana.

While it is excessive to read, as some critics do, a religious or mystical dimension into Sor Juana's love poems, it is equally wrong to deprive Sor Juana of a literal reading in favor of a forced symbolic or allegorical one when she records passionate human love—its hopes and despairs—between woman and man. The same disfavoring of sensual literality is normal in most readings of San Juan de la Cruz's poems modeled after the erotic Song of Songs, just as until Denys Page's *Sappho and Acaeus* in 1955, the lesbian element in Sappho's love lyrics was uniformly ignored or denied by serious European and American classical scholars. Even in the *Response*, Sor Juana's defiant defense (against her critics) of a woman's right to write, she is not immune to misreading for purposes of concealing eroticism. In the least-interesting, rhetorically polite, and pious beginnings of the *Response* (a section I take to be more satirically pious than genuine), Sor Juana Inés repeats the conventional dismissal of the canticles' surface meaning by quoting Jerome's warning, for "the young who read the Song of Songs will be harmed if they do not perceive that praise of a spiritual wedding happens to be expressed in carnal words" (*Response* 773).

In sum, if others force religion into her love poems or expunge the clear, profound expression of human love, reducing the surface text to mere symbolism, that is the problem of the overintentional reader. Sor Juana would have none of that interference, that interpretive judgment that carried with it praise, prescription, and proscription. In reality, less than a tenth of Sor Juana's poems are religious, and even these are largely occasion poems. She stood her ground against the censorship of the clergy, and in *Response to Sor Filotea*, she upheld her right to write what she wished. Juana is not alone among those in the Church who wrote what she wished. Góngora and Lope de Vega are scarcely associated with the cloth, yet Góngora was a prebendary and Lope a priest—and they wrote whatever they cared to. Calderón de la Barca and Tirso de Molina who gave us the Don Juan figure were also in the Church. But they were men and in Spain, not in the provinces of New Spain. Clearly in her earlier years, Sor Juana too wrote what she cared to, following, at least outwardly, the conventions and tastes of the time. Yet when a gale of ecclesiatical intolerance struck her in the form of a bishop's admonitions, she recorded her long document of defiance, declaring "her room of her own." And she composed her response with acuity and strength three centuries before Virginia Woolf's critical manifesto.

A young writer in the library

Juana's literary precosity continued. At the age of eight, she wrote a *loa* (a "praise" or short dramatic poem serving as introduction to a sacred play) for a religious festival celebrated in a church in neighboring Amecameca. Her library books and her writing began to inhabit a room where they become her surrogate life, a life which she chose in lieu of the one with carnal and ordinary reality, a literary realm in which from flesh to spirit she created her own habitat. Her later "total antipathy for marriage" is all intriguingly contradicted in her marriage to the word, wherein she created lovers. Like Emily Dickinson, the nun of Amherst, her pen was passionately creative, and she was alive in its creations. These women inhabited New England attic or convent cell of the word.

Given the word as the immense worldly center of Juana's life, it was natural that she moved from her grandfather's library to the convent where she had one of the most complete and sophisticated private collections of books in New Spain. (Even here, the report of it is not confirmed. It was said to contain four thousand volumes, making it one of the primary collections, especially in mathematics and the sciences, in the seventeenth-century New World. There is a possibility that the four thousand were actually four hundred select books, but this would still have put her in possession of perhaps the largest personal library of the time.) Those books, which inspired her creation, also charted the borders of her solitude.

We are not certain of Juana's childhood after her eighth year. What is probable is that when she was about eight or ten, she left her mother's hacienda (now at Panoayán where she grew up) and went to the city of Mexico. There she lived in the house of her mother's sister María, who was married to Juan de Mata, a wealthy man close to the viceregal palace. Juana took possession of Mata's ample library. Again the fatherless daughter, beautiful, clever, poor but aided by relatives, found a fine place to escape into and nourish her obsession to read and know. In regard to the move to the capital, Alan Trueblood speaks of "Juana on the solitary course to which the superiority of her mind predestined her, a course followed henceforth with the avidity and tenacity of the inspired autodidact" (Trueblood 2).

Light in the palace court

After eight years of self-instruction—and in her autobiographical letter she writes wistfully of lacking fellow students and a teacher—in 1665, when she was still sixteen, Juana entered the viceroy's palace in the capital where she became a lady-in-waiting to the vicereine Doña Leonor Carreto, the marquise of Mancera. Sor Juana was fortunate, for the vicereine, who cared for literature on her own, was sensitive and attendant to the young woman's intelligence and talents.

At the worldly court Juana was a brilliant figure of wit, charm, beauty. Intellectually she was a protégée. At the same time, one learns from her autobiographical letter that amid the glamor and surfaces of court activities, she possessed a gravity and determination of iron. Throughout her life, later as a nun and perhaps even as a result of her convent life, she managed to maintain her spirit of remarkable independence. That stubborn intelligence showed itself to its fullest in her daring assertions and retorts to the criticisms and suggestions in her response to Sor Filotea—that is, the bishop. At the court she was, for some four years, Leonor Carreto's favorite amid the soirées, balls, and ceremonies and all the formal and informal rites that took place in that palace center of the world's largest empire.

One of the principal preoccupations of the royal court in the Americas was *galanteo*—courting, wooing, and all kinds of flirtations of the body and spirit. As for Juana's involvement with suitors, we have nothing more than later conjecture—no recollections or letters of the time. Most of the court gallants were married, however, and the eligible ones would hardly be interested in marriage—or, rather, having their mutual families arrange marriage—with a smart beauty who had no dowry, family distinction, nor even natal legitimacy. She was still the fatherless orphan. The unlikeliness of marriage, at least with a court figure, surely contributed to Juana's own adamant rejection of marriage and her ultimate choice to find her worldly and spiritual life in books that she could read in her own cell. But as she says, again citing Jerome, "deprivation is the source of appetite," and whatever the source, personal or imagined, her sonnets, such as "En que satisface un recelo" (In which she satisfies a fear), describe the full intensity of love that surrounded her in those years:

> This afternoon, my love, speaking to you
> since I could see that in your face and walk
> I failed in coming close to you with talk,
> I wanted you to see my heart. Love, who
> supported me in what I longed to do,
> conquered what is impossible to gain.
> Amid my tears that were poured out in pain,
> my heart became distilled and broken through.
> Enough, my love. Don't be so stiff. Don't let
> these maddening jealousies and arrogance
> haunt you or let your quiet be upset
> by foolish shadows: false signs of a man's
> presence; and as you see my heart which met
> your touch—now it is liquid in your hands.

One of the delightful stories, probably true, is recounted by her contemporary biographer, the Jesuit father Diego Callejas, based on the viceroy's recollection. (Even today the main sources for biographical information remain the *Response*, our richest source; the Callejas brief biographical essay based on the *Response*; and her poems.) The viceroy, wishing to test the diversity and amazing wisdom of the young woman, gathered all the men of letters at the university and in the city of Mexico, which included the forty leading theologians, scripturists, philosophers, mathematicians, historians, poets, and humanists. Through oral questions and disputations, the marquis of Mancera arranged to have these authorities engage the intellect of the young Juana—as the twelve-year-old Jesus engaged the doctors of the temple. The marquis said that the mind cannot conceive what he witnessed. Callejas tells us that she extricated herself from the questions and objections that each expert directed against her "in the manner of a royal galleon fending off the attacks of a few canoes."

Choosing convent walls to secure freedom

In 1667, at age nineteen and apparently at the height of her admiration by the literati and the court society, Juana Inés entered the convent of San José de las Carmelitas Descalzas. The discalced Carmelites in this austere order of shoeless nuns held to the position and aspirations of its two founding Spanish saints, the mystics Santa Teresa de Avila and San Juan de la Cruz, who battled with the then-dominant shoed monks and nuns in order to have a life that had few temptations of worldly goods and comforts. (In more recent times the Carmelites have adopted sandals as a sign of their shoelessness.) In that struggle, San Juan was imprisoned for nine months in a fish-closet enclosure, whipped weekly by the opposing faction of calced Carmelites, and wrote his poems of darkness, love assignations, and light in the reality of his suffering. Even when his body was consumed by skin cancer, he chose to take refuge in a monastery in Úbeda, in northern Andalusia, where he knew the abbot would be unsympathetic to him and he would be certain of dying with no tempting comforts of this world.

All the deprivations and physical castigations of the Mexican discalced nuns were probably too much for Juana, and after three months as a novice, she left. But she would be a nun. On February 24, 1669, she took the veil in the more permissive Convent of Santa Paula of the Hieronymite order (the order of Saint Jerome). She signed her profession of faith as the "legitimate daughter" of Don Pedro de Asbaje y Vargas Machuca. Given the pomp and gossip of the upper classes (and nuns in Mexico, opposed to their attendant servants or slaves, were almost exclusively from these classes), she had little choice but to lie about her birth. Though not always enforced, the convents had rules of "purity of lineage" for entry into their orders. She was nearly twenty-one. Thereafter she remained cloistered for life within the walls of Santa Paula.

After leaving the court, she was not, however, without her public admirers, and in spirit, apart from her private activities of reading and writing, she had an increasingly sophisticated cultural life in the convent. Sor Juana received the most distinguished guests of the city and the realm, including a succession of viceroys—and especially their wives, who were her friends and strong literary supporters in her cell. Her cell was her court. Her friendship with the viceroys also protected her and her writings against condemnations by the Church; specifically, against Núñez de Miranda, her confessor, and the more formidable Francisco Aguiar y Seijas, the misogynist archbishop of Mexico. In her quarters she wrote poems that found publication and wrote her plays, including the extraordinary *El divino Narciso* (The divine Narcissus) that was published in 1689 in Madrid. Her convent was her library, workplace, literary salon, and place for *tertulias* (literary discussions usually held in a café).

The word *cell* in Spanish, English, and other languages suggests a prison or at least a place of enforced confinement, submission to religious austerity, and a deprivation of profane goods and comforts. But this ecclesiastical term *cell* is misleading and deceptive in the instance of *los monasterios* (the monasteries and convents). The nuns of colonial Mexico, with the exception of discalced Carmelites, lived ordinarily under privileged conditions of the upper classes. Sor Juana's "cell," as we see in portraits made in her personal library, is sumptuously elegant, the walls lined with her handsomely bound books in which is seen an imposing, elegant clock. And the cell was not one room. Most cells in her Saint Jerome convent, founded in 1586, were two-story apartments, including the one sold to Sor Juana, which contained a large sitting room and study, kitchen, bathroom, as well as sleeping quarters for herself and for her servants.

As the cell was not a cell, neither were the vows of poverty anything but nominal as were the rules of communal meals. Nuns normally had between three and five servants and slaves to care for them. It is not clear how many servant-maids Sor Juana had, but it is known that she was attended by Juana de San José, a mulatto slave whom her mother had given to her when she entered the convent. The slave stayed with her for some ten years until Sor Juana sold her for 250 gold pesos to her sister Josefa.

Nuns in Mexican convents dressed elegantly, often wore tasteful and expensive jewelry. Their clothing matched their high position in society. From the splendid portraits of Sor Juana by Juan de Miranda and Miguel Cabrera, we see a strikingly beautiful and aristocratic woman, standing (in Miranda's work) and sitting (in Cabrera's) amid her possessions, decked in a magnificent white tunic with full sleeves, sewn from the most costly cloths obtainable, and gently holding an enormous rosary whose beads extend from her neck down to the hemming of her long gown. She is a princess-nun.

One of the questions that Juana's commentators raise and answer in unison is why an intellectual woman of a strong and independent nature, in whom nothing in "earlier life reveals a particular religious disposition" (Paz 105), should choose to cloister herself in a convent. The commentators I have in mind are Octavio Paz and Sor Juana's consummate translators in English, Margaret Sayers Peden and Alan S. Trueblood. At a time when the the Church controlled education, the convent was a place of learning and a haven. Trueblood observes:

> Though Juana's turning from the worldliness of the court to the seclusion of the cloister may seem abrupt and startling today, it would have appeared less so to her contemporaries. The city of Mexico was full of convents which housed women of the upper classes for whom marriage, for whatever reason, was ruled out. Juana had neither a dowry nor a pedigree. Since all education was the prerogative of the Church, the path of an

exceptional woman who had the temerity to value cultivation of her mind above all else, including marriage, inevitably led to the convent. A woman as clear-sighted as Juana could not have failed to see the fundamental incongruence between her brilliant but superficial situation at court and her profound *amor intellectualis*. (Trueblood 5)

The clearest statement of her intentions we must find and accept in her own words in the *Response*, in which she confesses her initial reasons for entering the convent, reasons she now deems (with painful irony) unworthy and prideful. As everything in this deeply ambivalent letter, we must accept her movement to destroy her initial creative aspirations and the conditions by which they were achieved, since thereafter she sets herself squarely on the way of self-annihilation. Yet as we acknowledge her ultimate abasement, whether its cause was desperation, spite, sorrow, resignation—or some mixture thereof—we must also see her grand intellectual plans and dreams when, *faute de mieux*, she entered the freedom of the convent as a place of letters. She entered the new setting, openly stating what practices she disdained:

> I became a nun, although I knew that it required certain conditions repugnant to my nature (I am speaking of incidental, not essential aspects); nevertheless, given my total antipathy for marriage, it was the least unreasonable and most suitable one I could choose as a means to my desired salvation. All trivial considerations gave way to this primary concern, which was to live alone, to have no obligatory work that would interfere with my freedom to study, or hear no noises of a community that would intrude in the calm silence of my books. (*Response* 776)

As a nun Sor Juana found the time and means to devote herself to letters as well as science. Besides a sober, inquiring mind, Juana possessed the best scientific instruments available in the New World. The importance of her scientific interests should not be underestimated. Even in the *Response* she tells how when one prelate, in the manner of the Inquisition, kept her from her books for three months, it did not stop her from reflecting on all human phenomena that God created. All things of the world became her letters and the great chain of being was her book. Everything she looked at, in the imagination or in the street, she analyzed: those imagined pyramids whose visual lines she tracked in their optical illusions, the changing spirals of girl's spinning tops that she measured by spreading sifted flour on the ground to record the lines, also the lines of her room, which made her calculate the spherical lines of the universe. She has fascinating observations about cooking in which she discovered the secrets of nature, how eggs hang together when fried in fat or oil and disintegrate in syrup, and she makes the following wry observation about her philosophizing while cooking: "If Aristotle had cooked, he would have written much more" (*Response* 791).

"Stupid men imputing shame / on a woman unreasonably"

Sor Juana was consciously a woman in her writing and accused men of imposing a colonial rule on her sex. Her social poetry dealt not with the nation but with the rights of the individual and specifically of a woman in a hostile society in which men appeared to have all the power and moral authority. Her most quoted poem is the *redondilla*, "In Which She Argues As Invalid the Pleasure and Blame of Those Men Who Accuse Women of What They Cause," which begins:

> Stupid men imputing shame
> on a woman unreasonably,
> although you never see
> you cause the things you blame.

The poem is repetitious in its cataloguing and, like other pieces in her poems and poetry, ostentatious in its historical and literary reference, yet for all that, it is powerful and significant. She argues convincingly in perhaps too many stanzas (seventeen). Nevertheless, the poem is extraordinarily effective and ends with a blast, defending the prostitute and the unjustly and hypocritically accused woman. The diction, Sor Juana's special genius, is at once ordinary direct speech and high rhetoric:

> Whose guilt is greater in
> this raw erotic play?
> The girl who sins for pay
> or man who pays for sin?
>
> So why be shocked or taunt
> her for the steps you take?
> Care for her as you make
> her, shape her as you want,
>
> but do not come with pleas
> and later throw them in
> her face, screaming of sin
> when you were at her knees.
>
> You fight us from our birth
> with weapons of arrogance.

Sor Juana Inés de la Cruz

Between promise and pleading stance,
you are devil, flesh, and earth.

Her words bristle. Octavio Paz points out just how far ahead
Sor Juana was in using the weapons of language against male de-
tractors of her sex: "It is surprising that in such a society, with its
combined Arabic and Roman-Christian heritage, Sor Juana could
have published her satire. More surprising still is that it could have
been read with sympathy. But it was an isolated outburst that had
no sequels until the twentieth century" (304).

Her anger against male injustices did not, however, prevent her
from writing some of the most tender and candid love poems in the
Spanish language. Those love poems were not beloved by Don
Manuel Fernández de Santa Cruz, bishop of Puebla, with whom Sor
Juana was to exchange those famous letters concerning a woman's
right to have her own intellectual life. His letter of admonishment,
which he signed Sor Filotea de la Cruz, putting women in their
subservient, silent place, provoked her own reply to Filotea.

As Juana Inés studied books in diverse fields, when she wrote
she used diverse forms and had many voices. She shared Quevedo's
gravity as well as his scatological, aggressive humor, which she
expressed in onomatopoetic sonnets in direct imitation of the Span-
ish master, using Quevedo's rhymes in a burlesque of outraged
indignation against those who think her, as a woman, incompetent.
Here and elsewhere, and especially in the *Response*, on all levels
she can hit back, and with ironic invective. In the burlesque sonnet
on herself, "Inés," she uses Quevedo's harsh rhymes to punch out
her critics, whom she elsewhere refers to as slanderers and liars.
She can be just as coarse, down to earth, and wildly funny as her
opponents:

When they revile you as sly and obscene,
you have no problem getting off the hook,
you launch into your gobbledygook,
knowing just how to wipe your asshole clean,

"What you see here is colorful illusion"

In perhaps her best-known sonnet, "A su retrato" (To her self-
portrait), Sor Juana paints a severe self-portrait, adopting the final
line (as I discuss in the Introduction) directly from a conventional
baroque love sonnet by Góngora; yet what in Góngora is essentially
polite and courtly, she makes demolishingly dark and empty: "is
corpse, is dust, is shadow, and is nothing." So the poem ends with
a Spanish declaration about death that conveys a depressingly stoic

picture of absolute nothingness. She has converted Góngora's *carpe diem* line, offered for purposes of winning over his reluctant gold-haired lady, into her personal restatement of Quevedo's austerely depicted doom. What is singular about Sor Juana's poem is how, in her confrontation with destroying time, she rips away the masks of flattery and self-deception, leaving her alone before the nihilistic truth of death. Even the title of the poem should be looked at with care. Her lines are not a self-portrait but a rejection of a falsely painted self-portrait. When the Neoplatonic philosopher Plotinos was asked to have his portrait painted, he said why make an illusion of an illusion. In her way Sor Juana, who also held to a philosophy of dream, a very harshly defined dream, gave an identical reply in her poem of self-portrait:

> What you see here is colorful illusion,
> an art boasting of beauty and its skill,
> which in false reasoning of color will
> pervert the mind in delicate delusion.
> Here where the flatteries of paint engage
> to vitiate the horrors of the years,
> where softening the rust of time appears
> to triumph over oblivion and age,
> all is a vain, careful disguise of clothing,
> it is a slender blossom in the gale,
> it is a futile port for doom reserved,
> it is a foolish labor that can only fail:
> it is a wasting zeal and, well observed,
> is corpse, is dust, is shadow, and is nothing.

Sor Juana's most ambitious poem, "Primero sueño" (First dream), fully in the Spanish baroque tradition of rhetoric, is a long, meditative, beautiful, difficult poem. Its often-commented-on difficulties, as in the gratuitously symbolic indirections and obscurities of Góngora whom she is imitating, is its least important and least successful quality. Yet for all its stylistic trickeries, her diction in this master work is amazingly inventive and devoid of cliché. In typical offhand modesty, she contends that "First Dream" is a trifle she wrote for her own pleasure—in Spanish *trifle* is rendered from *papelillo*, a scrap of paper—and the only work she did which did not come at the request of others (Response *803*). Apart from its conventional, false authorial modesty—a trait of the age practiced even by Fray Luis de León in the prologue to his poems—her observation really declares that "First Dream" was entirely her creation and that we should take it very seriously.

As in the first- and second-century Hermetic and apocalyptic traditions, the poem describes the voyage of her soul soaring among superlunary spheres, while the harborer of the soul remains behind in deep bodily sleep. As such it is a poem concerning ecstasy in its strictly etymological sense of *ekstasis* of the spirit: "being outside oneself" or "being elsewhere." She attempts to find some philosophical explanation for this world of deceptive appearances and dream just as did Calderón de la Barca in the late Spanish drama *La vida es sueño* (Life is a dream) and Palladas (c. A.D. 400) in late Alexandrian poetry in the midst of Christian iconoclastic destruction of classical civilization. In his quatrain, "A Pagan in Alexandria Considers Life under Christian Mobs Who are Destroying Antiquity," the poet ponders:

> Is it true that we Greeks are really dead
> and only seem alive—in our fallen state
> where we imagine that dream is life?
> Or are we truly alive and is life dead?
>
> (*Sappho 555*)

The theme of dream, appearances, reality, in one form or another, with diverse terminology and from diverse disciplines, is the oldest and most persistent of our metaphysical dilemmas. Sor Juana's sources are traditional ones (some given to her not by direct sources but probably through summaries in manuals): Cicero's account of the dream of Scipio the Younger; Philo, the source of much later mystical ascent, who tells us that the soul has wings to travel amid the choir of planets; the Gnostic works attributed to Hermes Trismegistus; Macrobius's commentary on Scipio's dream; Kepler's *Somnium*; Athanasius Kircher's *Iter extaticum*, 1660.

In the Gnostic "Origin of the World," Eve creates Adam (*The Other Bible* 70). She raises his inert clay form from the mud by uttering her word and instilling breath and life into him. Yet in Adam's afternoon stupor, before he wakes to snitch on Eve's Promethean act of seizing knowledge from the tyrant master, Adam has the absurd dream that Eve came from one of his ribs. There is Plato's world of appearances perhaps best charted in the dream levels of the Allegory of the Cave, there are Plotinos's illusions of illusions, and Cervantes's dream of Alonso Quijano dreaming he is Don Quijote who cannot distinguish windmill from monster. In our time there is Antonio Machado's dreaming real and symbolic interior landscape with his eyes wide open, and Wallace Stevens's insistent confusions of imagination and reality. The world's great dreamers, even when it is Quevedo in his Bosch-like nightmare of *Los sueños* (The visions), usually have good, open-eyed day vision (blind Homer, Milton, and Borges notwithstanding) and cannot or will not divide the mind's energetic lexical and spiritual activity

Sor Juana Inés de la Cruz

from the apparently visible world around of things they must perceive and describe. Woody Allen's play *God* poses questions of metaliterature and metaphysics in lines worthy of Sor Juana's ironic vision when she mixes philosophy and the humorous grotesque. He writes:

> It's bizarre, isn't it? We're two ancient Greeks in Athens and we're about to see a play I wrote and you're acting in, and they're from Queens or some terrible place like that, and that they're watching us in someone else's play. What if they're characters in another play? And someone's watching them? Or what if nothing exists and we're all in somebody's dream? Or, what's worse, what if only that fat guy in the third row exists? (*God* 137)

In Sor Juana, as in the universal questioning of dream and reality, the mind can neither grasp the meaning of external reality nor explain, rationally or intuitively, our inner metaphysical precincts. Spiritually we are a failure—though she expresses these ideas of failure in an art that is in itself a monument to woman's or man's power to create works of beauty. Finally, in a contemporary sense, Juana was supremely aware of the mind's arenas of the conscious and unconscious. The unconscious, which we may call dream, is in Spanish, *sueño*, meaning both sleep and dream. In speaking about the constant activity of her brain, she records that even during sleep her mind is working actively, debating, composing verses, and doing so with acumen and clarity (*Response* 791).

The bishop's letter that was Sor Juana's "crucible of torment"

The incident of the letters, as this exchange has been euphemistically called, masks a documentation of critical oppositions, defiance, and sorrowful resolutions in which ecclesiastical powers are in combat with a woman asserting the independence of her mind, her freedom to create profane works of art, and her right to study, learn, and express her acquired knowledge. Although Sor Juana submitted to authority following the creation of her *Response*, the writing and existence of the *Response* itself is the first document and manifesto of independence we possess, perhaps in any language, of the right of women to pursue lives of learning and to follow artistic and professional careers. It was not only a *carta* (letter) to Sor Filotea, dated March 1, 1691, but, with no excess in the simile, a Magna Carta of women's intellectual and artistic liberty in the Americas and elsewhere in the world.

The background and nominal wrappings of these letters reveal the evasions, flatteries, hypocrisies, and formulaic rhetoric of the day. Under the wrappings is a contest of wit and more significantly, a battle of will and power. The controversy began after Sor Juana wrote a theological letter commenting on a sermon given forty years earlier in Lisbon by Portuguese Jesuit Antonio de Vieyra. She sent her letter to the bishop of Puebla, Manuel Fernández de Santa Cruz. Santa Cruz had her letter published under the title *Carta atenagórica* (Letter worthy of Athena). With unctuous piety he also included an admonishing missive to her, signed, "Sor Filotea de la Cruz, November 25, 1690." He begins with much flattery for her finely cut quill that does honor to her sex. Then, systematically, he cuts her down. He praises her skill in verse meters yet wishes he could compliment her choice of subject, meaning her profane poems. He notes that he himself does not subscribe to the common-place view of condemning the practice of letters by women. He observes that Saint Paul did warn that women should not teach, "but he [Paul] does not command that they not study." And it was his wish (presumably the bishop's under the word of Paul) that she (Sor Juana) "avoid the risk of any presumptuousness in our sex, inclined as it is to vanity." The "our" of "our sex" is consistent with Santa Cruz's speaking through the pseudonym of Filotea. By posing as a "she" within that danger zone of vanity which is woman, he adds an obsequiously arrogant thrust to his dagger against womanhood. By citing Saint Paul, the bishop turned to the most significant abuser of women in western religions. Paul wrote the infamous lines: "But I suffer not a woman to teach, nor to usurp authority over the man, but to be in silence" (1 Tim. 12.12).

Santa Cruz observes that Sor Juana has spent much time with philosophers and poets. It would be better now if she would improve her occupation and upgrade her books. He points to the example of Justus Lipsius, a marvel of erudition, who edited Seneca, but who understood at the end of his life that scholarship not devoted to Christ Crucified is folly and sheer vanity. Finally, he admonishes her:

> It is a pity that so great a mind should stoop to lowly earthbound knowledge and not desire to probe into what transpires in heaven. But since it does lower itself to ground level, may it not descend further still and ponder what goes on in hell! And, if sometimes it enjoys sweet and tender conceits, let it apply its powers of understanding to Calvary, where, seeing how considerate the Redeemer was and how ungrateful the redeemed, it will have ample scope for reflecting on the excesses of infinite love and, not without tears, will find words of atonement for the highest degree of ingratitude. Or, at other times, let the rich galleon of your mind sail usefully forth upon the high seas of the perfections of God. (*Sor Juana Anthology* 202)

After these kinds of warnings, including the open threat of punishment in her afterlife, from his convent in Puebla, Fernández de Santa Cruz assures Sor Juana that he remains enamored of her soul, which is a spiritual love not subject to the vicissitudes of change. His salutation reads: "Your devoted servant kisses your hands. Filotea de la Cruz."

The strange case of Sor Juana and her friend and ally, the bishop of Puebla

How did this incident of the letters start? It began presumably with a friendship and understanding between Sor Juana and the bishop of Puebla that they were in accord in regard to the powers of the Jesuit master of Mexico, Aguiar y Seijas, the archbishop of Mexico City. Without that understanding, it is inconceivable that Juana, as politically sophisticated as she was in balancing crown and Church powers for her own protection, would have dared to send off a letter putting down a Jesuit hero, particularly one who for many years had had a personal and political bond of mutual admiration and support with the Mexican archbishop. Sor Juana's theological letter criticizing an old sermon by the Jesuit Vieyra, its unanticipated and appreciative publication by the bishop of Puebla, coupled with his admonition for her to reform her ways—essentially demanding her to give up secular study and profane writing—spoken in falsely polite, patronizing, and offensive language, all suggest that behind these letters were powerful motives, on both sides, which were surely perfectly apparent to the players in the politico-religious squabbles of the day.

Octavio Paz and Italian critic Dario Puccini have deciphered the letters and revealed the battle lines. Precisely because there were conflicting forces, and with Sor Juana engaged on one side in a war between two powerful clerics and their allies, the consequences for herself were horrendously out of proportion to the dull theological scrapping in her initial polemic on the Portuguese Jesuit missionary in Brazil. At least the suffering and abuse that the events inflicted on her also incited her to write the earliest literation document on a woman's right to know and to create in freedom. I would also say it is a perfectly realized document.

Before the missive was sent out, the adversaries, Puccini asserts, were Fernández de Santa Cruz, bishop of Puebla and Sor Juana's ally, and the enemy, Francisco Aguiar y Seijas, of Mexico City. The prize behind their rivalry was the archbishopric of Mexico City, the most potent ecclesiastical post in New Spain and the Spanish Empire. The figures could not have been more distinct. Santa Cruz was more popular and experienced. He was not a fanatic.

Aguiar y Seijas was, as his biographer Father José de Lezamis describes him, a man who was obsessed with an aversion to anything female—if a woman entered his house he would have the bricks she stepped on removed; he was a man who mortified his body to keep down his lust. And he was one whose fever for charity caused him to plunder those who were too weak to refuse his pious exactions. Furthermore, this man liked to burn books of secular literature, particularly books of plays (Sor Juana was well aware of his opposition to her dramatic works). He even praised God for making him myopic so he would be less likely to cast his eyes upon a woman. Paz says: "His charity was despotism, his humility pride, and his chastity a mental debauch" (409).

Aguiar y Seijas was bishop of Michoacán when the election for archbishop took place. Santa Cruz was chosen on the earlier ballots, but on the fourth and decisive one, apparently through the intervention of Jesuit powers in Madrid, Aguiar y Seijas won out. He was in power. So by attacking the Portuguese Jesuit Vieyra, Sor Juana was striking the Jesuit archbishop of Mexico. Paz concludes: "Sor Juana intervened in the quarrel between two powerful Princes of the Roman church and was destroyed in the process" (403). He speculates further that Santa Cruz wanted Juana to write a critique of Vieyra; and to protect himself from anything less than compliments of the highest piety, he in turn reprimanded his friend Sor Juana for her secular passion for knowledge. Thereby his own views and position were clear and safe from criticism. He used her polemical skills of theological debate in her missive on Vieyra, and she took the heat. After publishing her letter as a work worthy of wise Athena, his own letter to her under the pseudonym Filotea ignored the content of hers on Vieyra and focused on Juana's life in letters, which he demolished. He set her up, and she could not have "foreseen the prelate's cruel desertion" (Paz 414).

The *Response* and the silences

Amid the sorrowful reasoning in her *Response* in which she defends her rights to books and the pen, Sor Juana acknowledges her accusers, bows to them, and states that she has unworthily succumbed to the temptation of her books, learning, and writing, "an inclination that exploded in me like gunpowder," and that henceforth she would give it up. Indeed, she did. The pose of blatant self-modesty in her learning and writing is gone. Indeed, she will give up her intellectual life (while mouthing the expected ecclesiatical claptrap), making clear, however, throughout the letter, her real passion for knowledge. Before her abandonment of personal writing, she articulates in pained detail her feelings and position—her "trap

Sor Juana Inés de la Cruz

of faith" to cite Paz's superb subtitle to his study—that caused her
to choose this radical path of silence.

The *Response* contains Sor Juana's threat of silence, which
would be executed, but the threat is not the essence of the *carta*.
The letter is a biography of her mind, an assertion of her intellectual
and creative freedom, and a refutation of censorial intrusion. The
imminent negation of the ideal Sor Juana is an awful external conse-
quence of the conflict. If in the last four years Sor Juana becomes
the Sor Juana of life's negation and to the delight of her ecclesiastical
biographers she renounces her vital forces, and if in strange repen-
tance before she dies she writes her name on a document in her
own blood (wholly out of character with her reason and unfanatic
poise), we witness a poignant scene: a devastated woman of genius
obliged to abandon the life and art of the mind.

The *Response* is Sor Juana's highest moment of articulate intel-
lectual assertion. By one-third of the way through it, after she has
admirably argued for the necessity of accumulating secular knowl-
edge in order to handle the spiritual, she confesses her thirst for
knowledge and does so by comparing herself to Saint Jerome in his
sufferings, who labored in the pursuit of learning. She cites Jerome:
"How often I have despaired, how often I have dropped my labors
and picked them up again, driven by the hunger for knowledge."
Then after identifying the ways of Jerome, the patron of her order,
she claims, with scarcely concealed contempt and irony, that she—
even without the consolation of companionship that Jerome en-
joyed—has succumbed to the same "black inclination [for acquiring
knowledge] that has been so great as to conquer all else!" (*Response*
782) Moreover, without a trace of *pudeur*, she tells us that while
she may lack the knowledge and aptitude of Saint Augustine or
Aristotle, it is not for lack of study, for she has studied more than
both of them (795).

Juana Inés is unstoppable in her argument of personal and
historic self-justification. When she lists the great learned women
of the past, she includes Hypatia of Alexandria. The philosopher
Hypatia has traditionally been evoked as a symbol of surviving
Greek intellectual civilization in its last distinguished manifesta-
tion before succumbing to the brute barbarism of Christian bigotry
and iconoclastic violence. Hypatia, "the beautiful and wise philoso-
pher" (her works have not survived), said to be the last significant
Neoplatonist before the darkness of total Christianization, was
murdered by a mob of Christian monks in the first decade of the
fifth century. Sor Juana's identity with Hypatia is not casual.

As proof of the bitterness and regret that her exchange of letters
with Filotea has enraged in her, she states, referring to her original
letter printed as the *Carta atenagórica*, that had she known that

her letter, which she had sent out like a foundling Moses on the waters of a silent Nile, would have provoked such controversy and led to her being silenced, she would have strangled the child in her own hands as soon as it was born, for fear that, with all its blemishes, it might fall "into the the light of your knowledge" (*Response* 804). Her satiric, yes, visceral anger, is not suppressed. Following these lines, she makes explicit, in her most terrible declaration, her threat of literary suicide: "Unless you intervene with other instructions, I will never pick up my pen again" (804).

Santa Cruz had written his Filotea admonition to Juana in November 1690. Her response came in March 1691. The bishop did not reply. He left unanswered her declaration of a woman's intellectual rights as well as her refutation of his admonitions. Since a change of instructions from the forbidding bishop never came, Sor Juana Inés de la Cruz did not pick up her literary pen again. His strategies were perfect. Her actual *Response* was not published until 1700, five years after her death.

After the explosion of her defiance, Sor Juana's confessor Núñez de Miranda, a prestigious professor of theology whose mind was distinguished by its mediocrity and orthodox insistence on subservience, humility, and rejection of worldly activities, withdrew spiritual aid. He refused to see her. When at her request he returned to her, it was to confirm her silence. Sor Juana then resigned herself to defeat and to what Father Callejas, in Catholic apology, saw as a process of separation from her books toward a more spiritual phase of her life. It is said that she broke up her library, sold it, along with her musical and scientific instruments, and distributed the proceeds among the poor. During the last four years of her life, apart from a few insignificant jottings, she held to the self-flagellating pledge in the *Response* "not to take up her pen again." In that unresolved conflict (and sometimes identity) of nun and writer, the nun, the self-abnegating nun, triumphed in dark silence. Her creative spirit stifled, she performed religious duties instead.

There is at least one deviation from her decision of creative stillness. To return again to Kafka (who willed that his writings be destroyed but left the assignment of destruction to the one intellectual friend, Max Brod, his literary executor, who not only was certain to ignore these instructions but would, and did, spend his life gathering and publishing his work), there is a similar confusion of intention in Sor Juana Inés's silence. While she did not write anything new, she did not order her works into silence. Indeed, she oversaw and assiduously corrected the publication of the volumes of her collected works, which began a few years earlier in 1689 when her friend the countess of Paredes, the vicereine, published the first volume of her poems in Spain. As for the dwindling of her extensive fame in the Spanish world, her last years of resignation and the Church disapproval had nothing to do with it. Her fame disappeared because of a change in literary taste. The exit of the baroque and entry of neoclassicism effectively stilled the print of her writing for these centuries. Only in the twentieth century with the resurgence of Spanish baroque authors have her works returned to us. Such was also the fate of many underesteemed or nearly forgotten poets, including Luis de Góngora, John Donne, and Maurice Scève.

In the end, after her conflict with the Church over the freedom of her word, the writer-nun of the Americas chose a reality distinct from the word in her text or the thinker in her chair. Sor Juana's last literary adventure, the *Response*, led to renunciation and a literary death from which she could not return. In 1695 a plague was ravaging Mexico. The plague entered the convent. Ministering to her sick sisters, Sor Juana inevitably became its victim. On April 17, 1695, two months into the unidentified epidemic, while nursing her sister nuns, she died. The day after her death, agents of Archbishop Aguiar y Seijas came to the convent to remove all her jewels and 5,200 pesos for purposes of his charities. Following his death in 1698, a suit was filed against the Aguiar y Seijas to take back what could be recovered from the booty of the archbishop's greed.

It is not likely that Sor Juana deliberately exposed herself to the disease that struck her down. In essence her decision to help her sister nuns was a necessary, ethical act of life, in accordance with the voice in her poems. She removed herself from one dream to enter another dream of compassion in which she touched the reality of the sick and dying. When she entered not the first but last dream, of eternity or sleep or nothingness, the mature voice of Spanish poetry fell mute for centuries. Curiously the last high moment of poetry of the Spanish Golden Age was found in the first poetic figure of the New World.

After Sor Juana, Spanish poetry was a dull manneristic imitation of European authors. There were also imitators of Lope and Góngora, but the well had run dry. The Spanish nation had lost its vigor, and New Spain was not to produce another Sor Juana. A series of incompetent monarchs reigned over a Spain that was losing its dominion and prestige and suffered from intellectual and artistic sterility. A century later, Francisco Goya y Lucientes shines with the sharp light of nightmare and graceful tones of the pastoral vineyard. And then another wait. The Spanish romantics, as the Spanish neoclassicists, were secondary imitators. In the mid-nineteenth century, Spanish poetry came awake briefly in the *Rimas* of Gustavo Adolfo Bécquer; and prose prospered in the realistic grandeur of Galdós and Clarín. There was also Rosalía de Castro, who wrote uneven but moving poetry in *gallego-portugués* as well as Spanish. But the generational awakening came only at the beginning of the twentieth century when suddenly, Spanish poetry, again of the New and Old Worlds, experienced an extraordinary rebirth in the poetry of Antonio Machado, Miguel de Unamuno, Juan Ramón Jiménez, Federico García Lorca, Jorge Luis Borges, Rafael Alberti, Miguel Hernández, Vicente Aleixandre, Jorge Guillén, Pedro Salinas, Luis Cernuda, César Vallejo, Pablo Neruda, and Octavio Paz.

A su retrato

Este que ves, engaño colorido,
que del arte ostentando los primores,
con falsos silogismos de colores
es cauteloso engaño del sentido;
este, en quien la lisonja ha pretendido
excusar de los años los horrores
y venciendo del tiempo los rigores
triunfar de la vejez y del olvido,
es un vano artificio del cuidado,
es una flor al viento delicada,
es un resguardo inútil para el hado,
es una necia diligencia errada,
es un afán caduco y, bien mirado,
es cadáver, es polvo, es sombra, es nada.

A la esperanza

Verde embeleso de la vida humana,
loca esperanza, frenesí dorado,
sueño de los despiertos, intrincado,
como de sueños, de tesoros vana.
Alma del mundo, senectud lozana,
decrépito verdor imaginado;
el hoy de los dichosos esperado
y de los desdichados el mañana:
sigan tu sombra en busca de tu día
los que, con verdes vidrios por anteojos,
todo lo ven pintado a su deseo;
que yo, más cuerda en la fortuna mía,
tengo en entrambas manos ambos ojos
y solamente lo que toco veo.

To Her Self-Portrait

What you see here is colorful illusion,
an art boasting of beauty and its skill,
which in false reasoning of color will
pervert the mind in delicate delusion.
Here where the flatteries of paint engage
to vitiate the horrors of the years,
where softening the rust of time appears
to triumph over oblivion and age,
all is a vain, careful disguise of clothing,
it is a slender blossom in the gale,
it is a futile port for doom reserved,
it is a foolish labor that can only fail:
it is a wasting zeal and, well observed,
is corpse, is dust, is shadow, and is nothing.

To Hope

A green beguilement in our natural life,
mad hope and frenzy wrapped about with gold,
a dream by those awake, yet thinly cold
like dreams and treasures rife, with illusions.
Soul of the world, exuberant old age,
decrepit greenness of pure fantasy,
the now for which the happy ones rampage,
the future where the miserable would be.
Clutching your name, seeking your day as real,
they stick green lenses in their glasses, and
the world they see is painted by command.
But I, much saner in my state of mind,
keep both eyes focused on my hands. Not blind,
I only see what I can touch and feel.

87

Quéjase de la suerte: insinua
su aversión a los vicios y justifica su
divertimiento a las musas

En perseguirme, Mundo ¿qué interesas?
¿En qué te ofendo, cuando sólo intento
poner bellezas en mi entendimiento
y no mi entendimiento en las bellezas?
Yo no estimo tesoros ni riquezas,
y así siempre me causa más contento
poner riquezas en mi pensamiento
que no mi pensamiento en las riquezas.
Y no estimo hermosura que, vencida,
es despojo civil de las edades,
ni riqueza me agrada fementida,
teniendo por mejor, en mis verdades,
consumir vanidades de la vida
que consumir la vida en vanidades.

En que da moral censura a una rosa, y
en ella a sus semejantes

Rosa divina que en gentil cultura
eres con tu fragante sutileza
magisterio purpúreo en la belleza,
enseñanza nevada a la hermosura.
Amago de la humana arquitectura,
ejemplo de la vana gentileza,
en cuyo sér unió naturaleza
la cuna alegre y triste sepultura.
¡Cuán altiva en tu pompa, presumida,
soberbia, el riesgo de morir desdeñas,
y luego desmayada y encogida
de tu caduco sér das mustias señas!
Con que con docta muerte y necia vida,
viviendo engañas y muriendo enseñas.

She Complains about Her Fate: She Asserts Her Aversion to Vices and Justifies Her Pleasure in the Muses

Why persecute me, world? To what effect?
Tell me how I offend. My sole intent
is to fix beauty to my intellect,
not hang my intellect in beauty's tent.
I do not care for emeralds or for gold,
and so I feel a happier effect
by fixing emeralds to my intellect
than to affix my intellect to gold.
I do not care for beauty that the knife
of age cuts into booty for the public hall,
nor can perfidious wealth please me at all.
The best I find of all my verities
is to consume my vanities in life
and not consume my life in vanities.

In Which She Morally Censures a Rose, and Through the Rose Her Peers

Holy rose, who in genteel cultivation
you show in all your redolent finesse
a magisterial beauty in your station,
a snowy discourse in your loveliness,
a fearful sign to human architecture,
emblem of the vanity in grace's bloom,
whose being unites through trickery of nature
the joyous cradle and the sorrowing tomb.
How haughty in your pomp, how arrogant,
sovereign, while you disdain the risk of death;
and then, collapsing, shrinking, you are plucked
in feebleness of being, a withered plant!
And so through stupid life and dying breath,
in life you fool, in dying you instruct.

Escoge antes el morir que
exponerse a los ultrajes de la vejez

Miró Celia una rosa que en el prado
ostentaba feliz la pompa vana
y con afeites de carmín y grana
bañaba alegre el rostro delicado,
y dijo: Goza, sin temor del hado,
el curso breve de tu edad lozana,
pues no podrá la muerte de mañana
quitarte lo que hubieres hoy gozado;
y aunque llega la muerte presurosa
y tu fragante vida se te aleja,
no sientas el morir tan bella y moza;
mira que la experiencia te aconseja
que es fortuna morirte siendo hermosa
y no ver el ultraje de ser vieja.

Sospecha crueldad disimulada,
el alivio que la esperanza da

Diuturna enfermedad de la esperanza
que así entretienes mis cansados años
y en el fiel de los bienes y los daños
tienes en equilibrio la balanza,
que siempre suspendida, en la tardanza
de inclinarse, no dejan tus engaños
que lleguen a excederse en los tamaños
la desesperación o la confianza
¿quién te ha quitado el nombre de homicida?
Pues lo eres más severa, si se advierte
que suspendes el alma entretenida,
y entre la infausta o la felice suerte,
no lo haces tú por conservar la vida
sino por dar más dilatada muerte.

A Good Face One Should Choose Before Dying Rather Than
to Expose Oneself to the Outrages of Old Age

Celia looked at a rose proud in the field,
happily showing off its futile grace,
and, while adorned in rouge fully revealed,
it cheerfully was bathing its white face;
Courageously enjoy your destiny,
the brief migration of your fertile age;
then death that comes tomorrow will not be
in place to rob you of a joy, your wage
today. And though persistent death comes now
and your delicious life moves far from you,
and youth and beauty mix with death and fears,
see what experience informs, and how
it's best to die with youth and beauty too
than to observe the outrage of the years.

She Suspects That the Relief That Hope Gives
Is Dissimulated Cruelty

With my one daily malady of hope
you plot to entertain my graying years
and in the scheme of goods and hangman's rope
you keep the scale in balance for all spheres;
and always hanging there (in the delay
before it tilts one way), your trickery
you won't let dominate to a degree
of posing crude belief or grave dismay.
Who stole the name from you of homicide?
You're it—severely so, if well observed—
and in the air you hang my laughing soul.
While between losing and your lucky side,
you do not work to keep a life preserved
but to give tolling death a lingering toll.

En que satisface un recelo
con la retórica del llanto

Esta tarde, mi bien, cuando te hablaba,
como en tu rostro y tus acciones vía
que con palabras no te persuadía,
que el corazón me vieses deseaba,
y amor, que mis intentos ayudaba,
venció lo que imposible parecía,
pues entre el llanto que el dolor vería
el corazón deshecho destilaba.
Baste ya de rigores, mi bien, baste;
no te atormenten más celos tiranos
ni el vil recelo tu virtud contraste
con sombras necias, con indicios vanos,
pues ya en líquido humor viste y tocaste
mi corazón deshecho entre tus manos.

Que contiene una fantasía contenta con amor decente

Detente, sombra de mi bien esquivo,
imagen del hechizo que más quiero,
bella ilusión por quien alegre muero,
dulce ficción por quien penosa vivo.
Si al imán de tus gracias atractivo
sirve mi pecho de obediente acero
¿para qué me enamoras lisonjero
si has de burlarme luego fugitivo?
Mas blasonar no puedes satisfecho
de que triunfa de mí tu tiranía;
que aunque dejas burlado el lazo estrecho
que tu forma fantástica ceñía,
poco importa burlar brazos y pecho
si te labra prisón mi fantasía.

In Which She Satisfies a Fear
with the Rhetoric of Tears

This afternoon, my love, speaking to you
since I could see that in your face and walk
I failed in coming close to you with talk,
I wanted you to see my heart. Love, who
supported me in what I longed to do,
conquered what is impossible to gain.
Amid my tears that were poured out in pain,
my heart became distilled and broken through.
Enough, my love. Don't be so stiff. Don't let
these maddening jealousies and arrogance
haunt you or let your quiet be upset
by foolish shadows: false signs of a man's
presence; and as you see my heart which met
your touch—now it is liquid in your hands.

In Which Her Fantasy Is Contented with Decent Love

Don't leave me, shadow of my love, elusive
and obsessed image which I care for most,
handsome deceit for whom I'd be a ghost,
sweet fiction for which pain is not abusive.
If my own body of obedient steel
serves as a magnet fated to your grace,
why flatter me with lover's commonplace,
only to drop me, run, while I congeal?
And yet you cannot brag of anything,
of any triumph through your tyranny.
If you elude the narrow noose I've set
to capture your fantastic form, and spring
out of my arms, who cares? You flee, and yet
I've got you locked up in my fantasy.

93

De una reflexión cuerda con que mitiga el dolor de una pasión

Con el dolor de la mortal herida,
de un agravio de amor me lamentaba,
y por ver si la muerte se llegaba
procuraba que fuese más crecida.
Toda en el mal el alma divertida,
pena por pena su dolor sumaba,
y en cada circunstancia ponderaba
que sobraban mil muertes a una vida.
Y cuando al golpe de uno y otro tiro,
rendido el corazón daba penoso
señas de dar el último suspiro,
no sé con qué destino prodigioso
volví en mi acuerdo y dije: ¿Qué me admiro?
¿Quién en amor ha sido más dichoso?

Prosigue el mismo asunto, y determina que prevalezca la razón contra el gusto

Al que ingrato me deja, busco amante;
al que amante me sigue, dejo ingrata;
constante adoro a quien mi amor maltrata;
maltrato a quien mi amor busca constante.
Al que trato de amor, hallo diamante,
y soy diamante al que de amor me trata;
triunfante quiero ver al que me mata,
y mato a quien me quiere ver triunfante.
Si a éste pago, padece mi deseo;
si ruego a aquél, mi pundonor enojo:
de entrambos modos infeliz me veo.
Pero yo por mejor partido escojo
de quien no quiero, ser violento empleo,
que de quien no me quiere, vil despojo.

Concerning a Sage Reflection That Mitigates
a Passion

With the affliction of a mortal wound
I brooded on a sore offense of love;
to see if death would drag me underground
I tried to make it grow and loom above.
The separated soul in clouds of pain,
counted its anguish one hurt at a time,
and with each second it was darkly plain
a thousand deaths dug one life into grime.
And after blows of battering a skull,
the ruptured heart discerned a maddening sign
that it had come to its last hopeless sigh—
and yet by some prodigious destiny
I woke, sensing: Am I not wonderful,
and who in love has happiness like mine?

She Continues with the Same Matter and Ends
with Reason Prevailing over Pleasure

The ingrate dumping me I seek a lover,
seek me as lover, I'll throw him away.
I always worship one who runs for cover,
who worships me I bump out of my way.
Whom I beseech with love is hard as steel,
I'm hard as steel to you beseeching me.
Triumphant I want you who murder me,
I murder you who want my triumph real.
If someone wants me, my desire is gone.
If I want you, I crush my dignity;
and either way I end up feeling bashed.
I choose then as the better course to be
a violent curse on you who make me yawn,
than be for you who dump me vilely trashed.

Inés

Inés, cuando te riñen por *bellaca,*
para disculpas no te falta *achaque*
porque dices que traque y que *barraque;*
con que sabes muy bien tapar la *caca.*
Si coges la parola, no hay *urraca*
que así la gorja de mal año *saque;*
y con tronidos, más que un *triquitraque,*
a todo el mundo aturdes cual *matraca.*
Ese bullicio todo lo *trabuca,*
ese embeleso todo lo *embeleca;*
mas aunque eres, Inés, tan mala *cuca,*
sabe mi amor muy bien lo que *se peca:*
y así con tu afición no se *embabuca,*
aunque eres zancarrón y yo *de Meca.*

96

Inés

When they revile you as sly and obscene,
you have no problem getting off the hook,
you launch into your gobbledygook,
knowing just how to wipe your asshole clean,
and when you grab the world, no magpie can
dish our such bad-year garbage from its throat:
you thunder and the clatter fills a moat,
stunning the world like pounding on a can.
That rumble jumbles all, one tumbling turd,
A con game making you a sweet Rebecca.
Though you, Inés, a wanton cuckoo bird,
must know my love and how to spot a sin;
your bumbling passion stumbles, fails to win,
though you're a holy saint and I'm from Mecca.

Antonio Machado

(1875–1939)

Spain

Antonio Machado

The Generation of '98 and the politics of rebirth

The Generation of '98 had a violent political origin. In 1898 the United States and Spain were at war. When Spain was defeated, quickly and decisively, certain intellectual elements in the country began to waken from the lethargy of long national decline, of passivity and imitation of France, which earlier in the century had humiliated the nation with invading troops and the disasters of war. Goya responded with fury in engravings at the grotesque massacre of Spanish civilians and soldiers. After the turn-of-the-century generation of writers and thinkers became acutely aware that their country had now lost everything, there was again a response in the air—one that demanded change.

Nevertheless, a climate of defeat beset the nation. Along with military disgrace, Spain was reduced territorially to the Iberian peninsula—with the exception of a few strips of land in North Africa. Encased behind glass in the National Maritime Museum of Barcelona were emblems of the Imperial Armada. Yet after the centuries of decay, there were indeed few other signs of the golden chain of colonies, all now liberated and culturally rejecting Spain in favor of France. The *Siglo de oro* was long gone, and gold from the old Indian mines and plundered treasuries no longer poured in from the Americas to support an unproductive economy, one that could barely provide its people with bread.

While the new gods of the Industrial Revolution were winning Western Europe and North America to a faith in progress and prosperity, Spain was castles, beauty, churches, landless peasants in Andalusia, and a skeletal industry in the north. There remained the cartoon version of the nation, Bizet's colorful *Carmen*, a French dream of gypsies and toreadors, glittering, romantic, and utterly cheap and unreal. In truth the countryside was a medieval relic, feudal in land ownership, but at the same time, the village and city life fascinating for the emerging naturalist novelists, and for all those who wished to find a country naturally fixed in a time warp.

Popular culture was alive and even preserved by the insignificance of industry and the stagnating economy. (Unfortunately there is an inverse relationship of growth between folkloric culture and economic prosperity.) Antonio Machado's father, folklorist and founder of the Spanish Folklore Society, was the first anthologist of the lyrics of flamenco song. In the spring came the *Semana santa* (Holy Week) of Málaga, with its floats carrying embellished statues of the Virgin and accompanied by the *penitentes*, men parading with crosses in KKK-like white robes and high conical hats, alongside priests and uniformed *guardia civiles*. This was followed a week later by the celebration of the *Feria de Sevilla*, with its dancing *sevillanas* in the *casetas*, the bulls, and the aristocratic horsewomen riding as elegant, anachronistic dolls in the morning streets. Everywhere and in full strength was the *canción anónima* (popular song), which with the exception of a brief period of total Italianization in the early sixteenth century, had nourished even the most *culto* of Spanish poets. Yet "eternal" popular culture aside, the nation as a whole lay impoverished after its civil wars, divided between its traditionalist and Europeanizing tendencies, and above all, effectively ensconced behind the isolating walls of the Pyrenees.

Of this Spain drifting into the twentieth century, Arturo Barea wrote, "Her fertile but mismanaged lands were exhausted; the country was short of bread. And she was plagued by earthquakes, epidemics and flood which seemed to herald the Apocalypse in the eyes of the bewildered masses" (Barea 9). Fifty years of church burning and those exhausting Carlist wars between traditionalists and liberals (*liberal* as a political term was invented in Spain) had preceded the military defeat of 1898. Spain had dissipated its prestige and its hegemony—it was surely no longer the dominant power of Europe as when it ruled Austria, parts of Italy, the Netherlands, Portugal, most of the two continents of the Americas, and even the Philippines.

Yet from all the shock of external political and military disaster and the despair of internal stagnation, at this moment, curiously, there took place an enormous apparent contradiction: the sudden and dynamic beginnings of a new Spain. There was an influx of literary and social ideas from abroad; the Nicaraguan poet Rubén Darío came on the scene, carrying the fresh aesthetic of contemporary French poetry in his own dubious verse, which led to Spanish *modernismo*. More significantly, from a recognition of immediate and distant precursors, there was, at this unlikely moment, a revolution, an explosion of Spanish talent, a huge renascence in all the arts. Perhaps a just comparison can be made with the emergence of the great novel in nineteenth-century Russia at a time when the nation was similarly characterized by feudal land ownership, abysmal government, and conflicting Russian and Europeanizing cultural currents.

In Spain the phenomenon of its major painters was to distinguish the century's visual arts. There were Juan Gris, Joan Miró, Picasso, and Dalí. In music there were the composers Falla, Albéinez, and Granados, all very Spanish as they were European, and Andrés Segovia who made the guitar an essential Spanish and classical instrument. In Catalunia there was a parallel regional resurgence in the arts. Gris, Miró, and Dalí were Catalans; Picasso grew up, was trained, and first developed his talent in Barcelona; the eccentric, brilliant Catalan architect Antonio Gaudí was a secret world figure of architecture in the early part of the century.

In literature the sense of renovation was messianic. A group of literary men, who identified with the national problems, set out on quixotic missions to rediscover the soul of Spain. Students, artists, and intellectuals went abroad to bring back new ideas. Within Spain the provinces were discovered: landscapes in Machado, Azorín, and Unamuno and the popular song and *romances* (ballads) in Machado and later Lorca. Popular culture became legitimate raw material for art forms. The "primitive" authors were resurrected—the medieval poets Gonzalo de Berceo, Juan Ruiz the archpriest of Hita, and Jorge Manrique. Spanish philospher-essayists Miguel de Unamuno and José Ortega y Gasset were engaged in labors of reexamination and rebellion, critical introspection and revaluation.

The decay in the national life did not of course automatically disappear upon being articulated by a group of ardent scholars, artists, and philosophers. Azorín wrote essay after essay calling for hard work and the exertion of *la voluntad* (the will). In politics the figures of '98 had no single party or program—they did have an influential professor, Francisco Giner de los Ríos, founder of the Institución Libre de Enseñanza (Free Institute of Learning), which educated many leading intellectuals, including the Machado brothers. Azorín, with his usual thoroughness, listed the evils against which his generation was rebelling:

> The old times also mean the vicious practices of our politics, administrative corruption, incompetence, unlawful practices, nepotism, caciques, verbosity, the *mañana* attitude, parliamentary frauds, the overbearing quality of grandiloquence, the political expediencies which make those go astray who were quite prepared to do so, the falsified elections . . . all in a dense and impenetrable atmosphere, against all of this the Generation of 1898 protested. (Azorín 235–36)

Few have better expressed these conditions of dismay and hope than Antonio Machado in "Una España joven" (A young Spain), a poem infused with the spirit of '98. It also has generalized notions of Spain and all the strength, slogans, and banality of his more boisterous poems of '98—as opposed to the memory of interiorized landscapes and the particular, clear geographical images in Machado's other poems.

> It was a time of lies, of infamy. They dressed
> our sorely wounded Spain in Carnival costume,
> and then they made her drunken, poor, debased
> so that no hand might touch her open wound.
>
> Yesterday. We were barely youths, in an era—
> an evil hour—pregnant with grim prophecy.
> We wished to ride an unrestrained chimera
> while shipwrecks rotted in the sleeping sea.
>
> We left the squalid galley in the harbor,
> choosing to navigate a golden ship through gales
> out to the open ocean. We sought no shore
> but cast away anchor, rudder, and sails . . .
>
> (*Dream Below the Sun* 87)

This rhetorical ship-of-state poem, replete with clichés and bombast, continues. As one who loves Machado as much as Wang Wei or Cavafy, I reluctantly cite these not fully admired Spanish hexameters that happen, however, to be an excellent essay on Spain's glooms and hopes in those days. Machado wrote them in 1915 when Spaniards were obsessed with asking, What is Spain? Pedro Salinas, an outstanding poet of the Generation of '27 and also a seminal critic of Spanish literature, captures the spirit and preoccupations of the time:

> The national tragedy functions as a lens, catching the spiritual energies of the new writers and joining them in concentrated form on a single, shining focal point, *lo español*. For that which distinguishes the "man of '98" is that he thinks Spain, feels Spain, and loves Spain over and above all his other activities, converting it into a completely preferred subject of mental preoccupation, making it into the measure of his art, of his life. (Salinas 770)

The devotion of those of '98 to Spain had nothing to do with jingoism or exaggerated patriotism. It was precisely the hollow ring of the chauvinists' rhetoric that they abhorred and that Azorín decried. It is a sad irony that much of their writing today should appear so declamatory and chauvinistic. They were set on discovering the "eternal" elements in the Spanish tradition, and this

turned them to study Castile, its grave and hermetic plateaus, the
heart of Spain. Unamuno and Machado were the poets most associ-
ated with the discovery of Castile, the old cities, and the depopu-
lated *páramos* (the harsh steppes). In their enthusiasm for Castile,
however, the writers of '98 pointedly ignored Galicia, Catalunia
(busy with its own self-discovery), and even Andalusia until the
Generation of '27. Such provincialism amidst discovery is odd, for
in reality most of the major Spanish poets of the twentieth century
Siglo de oro are Andalusian—Machado, Lorca, Alberti, Cernuda,
and two Nobel laureates Jiménez and Aleixandre.

Miguel de Unamuno from the Basque country and Antonio
Machado of Sevilla are the only poets of the '98 Generation whose
fame still lingers—and Unamuno is remembered more as a philoso-
pher and novelist. In reality the overly fecund Basque author of
much banal "famous" poetry has been disesteemed and unjustly
so, for his few good poems not only express the Spain of his day but
are among the most individually fine poems in modern Spanish.
There is no poetic voice like his; just as in his novels, he is an
intuitively learned experimenter, stubborn, cranky, courageous. His
metalingual novels, like and before Pirandello's plays, invent roles
for characters, readers, and authors, all of whom slip in and out of
the work of art with complicating brilliance. But his poems are our
concern, and they are Unamuno and '98. One good example is
Unamuno's "It Is Night, in My Study":

It is night in my study.
Deepest solitude; I hear the pounding
in my turbulent chest—
it feels alone
and blanched by my mind—
and I hear my blood
whose even whisper
fills up the silence.
You might say the waterclock's liquid thread
is dropping to the bottom.
Here, in the night, alone, this is my study.
The books don't speak.
My oil lamp
cools these pages with a light of peace,
light of a chapel.
The books don't speak.
Sleeping are the spirits
of the poets, the thinkers, the learned.
It's as if cunning death
were all around me.
I turn at times to see if it's waiting there,

I squint into darkness.
Among the shadows I try to spot
its wary shadow.
I think of heart failure,
at my strong age. Since my fortieth year
two years have gone by.
Silence turns me about
to face a bullying temptation.
Silence and shadows.
And I tell myself, "Maybe soon
when they'll come to say
that supper is waiting for me
they'll find a body
colorless and cold
(the thing I was, waiting
like these quiet and stiff books,
blood already stopped,
jelling in the veins,
the chest quiet
under the weak light of soothing oil,
a funeral lamp."
I tremble as I end these lines
that don't seem
an unusual testament
but rather a mysterious presentiment
from the shade on the other side,
lines dictated by hunger
for eternal life.
I finished them and am still living.

Antonio Machado, who in his solitude sees very clear things that are not true

The Wang Wei of Spain, the meditative nature poet who per-
haps alone in the West has written poems about landscape in which
no speaker seems to exist, who is the metaphysical explorer of
dream, landscape, and consciousness below language, is Antonio
Machado. He began as a young Spanish poet in part influenced
by a movement misleadingly called *modernismo*, which despite
protests from some Spanish critics, has not only nothing to do with
the European and American modernism of Eliot, Borges, Beckett,
and Lorca but represents very much what modernism was thor-
oughly rejecting: *fin-de-siècle* aestheticism. Machado took the best
of *modernismo* and in disguised forms, it persists throughout his
poetry, including his sonnets, which appear late in his life as a poet.
Indeed, *modernismo* persists after the more declamatory aspect of
the '98 poet has totally disappeared. The sonnets, however, are their
own world, or better worlds. There are the whimsically beautiful,

erotic ones, the landscape memory ones, and among his last poems, those of the war, the civil war, which are personal, beautiful, tragic, and again, of memory.

Antonio Machado y Ruiz was born in Sevilla in 1875, the same year Rilke was born in Prague. Astrology and stars aside, there is in these poets a coincidence of some essential qualities. They are the quietest, most introspective and landscape-oriented writers of modern poetry. Landscape, or the open-eyed dream of it, does all. It is thing and symbol. Semioticians speak with restrained ecstasy about that moment of significance in a moment of communication when all codes are right, when semiosis takes place. For Rainer Maria Rilke and Antonio Machado, the evocation of the meaningful landscape, usually through some aspect of dream, is the instant of semiosis—when it all comes together.

Machado's childhood years in Sevilla pervade the early poems. Antonio was only eight when the family moved to Madrid, but images of the Andalusian city continue to lurk in his poems till the very end. Sevilla with its gardens, fountains, white walls, ruined churches, cypress trees, and solitary plazas was a city with nature in its center. Madrid never appears in the poems, although it is in Madrid that Machado became a poet. But there is a logic to the preference of Sevilla over Madrid. The most obvious reason is that Antonio Machado and his poet brother Manuel did not begin their careers as late Baudelairean city poets; rather, following turn-of-the-century measures of what poetry was, they were recorders of nature. It was Sevilla, not Madrid, that allowed them nature and the city at once.

But beyond the nature of the city is Antonio Machado's obsessive turn to memory. Machado writes that "love is in the absence." In fact the absent, remembered place is more significant than the place where one is. So in Madrid Machado recalls Sevilla. Only in Soria, unique in his experience, will he actually write about the Soria of the moment, in part, because this small provincial capital northeast of Madrid in Castilla la Nueva (New Castile) corresponds so completely to his Generation of '98 ideas of Castile, including its ruinous decadence, its folklore, its profundity. But once gone from Soria to Baeza in northern Andalusia, he will dream back almost exclusively to the years 1905–12 in Soria, where he discovered the land, where he met and married his very young wife who died a few years later. After Antonio left Baeza for Segovia in the north, there was the same transfer of vision to the earlier place. Now he recalls the south. And finally, in the terrible days of civil war, he returns once again to childhood Sevilla. In fact the last line found in a notebook a few days before he died in exile in Collioure, France, is "Estos días azules y este sol de la infancia" (These blue days and this sun of childhood). His own biographical poem "Retrato" (Portrait) points to his primordial landscapes—childhood Sevilla and young adult Castile:

> My childhood is memories of a patio in Seville
> and a bright orchard where lemon trees ripen;
> my youth, twenty years on the soil of Castile,
> my life, a few events just as well forgotten.
>
> (*Dream Below the Sun* 45)

In his later forties or early fifties, Machado wrote a sonnet recalling his father, a literary man who died young, and as usual, Machado plays with time so that in the last lines, his father's eyes will look upon the child speaker who is now suddenly, and movingly, the graying writer. The pathos of the poem is guided by the impossibility of the last scene, enhancing the sense of loss:

> Light of Seville . . . The great palacial house
> where I was born, the gurgling fountain sound.
> My father in his study. Forehead round
> and high, short goatee, moustache drooping down.
> My father still is young. He reads and writes,
> leafs through his books and meditates. Then springs
> up near the garden door, strolls by the gate.
> Sometimes he talks out loud, sometimes he sings.
> And now his large eyes with their anxious glance
> appear to wander with no object to
> focus upon, not finding anywhere
> to rest in void. They slip from past and through
> tomorrow where, my father, they advance
> to gaze so pityingly at my gray hair.
>
> ("Esta luz de Sevilla" [Light of Seville])

In the Madrid of his young manhood, Machado led a literary, bohemian life. He collaborated in newly founded periodicals, worked briefly as an actor, and took several trips to France where he met Rubén Darío and also Oscar Wilde after his release from English prison. On Machado's last trip to Paris, his crucial encounter was with Henri Bergson, the French philosopher of time, *durée* (duration), and mystical experience determined by the evasion of everyday's external, mechanical clocktime. No one person in life so marked the active thought of Machado as did the French philosopher.

Antonio published his first book, *Soledades* (Solitudes), in 1904 and an expanded edition, *Soledades, galerías y otras poesias* (Solitudes, galleries and other Poems), in 1907. His galleries were, like Borges's labyrinths, a symbolism for the passageways of his interior vision. These first books reveal the temptation, acceptance, and at the same time, discomfort with *modernismo*. Machado was struggling to suppress or go beyond the *modernismo* he recognized in those early poems, whose fullest incarnation was Rubén Darío's life and art. Both friends recognized their common grounds and their disharmonies. So in a series of mutual literary assassination poems, they each wrote elegies to the other very much alive poet.

Darío fixes Machado in a splendidly sensitive poem that reveals even then a profound and luminous figure, a timid and quiet man of good faith. Darío sends his young friend "off to the impossible" on a strange mythological steed. To be certain he would stay there and not alter his way of being, even in death or limbo, Darío puts Machado in the elegaic past, prays to his own gods, presumably those spirited *décadent* French poets who had nurtured the Nicaraguan poet; and to be absolutely sure that Antonio will not return or reform, he asks his gods to save him forever, to preserve him as he is then. In his "Oración por Antonio Machado" (Prayer for Antonio Machado), he portrays the poet:

> Mysterious and silent
> he came and he left us.
> You could hardly meet his gaze,
> it was so profound.
> He spoke with a touch
> of timidity and loftiness,
> and you could almost see the light
> of his thoughts, burning.
> He was luminous and deep
> as a man of good faith.
> He might have been a pastor of lions
> and, at the same time, of lambs.
> He scattered thunderstorms
> or carried a honeycomb.
> The wonders of life,
> of love and pleasures
> he sang in deepest poems
> whose secret was his own.
> Mounted on a rare Pegasus
> one day he went off to the impossible.
> I pray to my gods for Antonio.
> May they always save him. Amen.

> (*Obras: Poesía y Prosa* 53)

Soria and hills of blue ash

By 1907 Machado wanted a regular job and became a schoolmaster in Soria, in an *instituto* (a public high school) in which he taught French. His life's profession was the lowly schoolteacher in rural *institutos.* There in Soria he met Leonor when she was thirteen, married her two years later in 1909—he was by then thirty-three. In 1911 Antonio obtained a fellowship to study in France, and the couple went happily to Paris. It was then that Machado attended the lectures of Henri Bergson. But the next July Leonor became violently sick. On their return to New Castile, he nursed her as her health failed. She was only eighteen in 1912 when she died. In 1962 in Soria, I spoke at length to an old gentleman who some fifty years earlier had been at their wedding and who described how Antonio used to push Leonor in a wheelchair up into the hills during the last summer. Machado remembers those hills in a series of poems of self-deceptive memory and depressing awakening:

> "Leonor, do you see the river aspens
> with their firm foliage?
> Look at the blue and white Moncayo summits,
> give me your hand and let us wander."
> Through the fields where we have lived,
> edged with dusty olive groves,
> I am walking alone, sad, tired, pensive, old.
>
> *(Dream Below the Sun* 67)

Although after Leonor's death Machado immediately requested and obtained a new post and so left Soria forever, the obsessive memory and conscious daydream of Leonor and Castile stayed with him throughout his life.

The impact of Soria is recorded in *Campos de Castilla* (Fields of Castile), 1912, and especially in its expanded edition five years later when Machado had left the region. It is a volume of solitude, bare Castilian landscapes, memories of Leonor, and Spain seen through the critical, reforming eyes of a poet of the Generation of '98. The language is spare, exact, yet sonorous, with a grave emotion. Machado (unlike Lorca who learned from Machado's popularism) was never fond of the baroque or for that matter, of Góngora and Calderón, whom he considered excellent examples of late Golden Age excess. Machado's poems could be any village of Castile or Andalusia, and his presence is of the accurate solitary observer, as in "Noche de verano" (Summer night):

> It is a beautiful summer night.
> The tall houses leave
> their balcony shutters open
> to the wide plaza of the old village.
> In the large deserted square,
> stone benches, burning bush and acacias
> trace their black shadows
> symmetrically on the white sand.

Antonio Machado

In the zenith, the moon; in the tower,
the clock's illuminated globe.
I'm walking through this ancient village,
alone, like a ghost.

(*Dream Below the Sun* 55)

Baeza and dreaming elsewhere

After Leonor's death Machado spent seven years in Baeza, teaching in another rural Spanish *instituto*. He wrote abundantly, but the forms in tone were different. He expressed himself now in verses which, like later Lorca, were based on prosody of popular Spanish song. He wrote brief, aphoristic philosophical poems, and he wrote sonnets, the latter for the first time. Castilian gravity has given way to Andalusian irony and humor in the philosophical and allegorical verses, as in his parabolic "Consejos" (Advice):

Learn to wait. Wait for the tide to flow
as a boat on the coast. And do not worry
   when it buoys
you out. If you wait, you will know
   victory,
for life is long and art a toy.
And if life is short
and the sea doesn't reach your ship, stay
forever waiting in the port,
for art is long, and never matters anyway.

(*Dream Below the Sun* 83)

In Baeza Machado managed to obtain an advanced university degree in philosophy in 1919 by commuting to Madrid. At the time, José Ortega y Gasset was a Tob-like member of the examining board. Machado's interest in the degree was not to enhance his modest, high school teaching career. Rather, he had become addicted to philosophy and, he claimed, gave himself to reading only philosophy during these years. He writes long series of proverbial verse in the manner of one of his preferred poets, the medieval Spanish rabbi Sem Tob:

In my solitude
I see very clear things
that are not true.

(*Dream Below the Sun* 110)

or

111

Antonio Machado

The eye you see is not
an eye because you see it
but because it sees you.

(*Dream Below the Sun* 109)

or on the way to epiphany, always secular, always with Heraclitean
skepticism for absolute truths, yet always seeking:

Behind living and dreaming
is what matters most,
coming awake.

(*Dream Below the Sun* 113)

And also in Baeza he perfected the special dream focus in which
landscape provides the poet with the symbols to express nearly all
ideas and emotions. The simple Chinese device of using the outer
landscape to describe the inner landscape of the spirit is the oldest
technique of poets. Antonio Machado, however, prefaces a step to
the usual procedure, because even his outer landscapes have had
their origin in open-eyed memory dream. The poetic mechanism
is, in its three steps:

1. The poet *dreams of a remembered landscape,*
2. which he describes as an *outer landscape,* and
3. which he transforms into a symbol of his *inner landscape.*

Steps 1 and 3 are inner landscapes, with step 2 a mirror in the
outer world of steps 1 and 3. And at times Machado bypasses the
second step and passes directly from first to third. The strange
beauty of Machado's best poems may be followed logically if we
remember his method: The poet dreams a remembered landscape;
he then presents a temporal reflection of his dream—an outer land-
scape—to the reader who in turn reads back into it the original
dreamed landscape. Occasionally, as mentioned, the poet moves
directly from step 1 to 3, omitting step 2. Then the poet dreams of
his own inner landscape.

Precisely this poetic process, made explicit in his later philo-
sophical reflections on time and abstraction, permits Machado his
most mature work, to write poems of a secular mystical character.
The mystical nature of these poems lies in Machado's dream vision
and follows the familiar *vias* of the mystical process. The poet, as
it were, is blind before the world about him, blinded in an afternoon
of tedium in which sun and consequently time both seem to stop;
in this darkness the poet opens his eyes in dream to a world of light.
Through dream, his mind takes flight, he awakens, the world is

112

revealed in images of startling clarity, and the outer and inner worlds of symbolized nature join.

In one typical poem, "Desgarrada la nube: el arco iris" (The torn cloud, the rainbow), we have an analogue of San Juan de la Cruz's awakenings. Here dream, landscape, and a metaphysical equivalent to the instant of mystical astonishment (*asombro*) in the Spanish saint are all present:

> The torn cloud, the rainbow
> shining now in the sky,
> and the fields wrapped
> in a beacon of sun and rain.
>
> I awoke. Who is darkening
> the magic crystals of my dream?
> My heart was beating,
> aghast and bewildered.
>
> —The lemon grove in blossom,
> cypresses in the orchard,
> green meadow, sun, water, rainbow.
> The water in your hair!—
>
> And all in my memory was lost
> like a soap bubble in the wind.
>
> (*Dream Below the Sun* 33)

After citing a landscape that is emerging from a sky of rain, the poet himself awakes, emerging from dream. It is stated abruptly: "I awoke." The dream was a preparation, as was the stormy landscape with its beach of sun. His awakening leaves him astonished and dumb. Like San Juan in the "Cántico espiritual" (Spiritual canticle), when after the darkness of the former dream he sees, he is barely capable of speech and is given to exclamation. No verbs, and each thing of nature carries the force of great clarity and importance. It is enough merely to cite the existence of these things of nature, quickly, without qualification or explanation. Similarly, San Juan writes in "Cántico":

> O birds on easy wings,
> lions, stags, leaping fallow deer,
> mountains, valleys, shores,
> waters, winds, passions
> and terror in the watchful nights.
>
> (John of the Cross 51)

Machado catalogues his vision:

Antonio Machado

> —The lemon grove in blossom,
> cypresses in the orchard,
> green meadow, sun, water, rainbow.
> The water in your hair!

After two stanzas of darkness and illumination, the third stanza of vision is not an instant of ineffable revelation—the poem with its words exists—yet it is limited in these four lines to nouns, to things, except for "green" which as a quality inherent in the meadow is more substantive than adjectival in function. Then in the poem's last lines, the memory of the vision is lost, and he wakes a second time to the world *without* vision or memory:

> And all in my memory was lost
> like a soap bubble in the wind.

The one word *hair* of "the water in your hair!" equates the vision with love. When Machado begins to write sonnets, we find that the sonnet leads him to a fluent yet intensely clear vision of love and nature. In the sonnet "Por qué, decísme, hacia los altos llanos" (You ask me, why my heart flies from the coast), he tells us that it is not coastal Andalusia and its fertile lands but the austere north and the starkly clean landscape of Soria where his heart lives. There he found one person—whom he translates into a landscape in order to represent his love:

> My heart is living, yes, where it was born,
> but not to life—to love, the Duero near,
> the whitewashed wall and cypress in the sky!

By now Machado was writing sonnets of immaculately bright nature images. The sonnets are dream games, with love mirrored on the land; the metaphysic of time distorts and creates everything, with the emphasis on the *thing*, in soundless, endless Spanish afternoons where time halts. All this we *see*, and in Machado, as in Chinese poetry, we always see. From the sequence "Los sueños dialogados" (Dreams in dialogue), the sonnet "Cómo en alto llano su figura" (How suddenly her face on the plateau) has the dreamed land, the love, the suspension of time:

> How suddenly her face on the plateau
> appears to me! And then my word evokes
> green meadows and the arid plains below,
> the flowering blackberries and ashen rocks.
> Obedient to my memory, the black oak
> bursts on the hill, the poplars then define
> the river, and the shepherd climbs the cloak

of knolls while a town balcony shines: mine,
ours. Can you see? Remote, toward Aragon,
the sierra of Moncayo, white and rose.
Look at the bonfire of that cloud, and far
shining against the blue, my wife, a star.
Santana hill, beyond the Duero, shows,
turning violet in soundless afternoon.

Segovia's Street of Abandoned Children

From Baeza in 1919 Machado went north to take a new teaching
position in Segovia, just a few hours by train from Madrid, and there
he was able to go each weekend to Madrid where he collaborated
with his brother Manuel in several plays. He also had more intellec-
tual companionship among his fellow teachers of literature and
philosophy and through his weekend trips, had again joined the
literary life, of his own choosing, in the capital. The best portrait
of Don Antonio in his Segovia days appears in a remembrance by
John Dos Passos. As a young man in his early twenties, Dos Passos
spent some days and evenings talking with Machado in Segovia. It
was in 1919. Thirty-nine years later I wrote to him and to Machado's
old friend Juan Ramón Jiménez, who was then near death, asking
whether they might write a reminiscence of Machado for a publica-
tion. They each wrote new pieces on Machado, which I received
almost by return mail. In their memoirs, time has sharpened mem-
ory and its images—as it should in treating Machado. Dos Passos
recalls:

Though I never knew Antonio Machado well my recollec-
tions of him are so sharp as to be almost painful. I remember
him as a large sad fumbling man dressed like an oldfashioned
schoolteacher. Stiff wing collar none too clean; spots on his
clothes, and the shine of wear on the black broadcloth. He had
a handsomely deep voice. Always when I think of him he is
wearing the dusty derby he wore the evening we walked around
Segovia in the moonlight.
Segovia is one of the walled mountain towns of old Castile.
It is full of arches. A Roman aqueduct stalks across the city.
There are Romanesque façades, squat towers, broad portals, all
built of an umber and honeycolored stone. Every detail of the
carved stonework stood out sharp in the flaming moonlight. It
was unbelievably beautiful. I remember how pleased Machado
was with the names of the streets and the churches. *San Millán
de las Brujas*—Saint Millan of the Witches—delighted him
particularly.
Machado himself was living then in a shabby lodging on a
street called *Calle de los Desamparados*—Street of Abandoned

Children. He couldn't have had an address more characteristic
of him. A lonely widower, in his forties I suppose, he gave the
impression of being helpless in life's contests and struggles, a
man without defenses. There was no trace of worldliness about
him. Long ago he had accepted the pain and ignominy of being
what he was, a poet, a man who had given up all hope of reward
to live for the delicately imagined mood, the counterpoint of
words, the accurately recording ear. (*Dream Below the Sun* xiii)

In Segovia in these later years he found a new love, Guiomar
(Pilar de Valderrama), a poet, a married woman with three children,
mostly separated from her diplomat husband at a time when there
was no divorce in Spain. They met by chance in Segovia in 1928
where she had come with her husband for some days of sojourning.
Thereafter they met regularly and inconspicuously in Madrid—
usually in an obscure restaurant—until civil war separated them.
An element of immediate erotic drama, not found in earlier poems,
now enters Machado's poems: "in the cold mother-of-pearl / of your
earring in my mouth." In the last sonnets of the war, he has the
vision of Guiomar, appearing on a *finisterre*. He admits, however,
it is

> a love that came to us in life too late.
> Our love's a hopeless blossom on a bough
> that now has felt the ax's frozen blade.
>
> ("De mar a mar" [From Sea to Sea])

Machado's late love had all the intensity, fantasy, frustration,
absence, separation, and dreams of romantic love. If we are to be
believe Valderrama's volume of memoirs, the love was always dis-
creet and never consummated, and while she avoided any trysting
place that would bring public notice, she also called off any meeting
where they would be entirely alone, leading to possible scandal. She
was also conservative politically, as was Antonio's brother Manuel
Machado, who was to side with Franco in that fratricidal war;
Antonio, committed as he was to liberal democracy and later to the
Republic, never knew Manuel as anything but his closest friend
in the world (indistinguishable from himself, he would say), and
similarly, despite Valderrama's politics and "public" prudishness,
Antonio would not be deterred from his longing for her, even during
the war when she had escaped, definitively, to the haven of Portugal.

Machado's love letters to Guiomar were published in 1950 by
Concha Espina in a book with the flashy title of *De Antonio Ma-
chado a su grande y secreto amor* (From Antonio Machado to his
grand and secret love), and although the letters are authentic, in his

own handwriting, the Spanish press in the Franco era predictably
condemned their publication as unworthy sensationalism. The only
"sensational" revelation in the letters is that Machado definitely
expresses his enthusiastically adolescent and wearily sad love for
an absent woman. Since, as Tomás Navarro Tomás observed, the
true biography of a poet, and particularly of Antonio Machado, is
to be found in his poetry, Machado's mature ambiguities in his love
for Guiomar are contained in some of his richest late poems. The
ambiguity is the obvious one. He needs Guiomar. He worships her.
She is real and unreal. Real is his fantasy. And that fantasy, he
recognizes perfectly well is a necessity of his need, not based on the
real Guiomar but on her creation through her unattainability and
absence. He needs to dream in peace his genuine false dreams where
historical truth, or any aberration, does not disturb the truth of
the passion. And the poems, uneven like a journal, without the
tenderness, nostalgia, and remembrance of those poems written
after the death of his child bride, are immediate, fanciful, incredibly
young as only a courtly love medieval troubadour might be. But
they are never sentimental, and they are always tempered with that
measure of irony and humor, telling us that while Guiomar really
exists and she is not a recalled figure of the past, she is also hope-
lessly away. Resigned to this knowledge, Antonio is joyfully, fu-
tilely inventing her:

> Your poet
> thinks of you. Distance
> is of lemon and violet,
> the fields still green.
> Come with me, Guiomar.
> The sierra will absorb us.
> The day is wearing out
> from oak to oak.
>
> (*Dream Below the Sun* 133)

Chinese as ever, Machado uses the condition of external nature
to express his passion. We see the two faces of Machado the lover—
which are in harmonious contradiction: in brief, epigrammatic lyr-
ics of love as self-conscious illusion; and then, in fuller poems, love
as the erotic, earthly creation of a real woman with kissable lips
and breasts, for whom he longs in a real bed, in a single, burning
night. The first is conceptual, and in it the Andalusian is laughing
proverbially at his self-deceptions. Machado distances himself from
this philosopher by creating a third-person narrator to speak in
wistful generalizations:

117

Antonio Machado

All love is fantasy,
and he invents the year, the day,
the hour and its melody;
invents the lover too, and even
the beloved, which is no reason
against the love. Though she
never existed nor can be.

(Dream Below the Sun 130)

When Machado speaks or, as the title of the sequence of poems "Canciones a Guiomar" (Songs to Guiomar) suggests, when he *sings* to his lover, then he is wholly poet and the woman, attainable or not, is wholly woman:

Today I write you from my traveler's cell
at the hour of an imaginary rendezvous.
A downpour breaks the rainbow in the wind
and its planetary sadness on the mountain.
Sun and bells in the old tower.
O live and quiet afternoon,
opposing its *nothing flows* to *panta rhei*;
childlike sky your poet loved!
Here is our adolescent day,
your eyes bright, muscles dark,
when by the fountain you felt Eros
kissing your lips, squeezing your breasts!
Everything in April light is a transparency.
The now in yesterday, the now that still is now
singing and narrating time
through these ripe hours,
burns into a single noon
that is a choir of afternoons and dawns.
Guiomar, I remember and crave you.

(Dream Below the Sun 135)

In Segovia, after the publication in 1924 of the first edition of *Nuevas canciones* (New songs), which are color patches of memory of other places, largely in succinct, popular-song prosody, Machado assumed the task of his imaginary poet-philosophers, Abel Martín and Juan de Mairena. Independent of Fernando Pessoa, the Portuguese inventor of poet voices with their own names and biographies, Machado created a gallery of other faces to comment on the world and himself. Only after 1936, at the outbreak of civil war, did the poet publish poems which were not through the intermediary of his apocryphal poets. Many of the poems by his apocryphal poets were sonnets.

Antonio Machado

Antonio becoming sonnetized

In the last years of his life, Machado turned to the sonnet form. There is a struggle going on in Machado between his aversion to certain tendencies in Spanish poetry, to superficial Spanish *modernismo* that he links with the sonnet of Ronsard, Rubén Darío, and even his brother, the modernist Manuel Machado; and at the same time, he reveals his attraction to the form, and so much so that he imitates lines from Dante and begins one sonnet with Dante's *Nel mezzo del cammin* of the *Inferno*. The sonnet won out, for he was to use the form in diverse ways, conceived by his imaginary poets or by himself, in all his later collections. Typical of his whimsical dogmatism, among his posthumous *Los complementarios*, he denounces the form for modern times as a used-up trinket, conceding that his brother Manuel Machado wrote some good ones. It is uncertain whether it is Machado or a prefatory resonance of one of his later voices speaking, Abel Martín or Juan de Mairena:

> The sonnet moves from the scholastic to the baroque. From Dante to Góngora, passing through Ronsard. It is not a modern composition, despite Heredia. The emotion of the sonnet has been lost. A skeleton remains, too solid and heavy for a contemporary literary form. One still finds some good sonnets among Portuguese poets. In Spain those of Manuel Machado are extremely beautiful. Rubén Darío never wrote one worthy of mention. (*OPP* 711)

The date of his mild diatribe is perhaps 1916, José María Valverde suggests, while he is still in Baeza. Soon he will write the sonnets in which he is "glossing Ronsard," dreaming of Dante the author of sonnets, hell, light, nightmare, and vision. In the subsequent sets of sonnets, Heraclitus becomes a familiar marker. Heraclitus (and his changing ashes of fire) is for Machado what he is for Borges: an obsession. Borges speaks of him so often that he is sometimes simply *El griego* (the Greek) as if there were only one Greek, or more enigmatically he calls him *Heráclito el oscuro* (Heraclitus the dark or obscure). Machado and Borges, both sworn to Heraclitean relativism, we know will never persuade us with absolutes and when they do decree we suspect their grin. Machado tell us:

> Confiamos
> en que no será verdad
> nada de lo que pensamos.

Antonio Machado

We know for sure
there never will be truth
in anything we think.

(OPP 309)

We can guess what he really has in mind when he contrasts
Calderón with the flow of things and consciousness in Heraclitus,
saying, "The whole charm of Calderón's sonnet—if it has any—
rests on its syllogistic correctness. The poetry here does not sing,
it reasons, discourses about certain definitions. It is—as all or al-
most all our baroque literature—left-over scholasticism" (*OPP* 317).
So while Don Antonio condemns the baroque sonnet for its
plodding, heavy ways, he disproves his disapproval of the form by
writing lyrical sonnets with the power of song. No one has made
the sonnet sing the way Machado has. His model for this is not,
however, popular Spanish song but Dante—another "habit" he
shares with Borges. He also translates the Shakespearean sonnet.
Indeed, he exchanges the Alexandrine of medieval verse and didactic
elegy—that dominate *Fields of Castile*—for the shorter eleven-syl-
lable sonnet line. The sonnet line in Spanish feels shorter than in
English (at least two syllables shorter) for the linguistic reason that
Spanish is more polysyllabic; it normally uses more phonemes to
put a word together.

The sonnet was Machado's compromise between the Alexan-
drine and the octosyllabic ballad. Endowing it with his epigram-
matic simplicity, Machado made of the sonnet a complete vehicle
for his final poetic expression, using it in sequences for his fields of
Spain, his woman in open-eyed dream, and his fields of war.

Antonio back in his Madrid cafés

On the day the Spanish Republic was declared in 1931, Ma-
chado and his students in Segovia climbed to the roof of the city
hall to raise the tricolor Republican flag. He transferred soon after-
ward to a newly opened school, El Instituto Calderón de la Barca in
Madrid. There must have been some witty god laughing at Machado
to have appointed the poet a *profesor* in a Madrid public high school
whose name was Calderón de la Barca, the great Spanish playwright
of *La vida es sueño* (Life is a dream), of the wondrous, allegorical
auto-sacramental, *El gran teatro del mundo* (The great theater
of the world), and the author of baroque sonnets that Machado
considered the epitome of foolish excess.

In the Madrid of 1931 to the war in 1936, Antonio was a more
successful man of letters and continued collaborating with Manuel
in those not overly significant but very popular plays. He lived with

120

José, his younger brother, the painter, and his family. Now at last truly back in Madrid, he retained qualities of the literary loner, keeping to his own older *tertulia* (a café literary group) in the midst of Generation of 1927 fervor. First of all he was no overt lover of Góngora or *neogongorismo*; curiously, however, the most significant new influence on his poetry at this time is (along with the abbreviated pigments of the Orient) the colorful sensuality and surrealism of Federico García Lorca. Lorca imagery and eroticism are in his love poems to Guiomar, and Lorca's mark is more clearly there than in his later elegy to the assassinated poet where he evokes Lorca's gypsy images. As for the woman Guiomar, his Muse— or maybe Muses—she remains in Madrid the secret woman, real, invented, absent, and desired.

Almost naked—like the children of the sea

When the Spanish Civil War began on July 18, 1936, Machado was in Madrid. He tried to enlist in the Republican army, but he was too old and moreover, not in very good health. Friends, particularly the poet Rafael Alberti, persuaded him by November to be evacuated to Valencia, and there, in Rocafort, a small village twenty minutes from the city of Valencia, he went together with his mother, his brother José, and José's wife and children. In Valencia he wrote poems about the luxuriant nature, about the Catalan-Valencian orchards and field, which provoked other scenes of childhood in Andalusia. By now the sonnet became the complete vehicle for most of his *Poesías de la guerra* (Poems of the war) in which pathos, horror, interludes of beauty, and recollection combine in fierce focus. Machado and Borges have been the two antiromantic dreamers in modern poetry, but in those days when dream meant memory, dream came and it was also resisted. Machado wrote, "I don't sleep / so I won't dream" (*Dream Below the Sun* 155). "La muerte del niño herido" (The death of the wounded child) has compassionate, surreal images of a bad dream in perhaps his only city poem of Madrid:

> Again the hammer through the night is heard:
> the fever in the bandaged temples of
> the child. "Mother, look, the yellow bird!
> and black and purple butterflies above!"
> "Sleep now, my son." The mother near the bed
> squeezes the little hand. "O flower of fire!
> Who can freeze you, tell me, O flower of blood?"
> In the bleak room a smell of lavender.
> Outside, the round full moon is whitening dome
> and tower across the city in its gloom.
> Somewhere a droning plane one cannot see.

Antonio Machado

Are you asleep? O flower of blood and gold.
The windows clamor on the balcony.
O cold, cold, cold, cold, cold!

In April 1938 Machado followed the government from Valencia to Barcelona. Louis MacNeice relates that he saw Machado during those last days in Barcelona, at a time when the Spanish poet was expending all his energy to the end of trying to save the remnants of the tormented Spanish Republic. He wrote regularly for *Hora de España* and *La Vanguardia* of Barcelona. Already in frail health, he was chain-smoking and scarcely aware that his clothes were covered with ashes fallen from his cigarettes. Ever since the exodus from Madrid, he had suffered from a heart ailment, which now caused a swelling in his feet and compelled him to walk with a cane.

During the last months in Barcelona, Antonio and a number of his friends used to have weekly reunions in a house outside the city. On a Sunday, January 11, 1939, the explosion of bombs from Italian airplanes constantly interrupted the singing that was going on inside the house. At least thirty bombers were in the sky all day long. Nevertheless, the music continued, Joaquín Xirau recounts, and on Monday, the several professors who were at the university gave their usual lectures at the university (Pradal-Rodríguez 12).

On January 22, a day ahead of the incoming Franco army, Machado and his family left Barcelona for Gerona in a government bus. Tomás Navarro Tomás delayed twenty-four hours, finally leaving with his wife the day Barcelona fell. They joined Machado at a farmhouse outside Figueras, twenty miles from the frontier. There, eighteen or twenty well-known Spanish intellectuals spent their last nights in Spain. On January 27, they boarded a military truck-ambulance and headed for the French border. One of the passengers in the crowded vehicle was Juan Roura-Parella, who related to me that in the cold and rain of that January evening, he witnessed the noblest action he remembered in his life:

> There was scarcely room for all the passengers in the vehicle. Personal belongings had to be left behind. When all were boarding, Machado insisted on being the last to find a seat. While his friends and relatives urged him to take a place, he remained in the patio and then insisted on being the last to enter the ambulance, saying, *Yo tengo tiempo, yo tengo tiempo* (I have time, I have time).[1]

1. This episode was related to me by Professor Juan Roura-Parella in Fall 1958 in Middletown, Connecticut, where we were both teaching at Wesleyan University. Roura-Parella examined this brief text in its written form for accuracy. The event took place at Cervia de Fer, near Figueras, in the Patio of an hacienda.

Antonio Machado

Each passenger was allowed to take only one small traveling bag. Since there was no room for his luggage, Machado left his suitcases by the roadside, containing all his unpublished writings of the last years. It is thought that among these lost papers was a songbook to Guiomar. We do not know, and probably will not, what writings were in the two, or possibly one, suitcases. The scene was described to me by Navarro Tomás:

> Machado sat opposite me in the crowded vehicle. We were all so numbed from the last sleepless nights and the most painful conditions of our traveling that none of us was able to utter a coherent sentence. During the trip, Machado sat with his head lowered, lost in deep reflection and a tremendous sadness. Occasionally, he mumbled a word to his brother José, who sat crammed next to him in the ambulance. When we reached the border at Port Bou, it was already night, cold, and raining heavily. The French police were preventing a crossing of the border between Port Bou and Cerbère. The accumulation of people and vehicles was so great that we had to get down from ambulance and walk half a mile by foot, in the rain, until the immigration office. Machado walked with difficulty. I had to help him, supporting his arm.
>
> I spoke to the chief customs officer and explained to him who Machado was, that he was sick, and that if he had to walk any further he would certainly die on the way. Fortunately, the officer, remembered his name from a Spanish textbook when he was studying the Spanish language, and was a man of understanding. He offered his private car to take Machado and his family to Cerbère.
>
> I was the only one who had any negotiable money, fifty prewar francs from a recent trip. With this money the writer Corpus Barga and I could go by train from Cerbère to Perpignan in search of financial resources for our immediate needs. Corpus Barga received a sum of money from a friend in Perpignan and returned to Cerbère to share this among his companions. With this same help I was able to go to Paris to seek aid from the Spanish embassy. The ambassador, Dr. Marcelino Pascua, with great urgency, cabled money to Machado at Collioure, so that, contrary to some reports, it can be said that Machado was not in financial straights during the last weeks of his life in France. (Interview at Columbia University, August, 1956)

Pradal-Rodríguez remembers: "Antonio Machado arrived at Collioure on January 29, 1939, drenched by a torrential rain. He had walked a long way and was so exhausted that he was obliged to take a taxi simply to cross the square and reach the hotel" (Pradal-Rodríguez 15). Most of the days that followed, Machado spent in his room, writing letters and gazing out of the window. He was able to go out a few times for a short walk on the beach—to see the sea of this Mediterranean village. Three decades earlier in Collioure, in the winter of 1909–10, not only had George Bracques and his compatriot Picasso invented cubism there, but in the late nineteenth century it had been a favorite site for the French impressionist painters to visit and record in paintings.

Antonio might have passed unnoticed if a little incident had not taken place at the Hotel Bougnol-Quintana where he and his family had rooms:

> A hotel employee found the name of Antonio Machado, "teacher," among the names of the latest guests. His schoolmaster, between two rules of grammar, pointed out the name and one or two of his poems. And so he went to ask if he were of the poet's family, and Machado confessed that he himself was the person to whom he was referring. This employee, Jacques Baills, was possibly Don Antonio's only friend (with the exception of his brother José) during the month at Collioure. There one imagines him, "mysterious and silent," with that "gaze you could hardly meet, it was so profound," as Rubén Darío pictured him one night of 1905; but with the immense sorrow of the lost war, with the kind of mute terror one has when catastrophe appears to have removed the meaning of one's existence. (Pradal-Rodríguez 15)

The poet was by now gravely sick. On February 22 he died and was buried the next day in the local Collioure cemetery. His hotel landlady, Señora Quintana, provided the plot. On February 25, his mother, in the adjoining room, died. Antonio Machado and his mother Ana Ruiz Hernández remain at *Collioure* today:

> And when the day for my final trip arrives,
> and the ship, never to return, is set to leave,
> you will find me on board with scant supplies,
> almost naked—like the children of the sea.
>
> (*Dream Below the Sun* 47)

In 1957 Juan Ramón Jiménez wrote his elegiac memoir of Antonio Machado. As in the prophetic poem "Portrait," Antonio Machado left naked and driven out, as Jiménez said, through the back gate:

> When bodily death came, he died humbly, miserably, collectively, the lead animal of a persecuted human flock, driven out of Spain—where he as Antonio Machado had had everything,

his dovecots, his sheepfolds of love—through the back gate. In this condition he crossed the high mountains of the frozen frontier, because such was the way his best friends, the poorest and most worthy, made the crossing. And if he still lies under the ground with those buried there away from his love, it is for the comfort of being with them, for I am certain that he who knew the rough uneven path of death has been able to return to Spain through the sky below the ground. (*Dream Below the Sun* xvi)[2]

That last line we have from Machado's pen was scrawled in a notebook found after his death. He wrote, clearly through the sun of Collioure and from his childhood memory in Sevilla:

Estos días azules y este sol de la infancia.

These blue days and this sun of childhood.

(*OPP* 658)

"My eyes in the mirror / are blind eyes looking / at the eyes I see with"

"I am never closer to thinking one thing when I have written the opposite," Machado wrote in *Los complementarios* (*OPP* 16). The mirroring of opposites is aphoristically contained in the brief tercet above, from Machado's *Nuevas canciones y cancionero apócrifa* (New songs and apocryphal songbook), anticipating the infinite regress of Borges's blind eyes and his hand fumbling in his mirrors; and as in Borges, the eyes in the mirror are material symbols of consciousness. Both men, the Andalusian and the Argentine, southerners and philosophers, laugh at the failure of their speech, using words to prove that the events of the mind are always beyond the fraility of language, and attempts to impose absolutes of truth upon elusive awareness are laughable, pompous nonsense. And they love to make that rich, insightful point of linguistic failure.

---

2. In 1957, while preparing the translations for *Eighty Poems of Antonio Machado*, I wrote to Juan Ramón Jiménez in Rio Piedras, Puerto Rico, asking whether he would not write a memoir of Antonio Machado for the forthcoming book. (John Dos Passos had already written his lucid portrait in response to a similar request.) Jiménez replied by telegram, saying: "I accept in principle." Two weeks later his memoir arrived in New Haven. It appears in its entirety, as does the Dos Passos portrait, in *Eighty Poems* and also in the expanded version. *The Dream Below the Sun: Selected Poems of Antonio Machado.*

Antonio Machado

So also like Whitman, Machado was comfortable with his contradictions. When he was writing against the form of the sonnet and its limitations, he was accepting those limitations, by studying the sonnets, translating them into Spanish from English, and preparing himself for his only work to survive the last years, *Poesías de la guerra* (Poems of the war), the larger part of which is a sonnet sequence. In the sonnets, he is always aware that he Antonio Machado is a speaker talking to another blind speaker, the reader, and he shares the roles of both figures in their experience, which is always a way, never an end. Machado's gods always save him from *truth* and other falsehoods.

Returning again to the Prague poet who shared with him his year of birth in 1875, Rainer Maria Rilke, Machado and Rilke were poets of solitude and landscape. Machado, as I read, hear, and see him, has been the silent laugh and eye of Western poets, rendering him Chinese in spirit and imagery. He described in pure-color planes (and never with the saturated Kodachrome of the early Stevens) the landscapes of monastic Castile and fertile Andalusia. He saw them through a metaphysical lens of open-eyed dream. What he saw, by extension, was also the soul of Spain made personal and particular— as the best poetry, religious or secular, political or social, inevitably is. More important, those outer landscapes of Spain's soul are also the silent fiery landscape of his solitude.

He communicated an image of his solitude with minimum means—and minimum loss. He understood perfectly the poems of the Tang dynasty, Buddhist nature poet Wang Wei, whom he surely never read. To his willing reader he bequeathed with unlimited generosity and modesty an intimate picture of an interior landscape.

El amor y la sierra

Cabalgaba por agria serranía,
una tarde, entre roca cenicienta,
El plomizo balón de la tormenta
de monte en monte rebotar se oía.
Súbito, al vivo resplander del rayo,
se encabritó, bajo de un alto pino,
al borde de una peña, su caballo.
A dura rienda le tornó al camino.
Y hubo visto la nube desgarrada,
y dentro, la afilada crestería
de otra sierra más lueñe y levantada
—relámpago de piedra parecía—.
¿Y vio el rostro de Dios? Vio el de su amada.
Gritó: ¡Morir en esta sierra fría!

Esto soñé

Que el caminante es suma del camino,
y en el jardín, junto del mar sereno,
le acompaña el aroma montesino,
ardor de seco henil en campo ameno;
que de luenga jornada peregrino
penía al corazón un duro freno,
para aguardar el verso adamantino
que maduraba el alma en su hondo seno.
Esto soñé. Y del tiempo, el homicida,
que nos lleva a la muerte o fluye en vano,
que era un sueño no más del adanida.
Y un hombre vi que en la desnuda mano
mostraba al mundo el ascua de la vida,
sin cenizas el fuego heraclitano.

Love and the Sierra

He was galloping over harsh sierra ground,
one afternoon, amid the ashen rock.
The tempest's leaden ball was heard rebound
mountain to mountain echoing with shock.
Suddenly, amid the glazing radiance
of burning lightning bolts, below high pines
his horse reared up beside a precipice.
He swerved back to the path, seizing the reins.
He looked. The sundered cloud came into view,
and in the rift the sharpened summits grew
of farther sierra peaks hanging above,
blazing. It seemed to be lightning of stone.
And did he see God's face? He saw his love.
He screamed: To die in these cold hills alone!

All This I Dreamt

The wanderer of the road becomes the road,
and in the orchard by the serene sea
a mountain fragrance follows him; grass mowed
across the pleasant fields is fiery hay.
The pilgrim on his lengthy journey reined
his heart in check. He found that it was best
for iron lines to wait and be contained
until the soul could ripen in his chest.
All this I dreamt: a homicidal time
floating us to our death or drifting (and
in vain) was just the peak of Adam's dream.
I saw a man who in his naked hand
revealed the coals of life, a constant flash
of Heraclitean fire, and yet no ash.

Cómo en el alto llano su figura

Cómo en el alto llano su figura
se me aparece! . . . Mi palabra evoca
el prado verde y la árida llanura,
la zarza en flor, la cenicienta roca.
Y al recuerdo obediente, negra encina
brota en el cerro, baja el chopo al río;
el pastor va subiendo a la colina;
brilla un balcón de la ciudad: el mío,
el nuestro. ¿Ves? Hacia Aragón, lejana,
la sierra de Moncayo, blanca y rosa . . .
Mira el incendio de esa nube grana,
y aquella estrella en el azul, esposa.
Tras el Duero, la loma de Santana
se amorata en la tarde silenciosa.

Por qué, decísme, hacia los altos llanos

Por qué, decisme, hacia los altos llanos
huye mi corazón de esta ribera,
y en tierra labradora y marinera
suspiro por los yermos castellanos?
Nadie elige su amor. Llevóme un día
mi destino a los grises calvijares
donde ahuyenta al caer la nieve fría
las sombras de los muertes encinares.
De aquel trozo de España, alto y roquero,
hoy traigo a ti, Guadalquivir florido,
una mata del áspero romero.
Mi corazón está donde ha nacido,
no a la vida, al amor, cerca del Duero . . .
¡El muro blanco y el ciprés erguido!

How Suddenly Her Face on the Plateau

How suddenly her face on the plateau
appears to me! And then my word evokes
green meadows and the arid plains below,
the flowering blackberries and ashen rocks.
Obedient to my memory, the black oak
bursts on the hill, the poplars then define
the river, and the shepherd climbs the cloak
of knolls while a town balcony shines: mine,
ours. Can you see? Remote, toward Aragón,
the sierra of Moncayo, white and rose.
Look at the bonfire of that cloud, and far
shining against the blue, my wife, a star.
Santana hill, beyond the Duero, shows,
turning violet in soundless afternoon.

You Ask Me, Why My Heart Flies from the Coast

You ask me, why my heart flies from the coast
back to Castile, to towering raw terrains,
why, near the sea, in fertile fields, I most
yearn to be back on high and barren plains.
No one chooses his love. It was my fate
that one day chose to send me to gray hills
where falling snows freeze and obliterate
the shadows of dead oaks—now winter still.
Out of that spur of Spain, rocky and high,
I bring you now, blooming Guadalquivir,
a sprig of rosemary, a pungent thorn,
My heart is living, yes, where it was born,
but not to life—to love, the Duero near,
the whitewashed wall and cypress in the sky!

Las ascuas de un crepúsculo, señora

Las ascuas de un crepúsculo, señora,
rota la parda nube de tormenta,
han pintado en la roca cenicienta
de lueñe cerro un resplandor de aurora.
Una aurora cuajada en roca fría
que es asombro y pavor del caminante
más que fiero león en claro día
o en garganta de monte osa gigante.
Con el incendio de un amor, prendido
al turbio sueño de esperanza y miedo,
yo voy hacia la mar, hacia el olvido
—y no como a la noche ese roquedo,
al girar del planeta ensombrecido—.
No me llaméis porque tornar no puedo.

¡Oh soledad, mi sola compañía!

Oh soledad, mi sola compañía,
oh musa del portento que el vocablo
diste a mi voz que nunca te pedía!
Responde a mi pregunta: ¿Con quién hablo?
Ausente de ruidosa mascarada,
divierto mi tristeza sin amigo,
contigo, dueña de la faz velada,
siempre velada al dialogar conmigo.
Hoy pienso: este que soy será quien sea;
no es ya mi grave enigma este semblante
que en el íntimo espejo se recrea
sino el misterio de tu voz amante.
Descúbreme tu rostro: que yo vea
fijos en mí tus ojos de diamante.

132

Lady, the Embers of a Shattered Dusk

Lady, the embers of a shattered dusk,
its storm clouds a monotony of brown,
have quickly painted rocks of ashen rust
on a far hill with blazings of the dawn.
It is a dawn congealed on frozen rock
that overwhelms the traveler with awe
and dread—more than a furious lion stalk-
ing the bright day, or great bears in the claw
of mountains. Seized by flaming love, with burns
and turbulence of dreams of hope and fright,
I'm walking toward the sea, oblivion,
and not like those huge boulders toward the night
as the dark somber planet turns and turns.
Don't try to call me back. I must go on.

O Solitude and Now My One Companion!

O solitude and now my one companion!
O muse of wonder offering the word—
I never asked for—to my voice! A question:
Who am I talking to? And am I heard?
Abstracted from the noisy masquerade,
I turn my sadness, punctured by no friend,
to you, lady of the veiled face, in shade,
who when you talk to me are always veiled.
Today I think: who I am I don't care;
it's not my grave enigma when I stare
into my inner mirror but the mystery
of your warm loving voice. Now clear the
   glare
and show your face to me. I want to see
your eyes made out of diamonds fixed on
   me.

Esta luz de Sevilla . . . Es el palacio

Esta luz de Sevilla . . . Es el palacio
donde nací, con su rumor de fuente.
Mi padre, en su despacho. —La alta frente,
la breve mosca, y el bigote lacio—.
Mi padre, aún joven. Lee, escribe, hojea
sus libros y medita. Se levanta;
va hacia la puerta del jardín. Pasea.
A veces habla solo, a veces canta.
Sus grandes ojos de mirar inquieto
ahora vagar parecen, sin objeto
donde puedan posar, en el vacío.
Ya escapan de su ayer a su mañana;
ya miran en el tiempo, ¡padre mío!,
piadosamente mi cabeza cana.

Primaveral

Nubes, sol, prado verde y caserío
en la loma, revueltos. Primavera
puso en el aire de este campo frío
la gracia de sus chopos de ribera.
Los caminos del valle van al río
y allí, junto del agua, amor espera.
¿Por ti se ha puesto el campo ese atavío
de joven, oh invisible compañera?
¿Y ese perfume del habar al viento?
¿Y esa primera blanca margarita? . . .
¿Tú me acompañas? En mi mano siento
doble latido; el corazón me grita,
que en las sienes me asorda el pensamiento:
eres tú quien florece y resucita.

Light of Seville, the Great Palatial House

Light of Seville, the great palatial house
where I was born, the gurgling fountain sound.
My father in his study. Forehead round
and high, short goatee, moustache drooping down.
My father still is young. He reads and writes,
leafs through his books and meditates. Then springs
up near the garden door, strolls by the gate.
Sometimes he talks out loud, sometimes he sings.
And now his large eyes with their anxious glance
appear to wander with no object to
focus upon, not finding anywhere
to rest in void. They slip from past and through
tomorrow where, my father, they advance
to gaze so pityingly at my gray hair.

Vernal

Clouds, sun, green meadow, and a villa set
all in confusion on the hill. The spring
placed in the light of these cold fields a net
of grace on river poplars ripening.
The valley roads lead to the river. There,
next to the water, love is waiting still.
Are fields dressed in a young, primordial air
for you, companion, now invisible?
And that perfume of beanfields in the wind?
And that white daisy, first one of the year?
Will you come *with* me? In my hand I feel
a double throb; my heart, undisciplined,
screams out to me, thoughts deafen me, I reel!
It's you who blossom newborn and rise here.

Rosa de Fuego

Tejidos sois de primavera, amantes,
de tierra y agua y viento y sol tejidos,
La sierra en vuestros pechos jadeantes,
en los ojos los campos florecidos,
pasead vuestra mutua primavera,
y aun bebeb sin temor la dulce leche
que os brinda hoy la lúbrica pantera,
antes que, torva, en el camino aceche.
Caminad, cuando el eje del planeta
se vence hacia el solsticio de verano,
verde el almendro y mustia la violeta,
cerca la sed y el hontanar cercano,
hacia la tarde del amor, completa,
con la rosa de fuego en vuestra mano.

Al gran Cero

Cuando el *Ser que se es* hizo la nada
y reposó, que bien lo merecía,
ya tuvo el día noche, y compañía
tuvo el hombre en la ausencia de la amada.
Fiat umbra! Brotó el pensar humano.
Y el huevo universal alzó, vacío,
ya sin color, desubstanciado y frío,
lleno de niebla ingrávida, en su mano.
Toma el cero integral, la hueca esfera,
que has de mirar, si lo has de ver, erguido.
Hoy que es espalda el lomo de tu fiera,
y es el milagro del no ser cumplido,
brinda, poeta, un canto de frontera
a la muerte, al silencio y al olvido.

Rose of Fire

Lovers, you are a weaving of the spring,
woven of earth and water, wind and sun.
The mountains in your panting chests, and spun
into your eyes the fields are blossoming.
Go out and walk with spring and share the season,
and fearlessly keep drinking the sweet milk
which the lewd panther offers you, the treason
of beasts, before she traps you in black silk.
Stroll when the axis of the planet bends
into the solstice days of summer, when
the almond trees are green and violets gone,
when thirst is near and water soaks the land.
Walk toward love's afternoon, fulfilled, and on
and on, the rose of fire inside your hand.

To the Great Zero

When *Being that is himself* made nothing, he
lay down to rest (and thoroughly deserved),
day owned the night, and man lost company.
Only through absence was his love preserved.
Fiat umbra! And human thought was born.
A universal egg arose, empty
and colorless and cold, deprived of form
and filled with an unsubstantial misti-
ness. Take the number zero, hollow sphere,
which, if you see it, will be standing near.
Now shoulders are the back of your wild
    beast,
a miracle of non-being born. Now feast,
drink, poet, and sling out a border song
to death, to silence and to oblivion.

La primavera

Más fuerte que la guerra—espanto y grima—
cuando con torpe vuelo de avutarda
el ominoso trimotor se encima
y sobre el vano techo se retarda,
hoy tu alegre zalema el campo anima,
tu claro verde el chopo en yemas guarda.
Fundida irá la nieve de la cima
al hielo rojo de la tierra parda.
Mientras retumba el monte, el mar humea,
de la sirena el lúgubre alarido,
y en el azul el avïón platea,
¡cuán agudo se filtra hasta mi oído,
niña inmortal, infatigable dea,
el agrio son de tu rabel florido!

El poeta recuerda las tierras de Soria

Ya su perfil zancudo en el regato,
en el azul el vuelo de ballesta,
o, sobre el ancho nido de ginesta,
en torre, torre y torre, el garabato
de la cigüeña! . . . En la memoria mía
tu recuerdo a traición ha florecido;
y hoy comienza tu campo empedernido
el sueño verde de la tierra fría,
Soria pura, entre montes de violeta.
Dí tú, avïón marcial, si el alto Duero
a donde vas recuerda a su poeta
al revivir su rojo Romancero;
¿o es, otra vez, Caín, sobre el planeta,
bajo tus alas, moscardón guerrero?

The Spring

More powerful than the war—its terror and crime,
when with the giant bustard's torpid flight
the ominous trimotor starts to climb
and over rooftops hovers in bleak fright—
today your cheerful salaam fires the plains,
the poplars guard your bright transparent green
in buds. The melting snow from high terrains
will flood red ice on lands gone drab and mean.
While mountains rumble and the oceans fume,
a siren wails alarm in deadly gloom
and the plane silvers a blue firmament;
untiring goddess, floating through the sphere,
immortal child, the wind stabs in my ear,
sounding your blooming rebec's harsh lament.

The Poet Recalls Lands of Soria

Its lanky profile wading in the pool,
rising into the blue with crossbow verve,
or landing on a patch of fragrant broom,
perched on a tower, shaped in a pothook curve.
It is the stork! And in my memory
your memory has bloomed and given birth
subversively. Today your stony sea
of fields begins the dream of frozen earth:
pure Soria, mountainsides of violet.
Warplane, let me know if the upper Duero,
your target now, remembers who its poet
once was—reliving its red ballads. Or,
under your wings, droning hornet of war,
are you not Cain again over the planet?

Amanecer en Valencia desde una torre

Estas rachas de marzo, en los desvanes
—hacia la mar—del tiempo; la paloma
de pluma tornasol, los tulipanes
gigantes del jardín, y el sol que asoma,
bola de fuego entre morada bruma,
a iluminar la tierra levantina . . .
¡Hervor de leche y plata, añil y espuma,
y velas blancas en la mar latina!
Valencia de fecundas primaveras,
de floridas almunias y arrozales,
feliz quiero cantarte, como eras,
domando a un ancho río en tus canales,
al dios marino con tus albuferas,
al centauro de amor con tus rosales.

La muerte del niño herido

Otra vez en la noche . . . Es el martillo
de la fiebre en las sienes bien vendadas
del niño. —Madre, ¡el pájaro amarillo!
¡las mariposas negras y moradas!
—Duerme, hijo mío. —Y las manita oprime
la madre, junto al lecho—. ¡Oh flor de fuego!
¡Quién ha de helarte, flor de sangre, díme?
Hay en la pobre alcoba olor de espliego;
fuera, la oronda luna que blanquea
cúpula y torre a la ciudad sombría.
Invisible avïón moscardonea.
—¿Duermes, oh dulce flor de sangre mía?
El cristal del balcón repiquetea.
—¡¡Oh, fría, fría, fría, fría, fría!

140

Dawning in Valencia from a Tower

These blasting winds of March, caught in the attic—
facing the sea—of time; the glowing plumes
of iridescent doves, tulips gigantic
here in the garden, and the sun that looms,
a ball of fire lost in violet brume,
lighting the earth of Valencia. Fury
of milk and silver, indigo and spume,
and white sails mingling on the Latin sea.
Valencia with its spring of fertile riches,
its orchards blooming and its fields of rice,
I'd like to sing you happy as you were,
mastering a river in your farming ditches,
taming a seagod in your salt harbor,
tangling centaurs of love in your rose trees.

The Death of the Wounded Child

Again the hammer through the night is heard:
the fever in the bandaged temples of
the child. "Mother, look, the yellow bird!
and black and purple butterflies above!"
"Sleep now, my son. The mother near the bed
squeezes the little hand. "O flower of fire!
Who can freeze you, tell me, O flower of blood?
In the bleak room a smell of lavender.
Outside, the round full moon is whitening dome
and tower across the city in its gloom.
Somewhere a droning plane one cannot see.
Are you asleep? O flower of blood and gold.
The windows clamor on the balcony.
O cold, cold, cold, cold, cold!

De mar a mar entre los dos la guerra

De mar a mar entre los dos la guerra,
más honda que la mar. En mi parterre,
miro a la mar que el horizonte cierra.
Tú, asomada, Guiomar, a un finisterre,
miras hacia otro mar, la mar de España
que Camoens cantara, tenebrosa.
Acaso a ti mi ausencia te acompaña.
A mí me duele tu recuerdo, diosa.
La guerra dio al amor el tajo fuerte.
Y es la total angustia de la muerte,
con la sombra infecunda de la llama
y la soñada miel de amor tardío,
y la flor imposible de la rama
que ha sentido del hacha el corte frío.

From Sea to Sea Between Us Is the War

From sea to sea between us is the war
now deeper than the sea. From my parterre
I watch the sky-bound water, Guiomar.
Then you appear upon a finisterre,
watching another sea, the sea of Spain
that Camões sang to us, a murky sea.
Goddess, your memory is a well of pain,
and can my absence be your company?
The war has cut a trench between our love.
Here is death's agony: sterile shadow
of a high fire and the dreamed honey of
a love that came to us in life too late.
Our love's a hopeless blossom on a bough
that now has felt the ax's frozen blade.

Federico García Lorca

(1898–1936)

Spain

Federico García Lorca

The Generation of '27, celebrating Luis de Góngora, with Federico García Lorca at the center

After the generation that produced Antonio Machado, Miguel de Unamuno, the *modernista* poet Juan Ramón Jiménez, the philosopher-essayist José Ortega y Gasset, the novelist Pío Baroja—whom Hemingway claimed as his master—and Ramón de Valle Inclán, the playwright of the *esperpento*, a new generation, very different in preparation and background, born around the year 1900, was waiting to take over. Its way was prepared by Machado and Unamuno, but the younger writers already saw their master liberators as friends neither to be emulated nor imitated.

The Generation of '98 had thrown off the immediate past. Now something more radically denunciatory and experimental was in the air. Marinetti had published his futurist manifesto in Paris in 1909. Cubism in painting was formulated in Collioure by a Spaniard and a Frenchman; Guillaume Apollinaire was there to describe and celebrate the new art of Picasso and Bracques and in his own work throw out all punctuation in one exasperated order to the printer when he published his wonderful book of poems *Alcools* in 1911. Tristan Tzara invented dadaism in Zurich in 1916, and after the great War, André Breton and company in Paris issued their manifestos of surrealism. Surrealism spilled over into most countries of Europe—with the exception of England, which was doing its own thing with help from the late symbolist city poets Laforgue and Corbière, who had actually preceded the stylistic uproar all over the Continent.

In Spain the poets Borges, an Argentine, and Gerardo Diego, a Spaniard, collaborated in the early twenties in their experimental *ultraísmo*, another anti-nineteenth-century, antisentimental, antidecorative, antigrammatical, and antipunctuation movement, which was at the same time pro-science and pro-machine and whose formulation on the page favored geometrical designs, as in concrete poetry and as opposed to traditional linear poetry. After those exciting and dynamic days, the leaders went on with their own personal styles, leaving most of the fun and protest experiment behind, once having cleansed their writing of the despised past with its affectations and ornaments. Although the "isms," which extended from Spain to Russia, soon disappeared, all subsequent poetry was affected by its initial energy and directions. Pedro Salinas, for example, at the heart of the somewhat later Generation of 1927 movement, published his first poems with ingenious images of electric princesses carrying swords in lightbulbs or white virgins who are targets (*blancos*) of the typewriter keyboard which, when touched by our fingers, utter metallic noises of *z,d,g,f*. . . . It is helpful to know that *blanco* means both "target" and "white," and that Underwood typewriters of the twenties (the poem's title is "Underwood Girls") had white keys.

The enduring Spanish *ismo* was *gongorismo*, and it pervaded the work of the 1927 poets. The scholar and sometime poet Dámaso Alonso took personal charge of it, organizing its literary politics and conferences. In a famous *congreso* (literary conference) in Sevilla, Lorca lectured on Góngora as did Ignacio Sánchez Mejías, a literary bullfighter whose subsequent death Lorca was to lament in his famous elegy "Llanto por Ignacio Sánchez Mejías" (Lament for Ignacio Sánchez Mejías). This lament was rendered in a magnificent baroque language clearly indebted to the same Góngora. Lorca's *Romancero gitano* (Gypsy ballads), 1928, his outstanding book of sequential poems, has Góngora's cold-metal surrealism. In *Romance de la Guardia Civil española* (The ballad of the Spanish Civil Guard), the *guardias* (police) are described as having souls of patent leather, and they pass by,

> . . . if they want to pass,
> concealing in their head
> a vague geometry
> of inconcrete pistols.

> (*Obras completas*, 15th ed. 453)

The image is typically Lorca, yet inconceivable before that period of Góngora emulation. Of course *gongorismo* was only one significant ingredient in the never-again-created wonder that was Federico García Lorca.

Federico García Lorca

Federico, who made me laugh like no one else and put us all in mourning for a century.

—Pablo Neruda

Federico García Lorca

From the beginning Lorca was a poet and playwright, and he wrote in both genres with equal dedication. To say this is not to suggest that there was not overlapping and sometimes conflict. From the earliest volume of poetry, *Libro de poemas* (Book of poems), 1921, to the *Gypsy Ballads* in 1928 and "Lament for Ignacio Sánchez Mejías," we see the poet moving from intimate, first-person poems toward the detachment and breadth of the theater, with its creation of characters and dialogue, narrated in the detached voice of a third-person speaker. There is a parallel development in the theater, not from first-person to implied narrator but from highly poetic to prose drama. The plays began as poetic drama, yet by the time of his last work, *La casa de Bernarda Alba* (The house of Bernarda Alba), completed just before his last fated departure to Granada, Lorca was able to tell his friends that *Bernarda Alba* did not have a single line of poetry in it. Then, curiously, having established his plays as prose plays rather than dramatic verse, his own poetry had no need to do what his theater was already expressing, and in his two important last collections, which were to appear posthumously, *El diván del Tamarit* and *Poemas del oscuro amor*, he is no longer a poet of the theater but returns to the intimate and personal mode of the first books, with all the maturity and passion of the master writer he was.

As for his extraordinary facility, Lorca insistently repeated, his gifts, grace, and ease came from total dedication and sweat. In a passage recorded by Gerardo Diego, Lorca eloquently describes the secrets, contradictions and labors of the poet:

But what can I say about Poetry? What can I say about those clouds, that sky? Look, look, look at them, look at it, and nothing else. You will understand that a poet can say nothing about Poetry. Leave that to critics and professors.

So that's it. Look. I have the fire in my hands. I understand it and work with it perfectly, but I can't speak about it without literature. I understand all poetics; I could speak about them if I didn't change my opinion every five minutes. I don't know. Maybe one day I'll very much like bad poetry as today I'm crazy about (we're crazy about) bad music. I will burn the Parthenon at night in order to begin to raise it up again in the morning and never finish it.

In my lectures I've spoken at times about Poetry, but the one thing I can't speak about is *my* poetry. And not because I am unaware of what I'm doing. On the contrary, if it's true that I am a poet by the grace of God—or the demon—it's also that I am so by the grace of craft and effort, and by being absolutely conscious what a poem is. (*Obras completas*, 15th ed. 167)

Federico García Lorca

Fuente Vaqueros and Granada

Federico García Lorca was born June 5, 1898, in the small town of Fuente Vaqueros (fountain of the cowhands) nor far from the small Genil river and from Granada. The village lay just off the main road between Granada and Córdoba. This is the *Vega*, that greenist of plains in Andalusia that Roman engineers and Arab horticulturalists turned into rich farmland. His father was a wealthy landowner, his mother a schoolteacher. Ian Gibson, Lorca's biographer, has destroyed the myth of the poet's childhood speech difficulties. His younger brother Francisco said he was "a precocious talker," and he certainly began very early, as a child, to put together plays.

Lorca said he inherited his passion from his father and his intelligence from his mother, who was also a musician. His biographers agree it was apparently a good, rich childhood, with all the unarticulated psychological forces of family relationships feeding into the complexities of his character. Till the very last days of his life, Lorca was very close to his brother, sisters, and parents. José Luis Cano tells us how from earliest childhood he was obsessed with nature and its small creatures:

> Federico was a contemplative, observing child. When he was not at play with other children, he used to watch for hours on end the little animals of which he spoke as though they were his friends, and also the plants and trees of his village. The world of Nature, in its variety and mystery, was for him a surprising world, a kind of strange paradise demanding his constant attention. (Cano 13)

In 1909 the family moved to Granada, a city of diverse beauty and ethnicities: Spanish, gypsy, Arab—the Arab civilization of eight hundred years. Spain was "reconquered" when the city of Granada fell to the armies of Fernando and Isabela. And not far behind—in historical fact and in Lorca's poems—Granada was also the city of Carthaginians, Greeks, Jews, Romans, Goths. In "Reyerta" (Quarrel) from the *Gypsy Ballads*, Lorca has the judge report a murder to the civil guards, by invoking the metaphor of the millennia of the region's peoples:

> Señores, civil guards:
> here the usual took place.
> Four Romans have died
> and five Cathaginians.
>
> (*Obras completas*, 15th ed. 429)

150

Federico García Lorca

For Federico, Granada was also the city of fine Andalusian culture, epitomized by his friendship with the composer Manuel de Falla, at whose house Lorca was a regular guest and with whom he would collaborate a few years later in the *Fiesta del Cante Jondo*. (It was also Falla who in 1936 on the morning of July 19, upon discovering that Lorca was imprisoned, went immediately to officials to seek his release.) Lorca was a talented musician, a musician before he was a writer.

Federico played the guitar and piano, studying classical music with Antonio Segura to whom he was to dedicate his first published book. Of course, he learned a repertory of classical pieces, including Albéinez and Debussy and also played folkloric songs from many parts of Spain; moreover, he rescued popular Spanish songs from oblivion, finding and transcribing them for later publication. He painted, drew, designed stage sets. Everything he set his hand to had his imagination, wit, and, as he liked to say, the art and perfection that came only with hard work. In truth the mature Lorca was incapable of imperfection in his poems in the sense that the craft, naturally and by his sweat was always there.

As early as 1915 Lorca began his studies formally at the University of Granada in philosophy and letters, where he eventually obtained a degree in law, which he never used. In June of 1916 with five fellow students, he took a study trip through Castile and Andalusia, led by his professor Martín Domíngez Berrueta. In Baeza he met Antonio Machado. One evening at the *instituto* where he had been teaching since leaving Soria after his young wife's death, Machado read from his *Campos de Castilla* (Fields of Castile); then Lorca, the *músico* in the group, played the piano, presenting classical pieces and some of his own compositions.

Little has been said of the influence of Machado on Lorca because Lorca, with all his *gongorismo*, surrealism, and experimentation, was not only of a later generation, but Machado himself kept aloof from the group of '27 by the nature of his own rural isolation and his suspicion of the "modern baroque." In reality there was not only cordiality between Machado and Lorca but essential ties. Lorca's immense reputation as a poet came with his *Gypsy Ballads* based on the popular traditional Spanish *romance* (ballad). Don Antonio chose the ballad form for his longest and most ambitious poem, "La casa de Alvargonzález" (The house of Alvargonzález), which appeared in *Fields of Castile*, 1912. The poem was key in Lorca's development. Dr. Roberto García Pinto, an Argentine writer who knew Lorca during his Argentine visit in 1933–34, informed me years later that one evening, with a group of friends, Lorca was asked to recite some of his own poems. Instead, for the next fifteen minutes, he recited Antonio Machado's "Alvargonzalez" ballad sequence. As for Lorca on Machado, many of Machado's late poems, especially the erotic, fantastic pieces on Guiomar, have a clear imprint of the color, passion, and whimsy of the younger Lorca. We all know Machado's poignant elegy for Lorca, using Lorcan images, written after word came in 1936 of Lorca's assassination.

In October of the same year of 1916, Berrueta took his students on a second, more extensive trip through northern Spain, including Salamanca where Lorca met Miguel de Unamuno. In all, the group made four journeys through Spain. Lorca's love for the newly discovered Galicia would eventually lead him back to Santiago where, with the help of friends, he wrote six poignant poems in *galego*, the Galician version of Portuguese. The following year Lorca published in Granada his first book, *Impresiones y paisajes* (Impressions and landscapes), a book of subtle prose reflecting both the beauty of the regions visited as well as protesting descriptions of urban decay and the poor as in his grim picture of the underfed children in the ruinous orphanage at Santo Domingo de Bonaval. At this time Lorca became fully committed to writing the first poems along with scenes for plays; he had begun the tasks that became his life. His first three literary works, however, were unsuccessful. *Impressiones y paisajes*, published in 1917, lived for a few months in Granada bookstores; his first play, *El maleficio de la mariposa* (The witchery of the butterfly), 1920, though produced in Madrid at an important theater, was an immediate failure; and *Libro de poemas* (Book of poems), published in 1921 in Madrid, was ignored by critics, though eventually praised by Adolfo Salazar, music critic for *El Sol*, Madrid's most prestigious newspaper. Lorca was discouraged by the play's failure, yet alive with his abundant new writings, friends, and the literary activities that had absorbed him since he had taken up residence in Madrid.

Madrid

In 1919 Lorca came to Madrid to study and live at the Residencia de Estudiantes. The "Residencia," or "Resi" as everyone called it then, was an enlightened continuation of Francisco Giner de los Ríos's Free Institution of Learning, which Antonio Machado and his generation had attended. The Residencia attracted the most interesting figures of the time to lecture there, from Spain and abroad, and we hear echoes of their presence as when Lorca quotes from talks by Le Corbusier on modern architecture or Louis Aragon on surrealism. It was also the residence of his close friends—the painter Salvador Dalí and filmmaker Luis Buñuel as well as the poets José Moreno Villa and Emilio Prados. His closest and enduring friends were the poets of the Generation of 1927, named for Gón-

gora, or sometimes "of 1925," the year that most of the poets of
that extraordinary group began to publish. They included Vicente
Aleixandre, Dámaso Alonso, Rafael Alberti, Pedro Salinas, Jorge
Guillén, and Luis Cernuda. To that vital gathering of poets we
should add Miguel Hernández, of the Generation of '36. Hernández
is Spain's last major voice in poetry of the century. Although he
knew Lorca, to whom he first wrote from the country asking for
his work, and Lorca helped and encouraged him decisively, there
remained a patronizing distance, in contrast to the much closer ties
Hernández had with Aleixandre and Pablo Neruda.

Having mentioned Neruda, for whose book *Veinte poemas de
amor y una canción desesperada* (Twenty poems of love and a
despairing song) Lorca did a series of accomplished ink drawings, we
should remember that in these years Spanish and Spanish American
poets were connected in both literature and place. Octavio Paz,
Jorge Luis Borges, César Vallejo, and Neruda were all in Spain at
different times and very close friends of the same Spanish mafia of
poets. Neruda and Lorca also were companions in Buenos Aires in
1933–34 when Lorca was in Argentina for his plays and later in
Madrid. Borges was part of the Spanish *ultraísta* group with Gerardo
Diego; Paz, Vallejo, and Neruda were in Madrid during periods of
civil war, and much of the best writing by Neruda and the last
poems of Vallejo were written in or about Spain.

Although in Madrid and by now fully committed to poetry and
theater, Lorca remained the musician and Andalusian, and in June
of 1922 he organized with Manuel de Falla the "Festival of *Cante
Jondo*" in Granada, an elaborate recital of flamenco song. Picasso
came from Paris to do the backdrop in the Moorish patio where the
festivities were held. Later the same year, Lorca delivered a lecture,
"The *Cante jondo*, Primitive Andalusian Song," and completed his
first extraordinary book of poems, *Poema del cante jondo* (Poem of
the *Cante jondo*), written in 1921, though, like other collections,
not published until much later, in 1931. In "Juan Breva" the *cantaor*
(flamenco singer) Lorca portrays the Andalusian singer, his orchards
and sea, and even makes an ingenious reference to Homer, with
humor and acuity, making what might have been an artificial or
pompous classical allusion connect the obscure Andalusian singer
with his ancient blind mentor:

> Juan Breva had
> the body of a giant
> and voice of a girl.
> Nothing like his trilling.
> It was the same
> pain singing

behind a smile.
It calls up lemon groves
of sleeping Málaga,
and in his wailing are
specks of marine salt.
Like Homer he sang
blind. His voice had
something of a lightless sea
and squeezed orange.

(*Obras completas*, 15th ed. 320)

The poet's lecture on the *Cante jondo* and his later "Architecture of the *Cante jondo*," his lectures on Góngora and on the *duende* (the ineffable source of the artist's inspiration), and many other talks and essays collected in his complete works make Lorca an outstanding teacher and scholar of Spanish poetry. His pieces are in the highest essayist tradition of Spain. Just as in England where the poets have been the enduring literary critics—Sidney, Dryden, Johnson, Coleridge, Arnold, Eliot—in Spain and Spanish America the poets Machado, Unamuno, Cernuda, Guillén, Alonso, Salinas, Bergamín, Bousóño, Paz, and Borges have given us the seminal studies on poetry in Spanish.

Federico had a good room in the Residencia where he lived for a decade. He liked to play an old Pleyel piano in the salon of the Residencia. José Luis Cano describes a typical session at the piano of the Residencia (a scene which was to be repeated in many cities and on many continents throughout Lorca's short life):

Federico liked to play alone or surrounded by friends who listened to him. Federico was indefatigable at the piano. He liked to begin by playing his preferred composers—Chopin, and Schubert, Mozart and Beethoven, Debussy and Ravel, Falla and Albéinez—but from them he went on to eighteenth-century *tonadillas* and folksongs of the nineteenth century from Castile, Galicia, Andalusia. He gave himself totally to the music and words of the song, which he sang in his warm, wet, somewhat husky voice; and when he finished, he looked staring and smiling at his listeners, as if saying to them, "This is Spain!" Often illustrious visitors at the Residencia, scholars and artists, listened ecstatically to that inexhaustible fountain of poetry and popular music, that richest treasure of the purest Spanish folklore. (Cano 36–37)

When not the piano it was the guitar through which Lorca allowed that deep river of Spanish song to flow. In all his habits, Federico was now in a fervor of creation. In 1924 he was writing the play *Mariana Pineda* and his *Gypsy Ballads*. Emotionally, his conflicts of bisexuality which had troubled him were clarified, if not pacified, as he accepted his dominant homosexuality. His "defect," as Mildred Adams in her warm biography refers to his homosexuality, was not unknown to his closest friends but given the time, he fearfully concealed it from his father—on whom he still depended financially—and of course from the larger Spanish society. He wanted to join his friends in Paris but had no money to do so. He was waiting for a literary success that would provide him with financial independence. Fame of almost a bullfighter's notoriety was about a decade away—not until after his return in 1934 from Argentina. Fame and literary success he wanted and yet curiously avoided, specifically by delaying publication of major books for years, the *Gypsy Ballads, Poem of the Cante jondo, Primeras canciones*, and *Diván del Tamarit*. The postponements, however, were not simply for reasons of perfection. Lorca, with his passions, depressions, good humor, felicity, and terrors, was a man of endless contradiction and complexity. His best friends, Aleixandre, Alberti, and Neruda, record how even in his apparently happiest, liberated moments, his eyes betrayed a reserve of sadness and fear.

His closest attachment, his passion, was the painter Salvador Dalí, six years his junior, whom he met in 1922 when he came to Madrid and took a room at the Resi. The affair lasted nearly six years. Lorca stayed with Dalí and his sister Ana María in Figueras in the Dalí summer house at Cadaqués on the coast. They collaborated. Dalí did the set designs for the Barcelona premiere of his verse drama *Mariana Pineda* in 1927, which received a moderate critical success. That same year saw the publication of his book *Canciones* in Málaga and an exhibition of his drawings in Barcelona. It was a year of being poet, playwright, painter, and as always, musician.

Dalí was very early, by inclination and by declaration in manifestos, a surrealist. The painter and the poet reinforced each other's surrealist fantasy. Lorca wrote a crucial surrealist poem, his "Ode to Salvador Dalí." But Dalí frequently reproached Lorca for not throwing off all signs of his earlier nonsurrealist art, as in his letter of 1928 after receiving a copy of *Gypsy Ballads*, which for the first time had established Lorca among the critics as the major poet of his generation. The book went through seven printings in the next eight years and became the most widely read volume of Spanish poetry in the century. Dalí was cool and scornfully critical of *Gypsy Ballads*, despite its neo-Gongorist, surreal imagery. It was not only too traditional, local, and tied to the past but failed to be governed by the "irrational," Dalí's code word for surrealism. Dalí, famous for his outrages, narcissism, and arrogance—usually excused as part of his act—was not aloof to the ordinary racism of the time. He accused Lorca of turning into a dark gypsy. The painter's letter ends with references to a poet "half-possessed by death," whom he, Dalí, loves for what the book reveals about him personally. "Goodbye, I BELIEVE in your inspiration, in your *sweat*, in your astronomical fatality" (Gibson, *Lorca* 216).

Lorca was not in full disagreement with Dali's criticisms. He worried about being labeled as a "popular" poet, one who had not labored to earn each word in his writings. In typical contradiction, he wrote to Jorge Guillén in 1927, before the book's publication, concerning the gypsy, his hero, artist, and outsider in the epic struggle against the police and the society it reflected. The ballads were already famous through publication in literary magazines and his many public and private recitations. He complained to Guillén:

> I am getting a little annoyed with that myth of *gitanería* (gypsyism). They confuse my life and my character. I do not want it at all. Gyspies are a theme. And nothing else. . . . Besides, this gypsyism makes it seem that I have no culture, education, and am a wild poet, which you know I am not. I don't want to be pigeonholed. I feel they are putting me in chains. No. (*Obras completas*, 15th ed. 1580)

And then, despite the needs of his own respectability, Federico rejected his own reservations, remaining loyal to his gypsyness. To his Chilean friend Carlos Morla Lynch, he wrote in 1934, "The gypsies are the ones who inspired my best book: the *Romancero*. Of all my works it is the one that satisfies me most. Perhaps it is the only one in which I don't find any flaws" (318).

Lorca's attachment to Dalí was perhaps the poet's first major erotic obsession in a life of intensely passionate relationships (well documented by Ian Gibson), the last of which was his happy and tragic friendship with Rafael Rodríguez Rapún. Gibson states that Lorca's passion for the painter did "lead to various attempts at anal intercourse" (Gibson, *Lorca* 165). Dalí, whose every act, however designed to shock, was equally humorous, witty, and ironic, informed the French poet Alain Bosquet:

> He was a pederast, as is well known, and madly in love with me. He twice tried to fuck me. That upset me a lot because I wasn't a pederast, and had no intention of giving in. Besides, it hurt. So the thing never happened. But I was deeply flattered from the point of view of my own prestige. Deep down in my being, I said to myself that he was a very great poet and that I owed him a bit of the Divine Dalí's asshole. (Bosquet 52)

Federico García Lorca

On the basis of letters to Lorca and a series of surreal prose poems to Saint Sebastian, who is clearly Lorca, Gibson concludes that "by 1917, Salvador was much more emotionally involved with Federico than he would later be prepared to admit" (Gibson, *Lorca* 182).

The year 1927 was a decisive year for Lorca. Not only did he formally establish himself as a playwright with the performance of *Mariana Pineda*, and as a poet with *Canciones*, but in December at the Ateneo in Sevilla, he gave his celebrated talk on Góngora at the festival in honor of the seventeenth-century poet. Dámaso Alonso arranged the resurrection of Góngora, and those aiding in the act were Rafael Alberti, Gerardo Diego, Juan Chabás, Jorge Guillén, José Bergamín, and the literary bullfighter Ignacio Sánchez Mejías. Lorca's talk was received with strong applause. He had prepared it assiduously over a period of some months, even rehearsed it a few days earlier with friends in Granada. After the formal presentations, Lorca was asked to read ballads from the *Gypsy Ballads*. In their enthusiasm the listeners lost control, tossing handkerchiefs and coats at him, as if celebrating the feats of a great torero. In the history of modern Spanish poets, these were marvelous, unique days of joy and exuberant creation by a group of cordial friends. Later that night the poets, who had dressed, according to instructions, in Arab robes, congregated at Sánchez Mejías's country place where they drank and recited. In his memoir *La arboleda perdida* (The lost grove), Rafael Alberti catches the spirit:

> What a night, amid poets and good friends! We drank. We recited our poems. Dámaso Alonso, the great commentator on Góngora, astonished us by repeating from memory the 1091 lines of the poet's *Primera soledad*. García Lorca gave some of those amusing theatrical bits of his. . . . When that choir of drunken Arabs was at its most absurd, Ignacio announced the arrival of the guitarist Manuel Huelva, accompanied by one of those geniuses of *cante jondo*, Manuel Torres, better known as "El Niño de Jerez," who died poverty-stricken in Triana some months later. . . . Manuel Torres knew neither how to read or to write, he could only sing. But that he could do—his singer's sense was perfect. That same night, with a wisdom and sureness equal to that which a Góngora or a Mallarmé would have displayed in talking of his aesthetics, Manuel Torres confessed to us that he did not let himself go with the current, the too widely known, the well ploughed fields; then he summed up in a strange and majestic manner that which he thought we would understand. "In *cante jondo*," he mumbled, his hands wooden on his knees, "what one always has to look for, until you find it, is the black torso of the Pharaoh." (Alberti 264–66)

Federico García Lorca

Federico felt that with the phrase "the black torso of the Pharaoh" (connecting *gypsy* with death, eternity, and the roaming Egyptian past of the word), Torres had explained the secrets of his *Gypsy Ballads*.

Lorca never lost his ties with Granada. He usually returned to the Huerta de San Vicente, the family place outside Granada on the Vega, for the summer where, despite being in the south, it is high, near the Sierra Nevada mountains, and cool. In Granada in 1928 he founded a sophisticated journal of the arts called *Gallo* (Cock). The avant-garde magazine attacked what was left of leftover romanticism, which made some people unhappy. When after four months and two issues Federico returned to Madrid, the magazine died for lack of a director.

In Madrid, Lorca at last had the forthcoming publication of *Gypsy Ballads* by the *Revista de Occidente* and acquired a new love, Emilio Aladrén, a young sculptor. The ballad book came out, and he was, as Ricardo Baeza had predicted in the *El Sol*, "enthroned" by the press and the public, despite the aforementioned sour letter from Dalí. Luis Buñuel, for whom anything less than prescribed surrealism was old-fashioned banality and compromise, wrote a diatribe against Lorca's Andalusianism in a personal letter to Dalí. In these attacks by Buñuel, who had never visited Andalusia, we have a reflection of the mutual disdain between north and south, which was normally an issue in fields other than literature. In literature one might expect jealousies and regional rivalries, since from Góngora, Zorrilla, and Bécquer to Machado, Jiménez, Cernuda, Alberti, Aleixandre, and Lorca, this largest and most Arabic of Spain's provinces dominated Spanish poetry. Yet in that fraternity of generations, of 1898, 1927, and 1936, there is, in reality, scarcely a hint of petty regional conflict. Perhaps Lorca himself betrayed the most self-conscious ambiguities, loving his Andalusian and folkloric richnesses, yet fearing provincialism. Lorca was also disturbed by the report of the film, *Un chien andalou* (An Andalusian dog), whose screenplay his surrealist "friends" Dalí and Buñuel wrote in December of 1928 in Figueras. Its description appeared in February 1929 in the *Gaceta Literaria*. The satiric Andalusian dog, depicted as weak and impotent, Lorca concluded, was aimed at him. To his friend Angel del Río in New York he rued, "Buñuel has made a shitty little film called *An Andalusian Dog*—and I'm the Dog" (Gibson, *Lorca* 229).

Meanwhile, Federico's new play, *The Love of Don Perlimplín for Belisa in His Garden*, which was scheduled to appear in Madrid, was at the last moment prohibited by the censors of the Primo de Rivera regime. For many reasons, including Emilio Aladrén's temporary desertion of the poet for a woman whom he eventually

158

married and the loss of Dalí, Lorca was seriously disturbed and depressed and sought escape, which came when his loyal friend, Professor Fernando de los Ríos, who had originally arranged for his coming to the Residencia, now arranged for him to spend a year abroad, mostly in America.

Lorca and Don Fernando left for Paris, went to London and Oxford where they spent a day with Salvador de Madariaga, and then from South Hampton sailed in the heat of the summer for New York.

New York

Like all his life experiments—with perhaps the exception of his later trip to Argentina and his years with the roving play company La Barraca, both of which were exceedingly happy experiments—Lorca's stay in North America was rich in pleasures and severe anxiety. Above all the journey led to a startling new literary production: his innovative volume, *Poeta en Nueva York* (Poet in New York), a collection of poems distinctly surreal, urban, modern, cinematic, and absolutely foreign to the Andalusian traditional verse forms of earlier years. The poems were a radical experiment which, at least in its surrealistic mode, now connected him with what some of his closest poet friends, Aleixandre and Alberti, were up to in Spain itself. He also wrote the sonnet "Adam," the first of those sonnets which, like the later *Sonetos del oscuro amor* (The Sonnets of dark love), would allude directly to homoerotic passions.

There were friends in America waiting for Lorca—the Spanish professors Federico de Onís and Angel del Río at Columbia, where he would be a student in English, and some Americans he had met in Spain. Dámaso Alonso would come later and even his friends Ignacio Sánchez Mejías and Andrés Segovia. New York was New York, meaning everything Spain was not. There was Wall Street and its Stock Exchange. Lorca was for hours with the crowds in the street outside the Exchange on the day of the crash. There was Harlem, the Chrysler Building, the Bronx Zoo, Brooklyn Bridge. There were peoples—blacks, Jews, the spirit of Walt Whitman, Armenians, Cubans, and children. Angel Flores recalls that Lorca loved Woolworth's and in his delight at all its mechanical wonders, took toys from the counter and spread them out on the floor. He loved how the blacks sang and danced. "Only our Andalusian *cante jondo* could be compared to them," he wrote home. There was the English language, which he attempted to learn by attending classes regularly, but English was not to be his. He did give lectures at Vassar and Columbia and traveled to northern Vermont for ten mostly rainy days where, in that Eden, he wrote poems in solitude.

159

Federico García Lorca

Mildred Adams, who had known Federico in Spain, was a devoted host to him in America. In her biographical study of the poet and playwright, she recounts how he responded, without English, to local Vermonters. After finishing his six-week language course at Columbia, Lorca had accepted an invitation to stay with his friend Philip Cummings and his elderly mother at Eden Mills in Vermont. There he walked through the almost autumn woods, discovering goldenrod, young dogwood, and the small things of nature that did not exist in Spain. The house was by a lake. Adams describes how Lorca used his music in Vermont to reach the villagers:

> The cabin had no piano, and Federico had come without a guitar. The two men sang familiar folk songs together, but Cummings wanted more than that. He was proud of his guest, and longed to share the guest's special skills with his Lake Eden neighbors. Language alone would not do it, even for two gentle schoolteachers who lived nearby, loved poetry, but knew no Spanish. Remembering the delight of the poet's music at the *Residencia*, "Felipe" persuaded Federico to sing for the village. The yellow-sided dance hall around the curve of the lake had a piano—not well tuned, but neither was the piano in the Hotel Washington Irving in Granada where he had played more than once. Cummings invited Stanton Ruggles who lived all the year in Eden village; "The Boy Stanton" invited his friends; so did the two retired schoolteachers, the Misses Tyler who lived further up the road behind their handmade stone wall.
>
> At four in the afternoon the village people came in, shy but curious. In a pattern which came to be repeated again and again in more sophisticated New York rooms Federico told them about the song he was going to sing and Cummings translated what he said into English; it would be the tale of the burro who carried vinegar for the village . . . or the one of the four mule drivers, or any other from the rich storehouse of Federico's memory. For the moment he forgot, as he always did, that his words were foreign to his audience. And by that charismatic miracle of charm, personal evocation, artistry which was his own great gift, he made the audience forget. They had been told what the song would be about—gestures, voice, and that ineffably vivid face conveyed even more than the friendly translator's words. Federico had never in his life failed to hold his audience, and those Vermont farmers in the bare Eden dance hall offered no exception. They cheered, they pounded the floor, they crowded around to shake his hand. He had won Eden. (Adams 107–8)

All commentators on his months at Columbia agree that Lorca attended only the summer language course and that there is no record that he was in any literature class. Perhaps he was not officially enrolled. In 1953–54 I was a student in Henry Wells's course in poetic drama. Wells told me that Lorca had chosen his class to attend because it was poetic drama, and he did so regularly, although he had virtually no English. He also recounted how he invited Lorca to his house. One evening, evidently before the well-known meeting of Lorca and Crane in Brooklyn, Henry Wells introduced Hart Crane to Federico in his apartment near Columbia. They shook hands, tried to speak to each other. They did not discover their imperfect French connection and then turned away to other friends. I often thought of that meeting through the years, when Lorca met Crane, each in his own language unsurpassed as a poet of his generation, and yet these two poets, almost the same age (Crane was born in 1899), could not discover their many common personal and literary causes. Lorca and Crane would have been friends. But language intervened. And nothing else. These were men whose life was language, and when apparently it wasn't there for them they were like those first to descend the Babelean tower, deracinated, separated, and confined to their solitudes.

New York was a strong, major, lonely, bizarre experience in his life and his work. *The Poet in New York* is one of the most original books in the Spanish language. There is Lorca's battle with the Babylonian metropolis, his compassion for the poor, the abandoned children, the people waking into dirty dawns like insomniacs just after leaving a shipwreck of blood. He wrote about the Brooklyn Bridge at the same time that Hart Crane, the man whose hand he shook meaninglessly in Wells's Manhattan apartment, was making Brooklyn Bridge the centerpiece of his great sequence about America called *The Bridge,* and almost at the same time that another lonely man, Vladimir Mayakovski, spent a year of exploration in New York, similarly deprived of English, and composed one of his fabulous poems, "To Brooklyn Bridge."

After three seasons in New York, Lorca was weary of language isolation and the metropolis, and he was ready for change. He had been looking for something to replace the life and vistas of his province of Granada, and after taking a train to Tampa, sailed for Havana.

Havana

The Hispano-Cuban Culture Institute had invited Lorca to give five lectures at their institute. Lorca left in early March and remained in Cuba till early June. As in New York, he was welcomed by friends of friends, who were loyal and hospitable. The most devoted of these was the family of Antonio Quevedo. They provided him with a place to come to daily for meals and friendship, where there was a place to write, a piano, an audience for his writing. Don Antonio's sons and daughters became his companions during the day and often during the very long nights that seldom saw Federico home before dawn. Perhaps the most important document on Lorca as a musician is contained in a letter from Manuel de Falla to the Quevedos in which the Spanish composer asks them to receive his "splendid collaborator in the matter of Spanish folk tradition":

> When God decides that an artist of such quality should be born, capable not only of assimilating the technique necessary for his work but of going beyond what in technique is merely mechanical (and this is the case with García Lorca in his arrangements of Spanish folk songs), we realize the enormous difference between that which is the product of teaching and that which wells up of its own personal, creative accord, stimulated by that teaching. (Quevedo 17–18)

The formal lectures were received enthusiastically, and Federico stayed on, for in Cuba he found another Andalusia—in the varied people, in the Cuban *son* music with its Afro-Cubano origins. Even the buildings on the tangled streets near his hotel recalled the streets of Granada. In Havana he wrote the first complete draft of his play, *El público* (The public or The audience), a fantastic, experimental work in which homosexual love, in a dreamlike, carnival ambience, is the subject. *The Public* contains a play within the play (the characters are Romeo and Juliet) and conscious borrowings from Shakespeare's *A Midsummer Night's Dream* and *Hamlet*. The play was too daring for Spain—it was a play to be booed, he would say, and it couldn't be performed in Spain. For decades after the poet's death, the play was thought to be lost, but like the *Sonnets of Dark Love*, it finally turned up.

Lorca seems to have written scenes for his surrealist drama, *Así pasen cino años* (When five years pass) and the poem "Iré a Santiago," (I will go to Santiago). His immensely important poem, written during this period, is "Ode to Walt Whitman," later included in *The Poet in New York*. We are uncertain where the ode was actually written, in Havana or, more probably, in New York. The manuscript copy is dated June 15, suggesting that it was completed, or at least copied, on board the ship home. It was published during his lifetime only in a limited edition of fifty copies in Mexico in 1933. The poem is ambivalent, probably reflecting Lorca's own unresolved conflicts as a "masculine" gay. It praises the "beautiful old Walt Whitman with his beard full of butterflies" while savagely attacking city *maricas* (effeminate gays) as degraders of an uplifting ideal pansexualism.

Federico García Lorca

Cuba was a liberation for Lorca. He was happy there as he had rarely been in his life. It was also a period of intense sexual activity. He was completely independent, unconcerned with critical comment and "spies"—no Buñuels to attack and satirize him in their art. His social conscience, as always, did not desert him—any more than in New York when he discovered the art and vitality of blacks while he inscribed mercantile and industrial nightmare in his poems. So amid his euphoria in tropical Eden, he was acutely aware of Cuba's poverty, corruption, and the military dictatorship of Gerardo Machado. His ever-present concern for the poor and the outsider, in Cuba as in Spain, did not impede him from being personally fulfilled in his own deliverance to the music, people, and the island's lush meadows and orchards.

Federico left Spain as the author of *Gypsy Ballads*, the most popular book of poetry in the Spanish language in his time. (There has been no rival since.) Now he gave himself to theater, comedy, and stark rural tragedy, and in a short time he would be Spain's most significant playwright at home and internationally. That reputation has also held firm. He failed in his efforts to legitimize *The Public* by having it produced in Madrid. But in December 1930, the Teatro Español produced his *La zapatera prodigiosa* (The shoemaker's prodigious wife), a play he had begun as early as 1924. This Andalusian comedy was not only a critical and commercial success, but with it he established ties with its premiere actress and producer, Margarita Xirgu, who was to be essential in the life of his succeeding plays. It was Xirgu who took his dramas to astonishing applause in Cuba and Mexico during the last months of his life, writing, wiring, phoning him to come to Mexico as he had promised. When he was ready to acquiesce, it was too late.

In the spring of 1931, the Republicans won a fierce election, King Alfonso XIII left the country, and democracy came to Spain with the Second Republic. Reform in every area was instant— education, law, land distribution, separation of church and state. But the cardinals and church leaders responded with prayers and intense political hostility to the "Marxist-Jewish-atheist" regime, as they saw the Republic (though there were no Marxists, probably no atheists, and certainly no Jews in its makeup). In a few years Jews in small numbers would, for the first time since 1492, begin to cross the frontier into Spain, fleeing from the Fascist states and their conquered territories into an independent Fascist state that no longer burned its Jews. The immediate strategy of the Church was to ally itself with the extreme right-wing movements that found their model in the emerging extremist political philosophies of Germany and Italy. By 1933 José Antonio Primo de Rivera, son of the former dictator-general, established the Falange Española,

Federico García Lorca

and its propaganda organ *El Fascio* appeared in Madrid. As the word *Fascio* suggests, the Falange was not a verbal victim, by association, of the bad odors associated with fascism. It proclaimed its association with the organization and ideals of Italian fascism by naming its main periodical *The Fascist*.

(The conquest by Falange blueshirt ideology was ultimately so total in Spain and the nation so isolated under Franco, that even in 1951, six years after World War II, I recall local mayors in the province of Granada, where I was living for a year, who were unembarrassed in praise of Hitler and Mussolini and expressed surprise, perhaps feigned, at disapproval of such loyalties. After all, the armies of Hitler and Mussolini, fighting with the rebels, were essential to Franco's victory over the Republic.)

For Lorca his great opportunity came in late November when the government asked him to assemble a theater company of student actors with the purpose of taking the Spanish classics to the small towns and villages, to put up stage and set in the public squares and provide free performances for local residents. It was called La Barraca (the barn or hut) and Lorca gave himself to it with all his talents and energy. With its first success it was of course attacked by the extreme Right as Marxist propaganda disseminated by immoral Jewish atheists. Lorca proved to be an able leader and a sternly exacting director of the young actors. In his blue boilersuit Lorca was changing his way of life. For three years he was to spend much of his time on the road with the Barraca; he learned as much as he gave, and in both the writing and production of his own plays, the disciplines he acquired contributed to his maturity as a playwright.

Meanwhile, he was preparing *Bodas de sangre* (Blood wedding), the first work in "a dramatic trilogy of the Spanish earth," to use the poet's words. Under Lorca's supervision, with his knowledge of timing, stagecraft, and direction, when *Blood Wedding* hit the stage, it was performed brilliantly. Attended by the poets of his generation, by Miguel de Unamuno and the Nobel Prize–winning, older playwright Jacinto Benavente, it was a mythical hit. Lorca was now the playwright of Spain, on the verge of financial independence, and ready to go off to Argentina where his work would dominate that city and his earnings inflate his pocket. The last years of his personal life were spent acquiring a constancy with his attachment to an engineering student, Rafael Rodríguez Rapún. Indeed, a difficulty in leaving Spain for Mexico in those last days when it was possible for him to do so was certainly enhanced by his unwillingness to be separated from Rodríguez Rapún, who still had university obligations.

Their relationship remains a mystery, as it should, since Lorca was discreet and most letters have not been preserved. They were with each other much of the time, and the *Sonnets of Dark Love* were probably addressed to Rapún. From the Federico García Lorca archive in Madrid, one letter written to Federico a few days after his departure for Argentina reads, "I remember you constantly. Not to be able to see a person with whom you have been every hour of the day for months is too much to be forgotten. Especially if towards the person in question you feel yourself drawn as strongly as I do towards you" (Gibson, *Lorca* 360).

Buenos Aires

Lorca was in Argentina from October 1933 to April 1934. Victoria Ocampo, founder of *Sur*, Latin America's most prestigious literary periodical, did a printing of *Gypsy Ballads* that was instantly a best-seller. At the time, none of his books were on sale in Latin America. When he died, much work was still unpublished—including all the plays (except for *Blood Wedding*), miscellaneous poems, *Diván del Tamarit*, and *Sonnets of Dark Love*. Lorca was not indifferent to publication. He often spoke about books he was about to publish. But it was hard to get the manuscripts from him. He left only copies of plays with friends, and in short he was much more interested in the serious act of writing than in seeing work through to the printer.

Argentina was glory, pesos, friendship. These were good years for Argentina. The problems in Spain of censorship and of a sector in the nation opposed to Lorca's art on moral and political grounds seemed laughable in Buenos Aires, whose theater was strong, varied, experimental, and eclectically international, as it still is. (Some years ago when I taught in Buenos Aires, it remained vital and international even amidst the horrors of the "disappearances" and the "dirty war.") Pablo Neruda was in Buenos Aires in those days. As was the habit of so many people with Lorca, they met and immediately shared a deep friendship. Later, Neruda wrote of hilarious happenings: an extraordinarily elegant joint speech on Rubén Darío before the P.E.N. Club banquet in which they spoke alternatively in renga rhythm, dazzling all with their verbal acrobatics; and Chaplinesque pranks and mishaps as when Neruda tried to undress a cooperative literary "golden girl" in a high tower over a swimming pool, only to be undone by his appointed sentinel, Lorca, who rolled down the tower's darkened stairs, causing the amorous couple to get up and rush to his aid.

When Lorca returned to Madrid in 1934, he had two good prolific years left to him. The Republic had passed into the hands of the far Right, there were thousands of political prisoners in jail, including Manuel Azaña, the Republic's first prime minister, whose arrest and charges were concealed by the censor. The National Socialist Party was in sole control in Germany and its human shadows in Spain labored avidly, wildly accusing all who were not with them to be Jewish Marxists implicated in nefarious conspiracies.

Yet the literary life of Madrid continued, as it did in all Europe, intensified by the politically intense air. And that generation of poets which began to publish a decade earlier was now at a peak of maturity and collaborative friendship. Neruda spoke of this period: "They were the great days of my life. It was such a splendid and generous rebirth of Spanish creative life that I never again saw anything that could approach it" (qtd. in Gibson, *Lorca* 404). Lorca's *Yerma* was produced, then condemned violently by the Right on unthinkably absurd moral grounds. Even his lovely Chekhovian play on old Granada society, *Doña Rosita la Soltera* (Doña Rosita the spinster) was abused by *parti pris* critics who seemed to yearn for his blood.

The terrible event for Federico in August 1934 was the death of Ignacio Sánchez Mejías, his literary bullfighter friend from the Góngora celebration in Sevilla, from New York days, from Madrid. Sánchez Mejías was forty-two when he returned to the ring. He was badly gored, and by a series of mistakes and the failure to get him from Manzanares to the Madrid hospital for thirteen hours after the goring, gangrene set in and he died. Lorca wrote his single most important poem, "Lament for Ignacio Sánchez Mejías," modeled after the "Coplas" of the medieval poet Jorge Manrique. The climactic lines of part two, "The Spilled Blood," epitomize Ignacio and Spain with its stark contrasts, its severity, its beauty, its tragedies:

> Oh, white wall of Spain!
> Oh, black bull of sorrow!
> Oh, hard blood of Ignacio!
> Oh, nightingale of his veins!
> No.
> I don't want to see it!
> There is no chalice to contain it,
> there are no swallows to drink it,
> there is no song nor deluge of lilies,
> no crystal to cover it with silver.
> No.
> I don't want to see it!!
>
> (*Obras completas*, 15th ed. 542)

The last verses of part four, "The Absent Soul," are often cited as a portrait of Lorca himself. The lines are right for Lorca's portrait:

Federico García Lorca

It will be long before is born, if such is born,
an Andalusian so dazzling, so rich in adventure.
I sing of his elegance with words that moan,
and recall a sad breeze through the olive trees.

(*Obras completas*, 15th ed. 545)

Sonnets of Dark Love

Sonnets of Dark Love were not published during the poet's life. The descendants of the family released them for publication in the literary supplement of the Madrid newspaper *ABC* on March 17, 1984, forty-eight years after the poet's death. They are now incorporated in his *Obras completas* (Complete works). The title was told to Vicente Aleixandre to whom he recited the poems a few months before his death. The "dark love" is surely an allusion to San Juan de la Cruz's "dark night of the soul," a notion reinforced by the lines "or let me live in my concordant night, / night of the soul forever dark, obscure." Juan de la Cruz is, I have always believed, even in his few poems, the poet most allied to Lorca, formally, by his darkness/light vision, by the absolute clarity and candor of his sensuality, by his passionate spirituality, by the severe rigor of his artistically spare yet full lines. The poets created each other. And in these poems of love they come closest. Only San Juan and Lorca have the sharp light of sexual openness of the Arabic *jarchas*, a sexuality absent from Spanish poetry after those tenth- and eleventh-century wondrous verses. While human love is a common mystical simile for union with the divine, San Juan goes further, giving us the penetration and climax of the lovers, in the first-person singular, speaking as the woman:

> O night that was my guide!
> O night more friendly than the dawn!
> O tender night that tied
> lover and the loved one,
> loved one in the lover fused as one!

(John of the Cross 49)

San Juan de la Cruz also has peace while making love, a silence of tenderness which Lorca perhaps wished but had not yet reached:

> Deep in the winevault of
> my love I drank, and when I came
> out on this open meadow
> I knew no thing at all,
> I lost the flock I used to drive.

(John of the Cross 49)

Lorca is more tormented. His love cannot be open—except in verse. In "El amor duerme en el pecho delpoeta" (Love sleeps on the chest of the poet), he writes:

> But, lover, keep on sleeping next to me.
> Hear my blood broken over violins!
> See how they watch and wait for us like hounds!

And toward the lover—who may not be like himself fully committed to that sterility of the seedless one referred to in the earlier sonnet "Adam"—he feels an inferiority, an inequality, an alienation because of his strange sex. He concedes that he may be a low beast. Nevertheless, in "Soneta de la dulce queja" (Sonnet of the gentle complaint), he asks for participation in his lover's waters:

> If you are now my only concealed treasure,
> if you are dripping pain, my cross and quiver,
> if I am just the dog of your high station,
> don't let me lose what is my rightful measure.
> Please decorate the waters of your river
> with leaves from my autumnal alienation.

Vicente Aleixandre later recalled that in 1937, in the midst of the war, Federico came to his place shortly before leaving for Granada. He then read Aleixandre the sonnets from his last work, which "we were not to see completed":

> He read me his *Sonnets of Dark Love*, with enormous passion, enthusiasm, happiness, torment, a pure and burning monument to love, in which the raw material is the flesh, the heart, the soul of the poet in the act of destruction. Personally surprised, I found myself staring at him and exclaming, "Federico, what a heart! How much one has had to love, how much one has had to suffer!" He looked at me like a child. As I spoke it was probably not me that was speaking. (Qtd. in García Lorca, *Obras completas*, 15th ed. 1831)

In extremist European politics of the 1930s and largely till our day, those not Fascists were labeled Communists, those not Communists were labeled Fascists. In Falange terminology, those who were not loyal "Blues" were enemy "Reds." So as the Popular Front prepared for the 1936 elections, which it was to win by a narrow margin, the *Azules*, the Blues, on the right prepared for civil war to save the country against the *Rojos*, the Reds, who were a coalition of center and left dominated by liberal democrats. On electoral victory, the Popular Front's first political action was to free all political prisoners. The conflict between ideologies increased by the day; there were assassinations, threats, hardening of positions. Military conspiracy was in the air. Lorca was always with the Republic, and his "Ballad of the Spanish Civil Guard" from *Gypsy Ballads* placed him, in the eyes of the Fascists, squarely with the Reds. In reality, he was impatient with those good friends, especially Rafael Alberti, who were pressuring him toward Communism. He commented that because of Alberti's deep involvement in politics, he doubted that the poet from Cádiz would write something worthwhile again. He told Dámaso Alonso, "I'll never be political. I'm a revolutionary, since all true poets are revolutionaries. Don't you agree? But political, never!" (Alonso 160–61).

In mid-June Lorca finished *La casa de Bernarda Alba* (The house of Bernarda Alba), the third rural drama in "the trilogy of the Spanish earth." Whenever he could, he read the play to friends. Vicente Aleixandre told me in 1962 about a phone call he received from Federico in early July. I was at Aleixandre's house on the small street Velintonia, later changed to Calle de Vicente Aleixandre after the poet won the Nobel Prize in the 1970s. Vicente was reminiscing, as he often did. During the Civil War he was the sick one, largely confined to bed, all because of an incorrect medical diagnosis and consequent wrong medicine, which for seven years kept him lying on the couch most days. He said, "Logically, I should have been the one not to survive the war, yet it was Miguel, Manolo and Federico, my three closest friends before the war, who died." Miguel was Miguel Hernández, Manolo was the poet and printer Manuel Altolaguirre, who survived in exile, only to be killed in a car accident on his return to Spain. Vicente then recalled the last words he would exchange with Lorca:

Federico called me shortly after noon. He said he had just finished a new play, *La casa de Bernarda Alba*, and wanted to read it to me. I asked him to come over. Then I remembered that Miguel Hernández was to come later that afternoon with some new poems. I mentioned Hernández to Federico, saying I was sure he would like to hear the play too. "No, I want to read it to you alone. Get rid of him." I said it would hurt Miguel, who was very sensitive, and I couldn't tell him not to come. "Tell him anything, tell him your mother died, tell him the planet just gave birth to a penguin and a minatour's head and you've been asked to verify them, think up something," Federico insisted, very excited. "I can't," I said. Federico's last words to me were, *"Bueno, en unos días te llamo y te lo leo."* (Okay,

I'll call in a few days and read it to you then.) A few days later he left for Granada. (Interview in Madrid, Spring 1962)

Hernández wrote an elegy for Lorca, as Machado did, on receiving word of his death.

Another unfulfilled appointment was with Pablo Neruda. It was not Lorca the grave Castilian of *Bernarda Alba*, but Federico the friend with whom he shared hilarity. Neruda writes, capturing the tragicomic moment, all portentous with the grotesque and with terrible ironies:

> A million dead Spaniards. . . . It all started on the evening of July 19, 1936. [July 13 is the more likely date.] A resourceful and pleasant Chilean, Bobby Deglané, was wrestling promoter in Madrid's huge Circo Price arena. I had expressed my reservations about the seriousness of that "sport" and he convinced me to go to the arena that evening with García Lorca to see how authentic the show really was. I talked García Lorca into it and we agreed to meet there at a certain time. We were going to have great fun watching the truculence of the Masked Troglodyte, the Abyssinian Strangler, and the Sinister Orangutan.
>   Federico did not show up. He was at that hour already on his way to death. We never saw each other again: he had an appointment with another strangler. (Neruda, *Memoirs* 122)

Amid the chaos, rumors, fear of a coup, Lorca announced on July 11 to his friends that he was leaving for Granada. He could work there in Granada, undisturbed, he said. Buñuel echoed the others, disagreeing, saying he'd be safer in Madrid. The next evening he read *Bernarda Alba* to the poets Guillén, Salinas, and Alonso. On July 13 he was leaving. He gave his friend Rafael Martínez Nadal, who took him to the station, a copy of *The Public*, asking him to destroy it if anything happened to him. Martínez Nadal had the good sense to ignore the order. Had Lorca planned his trip a week later, he could not have left for Granada and would certainly have survived the war. But on the July 14, the poet was already in the Huerta de San Vicente, with his parents.

Death by the olive grove

Lorca was not secretive about his presence in Granada. His visit, "before his forthcoming trip to Mexico" was announced in the newspaper *El Defensor de Granada* (at his request). He was seen in the city with friends. On July 18, 1936, General Franco in the Canary Islands announced the revolt. General Queipo de Llano seized control in Sevilla. The Republican leaders in Granada, believing the garrison loyal, refused to distribute arms to the people. On July 20, the insurgents took over, arrested government officials, and began a reign of terror, with the "black execution squads" acting with impunity. The mayor of Granada, Manuel Fernández-Montesinos, husband of Lorca's sister Concha, was arrested by his own officers. Lorca courageously went to the prison where his brother-in-law was held. He had with him a basket of food but couldn't get it to Manuel.

In the next days things got worse. Thugs came on August 9 to the family *huerta* and tied the caretaker to a tree and whipped him. Lorca intervened, and the thugs kicked him to the ground, with expected sexual insult. Before they left, Lorca was told that he was under house arrest and couldn't leave. Federico immediately called his friend the poet Luis Rosales, who with his brothers was a member of the Falange. He could trust him and asked for his help.

There are a number of published versions, all now very close, about the crucial meeting that took place at the *huerta* when Rosales arrived later that same day to counsel the family. Rosales taped his memory of the meeting in 1966 in Madrid. Four years earlier, in 1962, at the suggestion of Aleixandre, I spoke to Luis Rosales about Lorca for many hours in his Madrid apartment. What Rosales told me in regard to the actual arrest coincided exactly with the Gibson taping. I bring up the question of accuracy because of another event that occurred on the day before his arrest, in which the account differs on a crucial point. Let us first hear Rosales:

> Federico explained to me that some individuals had been there twice during the day, roughing him up and going through his private papers. . . . In view of this I promised to help in any way they thought I could. I am the only surviving witness of the discussion—Federico's parents and sister Concha have all died. Well, Federico discussed the various possibilities open to him and I put myself at his disposal. The possibility of getting Federico into the Republican zone was discussed. I could have done this fairly easily and had already done it with other people—and had brought people back from the Republican zone. But Federico refused. He was terrified by the thought of being all alone in a no-man's-land between the two zones. Nor would he consider going to seek refuge in Manuel de Falla's *carmen*. . . . He said that he would prefer to come to my house. And that's what we decided. He came that day. (qtd. in Gibson, *Lorca* 452)

Lorca was in the Rosales house for a week. He had some tranquility, played the piano, and did his best to entertain his hosts. But

171

Federico García Lorca

before daybreak on August 16, Manuel Fernández-Montesinos was executed. Lorca learned of it and must have known there was little hope for him. On the day before, a group had come to the *huerta* to arrest Federico. According to an exculpatory document Luis Rosales deposited in Molina Fajardo in 1983, Federico's sister, Concha, terrified, "blurted out that Federico had not escaped but was staying in the house of a Falangist friend, like him a poet" (qtd. in Gibson, *Lorca* 455). Twenty-one years earlier, in spring 1962, Rosales told me in Madrid about that day of August 15 when the squad invaded the *huerta*. He informed me, "It was "Federico's own mother Doña Vicenta who told the arresting group where he was. She did not want to give them the impression that he was hiding or had any need to hide." The discrepancy in Rosales's two versions is surely one of memory in regard to who, sister or mother, may have let the intruders know where Federico was. And in any case his statement was itself secondhand since he was not there. Whatever happened, nothing but loyalty was the Lorca family purpose and practice. Moreoever, the Falange police were on his trail and would have found the poet no matter what was said or not said. Immediately after the incident with the police, the Lorca house phoned the Rosales family.

The Rosales family members knew that they had to act quickly to move Federico to a safer place. Again Falla, who was deeply Catholic and venerated, came to mind. His *carmen* (estate) could not be violated—perhaps not even in those days. But it was too late. On the afternoon of the August 16, Federico was arrested and taken away. The succeeding events comprise, sadly, the most complete and violent drama in his life. Many details will never be known, but enough is there—perhaps too much—to inform us of the violation. In his *Assassination of García Lorca* and pioneer biography, Ian Gibson has assembled the known facts (many essential ones brought to light by the biographer) in the last pages of his narration. He tells us:

> But the enemy moved faster than the Rosales family. They looked for him first at the house of Luis's brother, Miguel, and realizing their mistake soon located him at I Calle de Angulo. On the afternoon of 16 August Federico was arrested and taken away. It was a large-scale operation mounted by the Civil Government: the block was cordoned off, police and guards surrounded it and armed men were even stationed on the rooftops to prevent the poet from escaping that way. (455)

The remaining steps to doom involve a number of stereotypical men whose names are known to us now only because they were

Federico García Lorca

implicated in the murder of Spain's most accomplished poet-play-wright. The two thousand plus recorded executions in the Víznar cemetery area where Lorca fell would otherwise not have called our attention to the names of the officials, since the same pattern of terror and brutal executions was occurring across the nation and persisted for three years of war and after the war. Much is signified by an incident that took place, a few days after the revolt began, in a meeting room at the University of Salamanca where Miguel de Unamuno was then professor and rector of the university. As a persistent, cranky outsider, critic, and dissident even in days of the Republic, the generals harbored some expectation that Unamuno might go along with their rebellion. He was introduced with cere-mony. The writer-philosopher, a few months from his own death by natural causes, got up, refusing collaboration, and declared (pun-ning on the Latin root of the verbs *vencer* and *convencer*), "Vencerán tal vez, pero no convencerán" (You will vanquish, perhaps, but not convince). One of the generals shouted, "Muera la inteligentsia!" (Let the intelligentsia die!) and then another yelled, "Viva la muerte!" (Long live death!). Death was thriving in Spain.

The leader of the men who came for Lorca was Ramón Ruiz Alonso, accompanied by Juan Luis Trescastro and Luis García Alix. Luis Rosales and his brother José were not at home when Lorca was seized. They went to the authorities and were lied to; they thought they still might have time to save Federico. The ultimate responsi-bility lay with the Governor José Valdés Guzmán, who was regularly ordering executions. He told José Rosales that Ruiz Alonso had given him a typed report with a long list of his charges against Lorca. (The pages stated that Lorca was a Red spy with a clandestine radio, that he transmitted information to the Russians, that he was the personal secretary of Fernando de los Ríos, and a lot of grave nonsense.) Valdés said that he as governor could not let Lorca be released until these serious charges were examined.

There is a story that Valdés asked General Queipo de Llano what to do with Lorca, and Queipo's reply was "give him coffee, plenty of coffee," code words for "execute." The decisive order did not come, however, from above or below. As with more than two hundred official executions already carried out in those few weeks, Valdés made the decision to kill Lorca.

Some time after 3 A.M. on July 18, the black squad left Granada with Lorca handcuffed to a Republican schoolteacher, Dióscoro Galindo González. They went out of town to the "Nationalist" execution site at Víznar. They were taken to the Colonia, a school-children's summer residence, now used for victims before execu-tion. Then, still before dawn, they were driven on the road to Alfacar by way of Fuente Grande (big fountain), which by its Arabic name

173

is Ainadamar (the fountain of tears). Just before reaching Fuente
Grande, the killers shot their victims—Lorca, the schoolteacher,
and two anarchist bullfighters. Their bodies lay next to an olive
grove. Lorca was not killed with the first fusillade. Later that morn-
ing Juan Luis Trescastro boasted that he had just helped to shoot
Lorca, "firing, for good measure, 'two bullets into his arse for being
a queer' " (Gibson, *Lorca* 468).

That same morning in Granada, Manuel de Falla went to the
civil government building. It was too late.

It was three weeks before a rumor of Lorca's death got to Madrid
and to the Republican newspapers. Antonio Machado was asked by
the editor of the periodical *Ayuda* to write something on Lorca.
Machado waited three more days until the rumor was confirmed
and then wrote his poem on the younger poet, *"El crimen fue en
Granada"* (The crime was in Granada).

> He was seen walking between rifles
> down a long street,
> coming upon the cold field
> which still held stars of dawn.
> They killed Federico
> as the light appeared.
> The squad of executioners
> dared not look him in the face.
> All of them closed their eyes.
> They prayed, Not even God saves you!
> Federico fell dead,
> blood on his face, lead in his bowels.
> Know that the crime was in Granada,
> Poor Granada, in his Granada!
>
> *(Dream Below the Sun* 145)

In his memoirs Pablo Neruda said of Lorca: "What a poet! I
have never seen grace and genius, a winged heart and a crystalline
waterfall, come together in anyone else as they did in him. Federico
García Lorca was the extravagant *duende*, his was a magnetic joy-
fulness that generated a zest for life in his heart and radiated it
like a planet" *(Memoirs* 122). And when he thought of the poet's
assassination, he wrote:

> It would never have crossed anyone's mind that they would
> kill him one day. He was the most loved, the most cherished,
> of all Spanish poets, and he was the closest to being a child,
> because of his marvelous happy temperment. Who could have
> believed there were monsters on this earth, in his own Granada,
> capable of such an inconceivable crime? (122)

Federico García Lorca

After Granada

The official government document, devised years after the Civil War, recorded that in August 1936 Federico García Lorca died of war wounds. In the poems and plays, death was a haunting, even obsessive figure. It was Federico's fate to be, for the Republic, for those opposed to the political forces of the thirties represented by the Falange, Germany, and Italy, and for modern literature, the Civil War's young martyr. The recent Saura film *Ay, Carmela!* is the first major film document in post-Franco Spain to treat the Civil War with no sense whatsoever of controversy or censorship. In the film, an entertainer of the troops recites Machado's lines of "The Crime was in Granada." In the first decades after the war, Lorca's books could not be printed in Spain, nor his plays performed, not even privately in *teatro de cámara* (chamber theater). Then there was a gradual loosening of restrictions, and imported editions of his work could be sold over the counter. In the mid-seventies, with Franco's death and the end of the dictatorship, streets all over Spain were renamed, carrying Lorca's name, and a special-issue, large postage stamp now bears his portrait.

Adán

Arbol de sangre moja la mañana
por donde gime la recién parida.
Su voz deja cristales en la herida
y un gráfico de hueso en la ventana.
Mientras la luz que viene fija y gana
blancas metas de fábula que olvida
el tumulto de venas en la huida
hacia el turbio frescor de la manzana.
Adán sueña en la fiebre de la arcilla
un niño que se acerca galopando
por el doble latir de su mejilla.
Pero otro Adán oscuro está soñando
neutra luna de piedra sin semilla
donde el niño de luz se irá quemando.

Soneto de la dulce queja

Tengo miedo a perder la maravilla
de tus ojos de estatua y el acento
que me pone de noche en la mejilla
la solitaria rosa de tu aliento.
Tengo pena de ser en esta orilla
tronco sin ramas, y lo que más siento
es no tener la flor, pulpa o arcilla,
para el gusano de mi sufrimiento.
Si tú eres el tesoro oculto mío,
si eres mi cruz y mi dolor mojado,
si soy el perro de tu señorío,
No me dejes perder lo que he ganado
y decora las aguas de tu río
con hojas de mi otoño enajenado.

176

Adam

The tree of blood moistens the morning of
the world where the new mother starts to
  groan.
Her voice leaves windows in the wound;
  above
the panes she leaves a diagram of bone.
While light pours in, it fixes and makes white
intentions of the fable now a chapel,
forgets the tumult of the veins in flight
toward the murky freshness of the apple.
Adam dreams through the fever in the mud
of a child coming near, galloping in,
red from the double throbbing of his cheek.
And yet another Adam of dark blood
dreams of a seedless moon of stone wherein
the child of light will burn week after week.

Sonnet of the Gentle Complaint

I am in fear of losing the sheer wonder
of statue eyes, and your rare voice that grows
into my night through which it places, under
my cheek, your breathing's solitary rose.
I am in grief that on this shore I stay
a leafless trunk, and what I miss the most
is not to have the flower, the pulp or clay
for my poor worm of torment, my poor ghost.
If you are now my only concealed treasure,
if you are dripping pain, my cross and quiver,
if I am just the dog of your high station,
don't let me lose what is my rightful measure.
Please decorate the waters of your river
with leaves from my autumnal alienation.

El poeta habla por teléfono con el amor

Tu voz regó la duna de mi pecho
en la dulce cabina de madera.
Por el sur de mis pies fue primavera
y al norte de mi frente flor de helecho.
Pino de luz por el espacio estrecho
cantó sin alborada y sementera
y mi llanto prendió por vez primera
coronas de esperanza por el techo.
Dulce y lejana voz por mí vertida.
Dulce y lejana voz por mí gustada.
Lejana y dulce voz amortecida.
Lejana como oscura corza herida.
Dulce como un sollozo en la nevada.
¡Lejana y dulce en tuétano metida!

Soneto gongorino en que el poeta
manda a su amor una paloma

Este pichón del Turia que te mando,
de dulces ojos y de blanca pluma
sobre laurel de Grecia vierte y suma
llama lenta de amor do estoy parando.
Su cándida virtud, su cuello blando,
en lirio doble de caliente espuma,
con un temblor de escarcha, perla y bruma
la ausencia de tu boca está marcando.
Pasa la mano sobre su blancura
y verás qué nevada melodía
esparce en copos sobre tu hermosura.
Así mi corazón de noche y día,
preso en la cárcel del amor oscura,
llora sin verte su melancolía.

The Poet Talks on the Phone with His Love

Your voice watered the sand dune of my chest
inside the wondrous phone booth made of wood.
South of my feet a place for spring to rest,
north of my brow a ferny blossom stood.
A pine of light there in the narrow space
sang without dawning or a seeded field,
and my lament, for the first time, was face
to face with crowns of hope a roof revealed.
A soft and distant voice poured over me.
A soft and distant voice I loved to hear.
Remote and tender voice and almost dead.
Remote like the dark wounded fallow deer.
Soft like a sobbing where a snowfall spread.
Remote, soft, placed in marrow quietly!

A Gongoresque Sonnet in Which the Poet
Sends His Love a Dove

This pigeon from the Turia which I send,
with gentle eyes and plumage of pure white,
pours out, on a Greek laurel tree, a blend
of a slow flame of love where I alight.
How candid virtue and her slender neck
—double lily of incandescent spume—
outline the absence of your mouth, and deck
it with a trembling frost of pearl and brume.
Raise up your hand and on its whiteness pause
and you will see what snowy melody
is spread in flakes on your full elegance.
And so my heart, both night and day, because
it is a prisoner in dark love's dance,
cries out in grief for you it cannot see.

El amor duerme en el pecho del poeta

Tú nunca entenderás lo que te quiero
porque duermes en mí y estás dormido.
Yo te oculto llorando, perseguido
por una voz de penetrante acero.
Norma que agita igual carne y lucero
traspasa ya mi pecho dolorido
y las turbias palabras han mordido
las alas de tu espíritu severo.
Grupo de gente salta en los jardines
esperando tu cuerpo y mi agonía
en caballos de luz y verdes crines.
Pero sigue durmiendo, vida mía.
¡Oye mi sangre rota en los violines!
¡Mira que nos acechan todavía!

Noche del amor insomne

Noche arriba los dos con luna llena,
yo me puse a llorar y tú reías.
Tu desdén era un dios, las quejas mías
momentos y palomas en cadena.
Noche abajo los dos. Cristal de pena,
llorabas tú por hondas lejanías.
Mi dolor era un grupo de agonías
sobre tu débil corazón de arena.
La aurora nos unió sobre la cama,
las bocas puestas sobre el chorro helado
de una sangre sin fin que se derrama.
Y el sol entró por el balcón cerrado
y el coral de la vida abrió su rama
sobre mi corazón amortajado.

Love Sleeps on the Chest of the Poet

How much I love you you will never know
because you sleep on me and are asleep.
I hide you as I sorrow, held below
a voice of steel, penetrating me deep.
A pattern stirring flesh and star alike
is digging through my agonizing chest,
and dark confusing words have been a spike
biting the wings of your stark wit. Obsessed,
waiting for your body and my agony,
crowds of people in the gardens leap around
on horses luminous with manes of green.
But, lover, keep on sleeping next to me.
Hear my blood broken over violins!
See how they watch and wait for us like hounds!

Night of Sleepless Love

Climbing the night, we two in the full moon,
I wept and you were laughing. Your disdain
became a god, and my resentments soon
were morning doves and moments in a chain.
Descending night, we two. Glass pain. And you
were weeping through profound remoteness, and
my grief was crowds of agonies that grew
on your debilitated heart of sand.
The dawn sewed us together on the bed,
our mouths joined to the frozen spurting of
interminable blood. Sun pierced a cloud,
came through the shuttered balcony and spread.
Then life's coral opened its branch above
my heart embedded in its funeral shroud.

Llagas de amor

Esta luz, este fuego que devora.
Este paisaje gris que me rodea.
Este dolor por una sola idea.
Esta angustia de cielo, mundo, y hora.
Este llanto de sangre que decora
lira sin pulso ya, lúbrica tea.
Este peso del mar que me golpea.
Este alacrán que por mi pecho mora.
Son guirnalda de amor, cama de herido,
donde sin sueño, sueño tu presencia
entre las ruinas de mi pecho hundido;
Y aunque busco la cumbre de
       prudencia
me da tu corazón valle tendido
con cicuta y pasión de amarga ciencia.

El poeta dice la verdad

Quiero llorar mi pena y te lo digo
para que tú me quieras y me llores
en un anochecer de ruiseñores
con un puñal, con besos y contigo.
Quiero matar al único testigo
para el asesinato de mis flores
y convertir mi llanto y mis sudores
en eterno montón de duro trigo.
Que no se acabe nunca la madeja
del te quiero me quieres, siempre ardida
con decrépito sol y luna vieja;
Que lo que no me des y no te pida
será para la muerte, que no deja
ni sombra por la carne estremecida.

Wounds of Love

This light, this conflagration that devours.
This dingy countryside encircling me.
This pain around one theme, an agony.
This agony of heaven, world, and hours.
This elegy of blood that decorates
my now unthrobbing lyre, my moist firebrand,
this gross weight of the sea that pounds me and
this scorpion in my chest that amputates,
all these are wreathes of love, a bed of wounds
where dreamlessly I dream your presence ashen
amid the ruins of my sunken chest.
And though I call the peak of prudence best,
your heart gives me a valley spread with passion
of bitter science where the hemlock blooms.

The Poet Says the Truth

I want to cry my sorrow and unveil
it so that you will love and cry for me
in the oncoming night of nightingale;
with dagger, kisses and with you I'll be.
I want to kill the only witness to
the assasination of my flowers. Then heat
and turn my misery and sweat into
an everliving mound of muscular wheat.
Let the entangled yarn perceive no end
of *I love you, you love me*, always flame
with its decrepit sun and ancient moon;
let what you may not give (or I not bend
to beg) belong to death that cannot claim
a shadow of our quivering flesh immune.

El poeta pregunta a su amor por la "Ciudad Encantada" de Cuenca

¿Te gustó la ciudad que gota a gota
labró el agua en el centro de los pinos?
¿Viste sueños y rostros y caminos
y muros de dolor que el aire azota?

¿Viste la grieta azul de luna rota
que el Júcar moja de cristal y trinos?
¿Han besado tus dedos los espinos
que coronan de amor piedra remota?

¿Te acordaste de mí cuando subías
al silencio que sufre la serpiente
prisionera de grillos y de umbrías?

¿No viste por el aire transparente
una dalia de penas y alegrías
que te mandó mi corazón caliente?

Soneto de la guirnalda de rosas

¡Esa guirnalda! ¡pronto! ¡que me muero!
¡Teje deprisa! ¡canta! ¡gime! ¡canta!
Que la sombra me enturbia la garganta
y otra vez viene y mil la luz de enero.

Entre lo que me quieres y te quiero
aire de estrellas y temblor de planta,
espesura de anémonas levanta
con oscuro gemir un año entero.

Goza el fresco paisaje de mi herida,
quiebra juncos y arroyos delicados.
Bebe en muslo de miel sangre vertida.

Pero ¡pronto! Que unidos, enlazados,
boca rota de amor y alma mordida
el tiempo nos encuentre destrozados.

The Poet Asks His Love about the "Enchanted City" of Cuenca

Cuenca. How did you like how drop by drop
the water carved this city in the pines?
Did you see dreams, faces and roads, the signs
and walls of pain where gale-winds whip and chop?
Did you absorb blue slopes made of the broken
moon which the Júcar soaks with glass and trills?
And were your fingers kissed by florid buckhorn
playing its crown of love on rocky hills?
Did you remember me when you were climbing
up to the silence suffered by the snake,
a prisoner of crickets and black sighs?
In lucid air did you observe a shining
dahlia of joys and pains, coming awake,
sent by my heart with fire into your thighs?

Sonnet of the Garland of Roses

This garland! Hurry! I'm about to die!
Weave it swiftly! Sing! Moan! Sing!
The shadow on my throat moves darkening
and January light comes endlessly.
Between how much you love me and how I
love you, a trembling plant and wind with stars,
a windflower's thickness is erect, with far
moaning of an obscure and year-long sigh.
Enjoy the morning landscape of my wound,
break open reeds and rivulets in the void.
Drink up the blood poured on our thighs made of
a honey. Quick! So bound together, found
as one, soul eaten live, mouth cracked with love,
time will waylay us thoroughly destroyed.

Ay voz secreta del amor oscuro

Ay voz secreta del amor oscuro
¡ay balido sin lanas! ¡ay herida!
¡ay aguja de hiel, camelia hundida!
¡ay corriente sin mar, ciudad sin muro!
¡Ay noche inmensa de perfil seguro,
montaña celestial de angustia erguida!
¡ay perro en corazón, voz perseguida!
¡silencio sin confín, lirio maduro!
Huye de mí, caliente voz de hielo,
no me quieras perder en la maleza
donde sin fruto gimen carne y cielo.
Deja el duro marfil de mi cabeza,
apiádate de mí, ¡rompe mi duelo!
¡que soy amor, que son naturaleza!

El poeta pide a su amor que le escriba

Amor de mis entrañas, viva muerte,
en vano espero tu palabra escrita
y pienso, con la flor que se marchita,
que si vivo sin mí quiero perderte.
El aire es inmortal. La piedra inerte
ni conoce la sombra ni la evita.
Corazón interior no necesita
la miel helada que la luna vierte.
Pero yo te sufrí. Rasgué mis venas,
tigre y paloma, sobre tu cintura
en duelo de mordiscos y azucenas.
Llena, pues, de palabras mi locura
o déjame vivir en mi serena
noche del alma para siempre oscura.

186

O Secret Voice of Dark and Obscure Love!

O secret voice of dark and obscure love!
O bleating yet no wool of sheep! O wound!
O needle prick of gall, camelia drowned!
Brook without sea, city no wall above!
O mammoth night yet profiled iron stripe,
celestial peak of erect agony!
O dog in the heart, voice trailed by misery,
unbordered silence and a lily ripe.
Get away from me, hot voice of ice and stone,
don't let me wander lost in underbrush
where flesh and heaven moan deprived of
    fruit.
Leave the harsh ivory of my head alone,
take pity on me, crack my grief! and rush
to me. I'm love. i'm nature in my root!

The Poet Asks His Love to Write to Him

Love of my inner flesh and death alive,
I'm waiting for your written word in vain
and think: like a wild blossom without rain,
if I must live in me without you live,
I want to lose you. Winds don't die. Yet still
the dumb stone neither knows nor shuns its shade.
The inner heart needs not a drop or spade
of frozen honey for the moon to spill.
I suffered you and my own veins I tore,
tiger and dove around your waist, and fell
in a hot duel of lilies and our bites.
Now fill my madness with your words, or else
let me live on in my concordant night,
night of the soul forever dark, obscure.

Jorge Luis Borges

(1899–1986)

Argentina

Jorge Luis Borges

In 1899, still with a foot in the nineteenth century, Jorge Luis Borges was born

During the war of the Malvinas between Argentina and the United Kingdom, someone asked Borges his opinion on the conflict. Being a friend of the English language, of Whitman, Melville, and Chesterton, an Argentine from an old military and conquistador background but whose paternal grandmother Fanny Haslam was from Staffordshire, and being a retired professor of Anglo-Saxon living in a country where a good Argentine university student might have the name Nelly Shakespear (such was my student's name in 1974), having been a lifelong dissenter who denounced the military junta before it launched the invasion, Borges had reason for ambiguity. His answer would be serious—he was always serious—yet never without humor, irony, paradox. Like his preferred late translator Anthony Kerrigan, who despite pain laughed and joked his way to the grave, Borges was incapable of boring gravity or verbal numbness. As to his sentiment on the conflict, he replied ruefully, "This awful war is a struggle between two old bald men, fighting over a comb."

The words of Borges in conversation and those found in his books come amazingly from a single generating source. The speaking man and his printed pages are the same. His conversation is an oral disclosure of the same creative activity that concludes in written texts. This unique Borgesian voice dominates the person and his printed words. His mid-life blindness only clarified the union of tongue and pen. In his early fifties when Borges went blind, he had to dictate his writings, which was appropriate to his poetry, because, given his fabulous memory—the true Irineo Funes, the Memorius, was Borges—he could compose and polish a sonnet while sitting in a bus or walking down the street.

This unity in Borges of speaker and writer, of voice and print, recalls a parallel in the Chinese perception of Wang Wei, the Tang poet and painter. Song dynasty commentators saw a unity of poem

191

and painting in Wang Wei and declared: "His poems are silent paintings, his paintings spoken poems." It would subvert the integrity of Borges's miracle to insist on an elemental distinction between spoken voice and written text, as it would be injurious to separate the Sophist voice of the peripatetic Socrates heard in the streets of Athens from the one recorded by his scribe Plato in the *Crito* and the *Apologia*. We guess the dialogic genius of sages— Isaiah, Lao-tzu, Socrates, Jeshua the Messiah—who are known only through their scribes. We depend on the scribes of voices. In the instance of Borges, the identity of the voice and the pen is witnessed through the experience of a legion of friends, casual audiences, and recording devices. Even on the last day on his deathbed, when he uttered, "This is the happiest day of my life," his word in life and art were kindred.

Borges's speech authenticated his writing, his writing authenticated his speech. To have heard him was to read him. To have read him was to hear him. During the two decades I knew Borges I was constantly surprised by the way the poet gave his voice away. When he was addressed by an unknown voice, he had little idea who that person was. Unfailingly he spoke to each unseen person with intimacy and with an elevating assumption of confidence, whether the unknown speaker was a journalist, a doorman, a student, a writer, a clerk.

Whether spoofing or grave, laughing or weary, Borges spoke literature. Whether you were chatting with him in Maxim's restaurant in Buenos Aires, up from Maipú Street where there was good food (and usually a few aging German Nazis sitting in the back), or you were with him for hours on a plane or waiting for a plane, or he confided in you after midnight in the Saint James café on Córdoba Street, all those voices spoke nothing but literature. I don't mean that Borges was talking about literature—one of his preferred "habits"—but that his voice *was* literature. There was rarely a sentence that passed through his mouth, even the most ordinary, which should not have found itself on some permanent page for the rest of us. He spoke about his English as bookish, and it was, yet not because it was stilted or unnatural or derived from books, but because, like his speech in Spanish, it was unfailingly worthy of books.

Borges's poetry has been splendidly translated into English by Robert Fitzgerald, Mark Strand, John Hollander, John Updike, Alastair Reid, and Richard Howard. Borges comes through in English both in informal poems and what he liked to call his Whitman kind of free verse. Yet to most of the world that loves Borges, the poetry is half in shadow—unlike the perception of Federico García Lorca who is always poet and playwright. Probably because his stories, his parables, his essays—often all mingled in one—have, like Kafka's fantastic fiction, made him one of the master prose writers of the century, Borges's poetry, beyond his Spanish readers, seems secondary. It is a mistake. Even Borges thought himself first a poet, and he was publicly unreliable about his own writing (he regularly badmouthed it, offering to conspire with those against it, saying its reputation was all a big mistake, one he was grateful for, but a mistake). In reality for most of the first decade and last two decades of his very active writing career, he wrote largely poetry.

That career began in Europe where he lived from 1914 to 1921, the last two years in Spain where, like others, he was taken by the radical social experiments in Russia and where he had collaborated with the "ultraist" poets associated with Gerardo Diego and his mentor Rafael Cansinos-Asséns. Borges remarks that Cansinos had coined the word *ultraísmo* for that experimental poetry that occupied a place between Dada and surrealism. (Rodríguez Monegal suggests that it is not certain whether or not Cansinos invented the movement, but promote it centrally, he did.)

Borges's wanderings began as a child in the paradise of his father's library and continued in his bookish habits as he acquired French, Latin, and German (in addition to native Spanish and English) before returning to Buenos Aires. It was with Cansinos in Madrid that he found the figure who was to confirm his own obsessive dedication to the words and thought of the West and the East.

In his *Autobiographical Essay*, Borges tells us how as a young man in Madrid, he would do his own reading and writing during the week and live for the literary *tertulia* centering around Cansinos-Asséns at the Café Colonial. It began at midnight and lasted till daybreak. Although Cansinos and most of the group were experimental writers, the "dictator," as Borges called him, would not let the conversation drift to contemporary writing. He had translated De Quincey's *Opium-Eater*, the *Meditations of Marcus Aurelius* from the Latin, versions of Goethe, Dostoyevski, and the *Arabian Nights* whose version Borges considered better reading than Burton's or Lane's, which he also admired. All his life, Borges wrote, he had tried to be a Jew, and claimed Jewish blood on his military Acevedo side. Cansinos went further. He studied for the priesthood, "but having found the name Cansinos in the archives of the Inquisition, he decided he was a Jew. This led him to the study of Hebrew, and later on he even had himself circumcised" (*Essay* 221). Borges confesses, "I was stimulated by him to far-flung reading. In writing, I began aping him. He wrote long and flowing sentences with an un-Spanish and strongly Hebrew flavor to them" (222). Later, after translating Kafka's parables and *The Metamorphosis*, Borges confessed that he had become "the sedulous ape" to Franz Kafka.

In the Argentine poet, below the labyrinths, below the nightmare, below even the algebra of dream, there is a great library and its memory. In Buenos Aires he was actually to spend nine years in the basement of the Miguel Cané library, with a dismal job which permitted him, however, to have time to write the stories that were to bring him his first fame. The interior library is not orderly, but his access to it through memory is flawless, and he has relied on it during his sighted years and blind years for his erudite and allusive thought and writing. His description of Cansinos-Asséns's library gives us a clue as to just how Borges was buried among the bookshelves and how, as a result, he became the thinker and writer he was, spread over centuries and continents:

> Once, I went to see him and he took me into his library. Or, rather, I should say his whole house was a library. It was like making your way through a woods. He was too poor to have shelves, and the books were piled one on top of the others from floor to ceiling, forcing you to thread your way among the vertical columns. Cansinos seemed to me as if he were all the past of that Europe I was leaving behind—something like the symbol of all culture, Western and Eastern. (*Essay* 222)

Jorge Luis Borges was born in the nineteenth century. He liked to say he was "a nineteenth-century man, barely." Actually, Borges stepped into all waters of time and non-time: whether by way of Virgil's Latin ("a marble language," he called it); the escape from time of the Buddha; or a medieval Sufi mystical poet; or by way of his immersion in Old English kennings where he followed "seastallion" ships across the "whale's road" sea; in the Gnostics of Alexandria and Syria who reversed essential concepts of Jews and Greeks (and their offspring Christians and Romans); in the letters of the Kabbalah, which saw mind and universe as word system; in Cervantes who dreamt up Alonso Quijano, a dreamer who thought he was Don Quijote; in that realist and symbolist of the whale, Melville; and in the detective mind of Poe and the perfect translation of *Quijote* by his mad Frenchman Pierre Menard who invented reader reception theory. By his immersion in so many times, Borges in our century became its most innovative master, without succumbing to any transient fashionable "isms," and while he did much to invent our century, he kept himself firmly, in his rereadings, writing, and *charlas* (chats), at a tilt to the world. He was firmly here and elsewhere.

Jorge Luis Borges in his father's library

Jorge Luis Borges was born in Buenos Aires, spending his childhood in Palermo, which he described as the frayed northern outskirts of the city. In Palermo were the "streetcorner men" or *compadritos*, the hoodlum knifefighters whom he was to turn into dramatic figures in many of his stories. But that raw life he discovered much later. His family was of the "shabby, genteel people," and he lived not out in the barrio with the *compadritos* but essentially indoors, in a double museum.

The first museum was an ancestral and military memory, with daguerreotypes, pictures, uniforms, and tales of officers who fought the nineteenth-century liberation and civil wars. On his mother's side was Colonel Isidorio Suárez who fought for independence at Junín, and on his father's side, similar images and tales of the military. Most colorful and essential for the family tableau was his grandfather, Colonel Francisco Borges, whose wife was the English woman Fanny Haslam. After the defeat at La Verde in 1874, Colonel Borges, in his white poncho and with arms folded, rode out on horseback toward the enemy lines until two Remington bullets caught him and he fell, near death. In the seventeenth century his conquistador ancestor Jerónimo Luis de Córdoba founded the city of Córdoba. A statue of the conqueror, soberly mounted on a horse radiating equestrian authority and glory, graces a central plaza in Córdoba.

The second museum was not of stone and steel either and was definitely more lively, its histories more mythological and fantastic. That museum (in Greek the *mouseion* was the library in Alexandria) was his father's personal library. The library gave Borges his profession, his speculation, and it contributed, along with unfriendly genes, to his deteriorating eyes. Borges read his first books in English, and they were from Jorge Guillermo Borges's collection: *Huckleberry Finn*, Wells's *First Men in the Moon, Treasure Island*, Burton's *A Thousand Nights and a Night*, and works by Lewis Carroll, Poe, Longfellow, and Dickens. His father was a lawyer, professor of psychology and English, and writer who had published poetry, stories, essays, and a novel. Jorge described him as a "philosophical anarchist" with very bad eyesight. His father's mother, Fanny Haslam, had been a great reader and through her came the line of bookish English as well as the living presence in the house of the English tongue. Despite insistence on the past, Borges was never one to sentimentalize and describes Fanny's quirky, almost flippant leavetaking:

> When she died at the age of ninety, in 1935, she called us to her side and said, in English (her Spanish was fluent but poor), in her thin voice, "I am only an old woman dying very, very slowly. There is nothing remarkable or interesting about this." She could see no reason whatever why the whole household

should be upset, and she apologized for taking so long to die. (*Essay* 206)

Two of the most Argentine emblems—like flamenco and the bullfight in Spain—are the tango and the gaucho. (The bullfight does not exist in Argentina, which is a unique absence among the larger countries of Spanish America.) Borges always had ambivalent feelings about the tango and was more interested in its quicker version, the *milonga*, which he felt had not been corrupted by Carlos Gardel, commercialism, international steamships, and Paris *boîtes*. He wrote and published *milonga* lyrics about the heroic, knife-wielding outlaws he was fixed on, and was happy when composers made them into popular songs. The original tango, with its off-color words, its toughness, passion, and melodrama, he recalls as part of the ritual of the bordellos of Argentina. As a boy in Palermo, he saw working-class men dancing the tango in the street, not with women but with each other. They were practicing the steps to gird up their courage for the encounter inside with the prostitute entertainers.

Gauchos were first known to him through books. He saw his first Argentine cowboys in 1909 on a trip northwest of Buenos Aires. The boy discovered that the farmhands on the pampa were gauchos. In his autobiographical essay he writes, "Once, I was allowed to accompany them on horseback, taking cattle to the river early one morning. The men were small and darkish and wore *bombachas*, a kind of wide, baggy trouser. When I asked them if they knew how to swim, they replied, 'Water is meant for cattle' " (*Essay* 213).

By 1914 his father's eyesight was so poor he couldn't read, and he had to retire from his legal work. It was a time when the Argentine peso was hard currency, and Jorge Guillermo decided to take his family to Europe, place Borges and his sister Norah in school in Geneva, and have his eyes treated by a famous Geneva specialist. There is no question that young Borges's worldly curiosity for foreign texts and ancient events, initially stimulated by the existence of his father's library, was now enhanced by the parental decision to go abroad. During seven years he learned languages, collaborated in the inception of a literary movement, added nations to his wanderings, and drew diverse books into the labyrinths of that fabulous interior library, which he was to reread and recall all his life. On the way to Geneva, the family stopped a few weeks in Paris. To give some idea of Borges's fearful memory and other aspects of the mature Borges, I turn to a conversation in 1976 that takes us directly back to those weeks in Paris of 1914.

A few friends were in my living room–barn in Bloomington, Indiana, including the Italian writer Giorgio Bassani, whose novel *The Garden of the Finzi-Continis* had just come out as a De Sica

Jorge Luis Borges

film. Bassani informed Borges that he was his first translator into Italian. Borges learned much from those authors whose first rewording into Spanish had been his, Whitman's, and Kafka's, and he told Bassani how translation and translators had always interested him. Then to illustrate, he recounted how once at a party, he had been introduced to John Dos Passos, and thereafter that evening Dos Passos introduced him proudly to others as the man who had translated his work into Spanish. Borges was pleased and flattered with this generous and gratuitous distinction, and why not? "I admired Dos Passos' books," he said, "though I never translated a line of them into Spanish."

A few minutes later I led Borges to a friend, Matei Calinescu, and they began to chat as if they'd been at it for years. On discovering that Calinescu was Romanian, Borges said, "Some years ago I was in Paris, I was just fifteen, and my parents had gone to an opera I was not interested in hearing. I was alone, reading a novel set in Bucharest, by a minor Romanian woman novelist. It had a poem in a pseudofolkloric style that she had interspersed in the French text with a few untranslated Romanian words. Could you tell me what they mean?" he asked Matei. Then, as if reading from a page, he recited a longish, rhyming, insignificant ballad (which he had read through sixty-two years earlier), stopping at the unknown words.

The next day Calinescu went to the library, located the pre–World War I French novel with its banal poem and its Romanian words obscure to Borges.

Geneva and Madrid

In Geneva Borges studied at the Collège de Genève where he was not only immersed in French but became deeply grounded in Latin. After all those declensions and conjugations, the next step was German, which he learned on his own with a dictionary, the poems of Heine, and later the works of Schopenhauer. He also met Walt Whitman in Switzerland, through a German translation beginning, "Als ich in Alabama meinen Morgengang machte" (As I have walk'd in Alabama my morning walk). Whitman was not only a great poet but "modern poetry," and for a while the *only* poet. All poets in the world were only a preamble to Whitman. For Spain and Latin America, Walt Whitman was what Poe was for France and Europe: the beginnings of modernity. From Whitman, Borges got a sense of freedom, the enumeration of things, the reality of the ordinary, all of which served him in his fiction and in all his poetry, from the first collection, *Fervor de Buenos Aires* (Fervor of Buenos Aires), 1923, until his last book, *La cifra* (The cipher), 1984. Even in the posthumous poems the voice of Whitman is there. But

Borges's attachment to Whitman was ambiguous, for his human attachment was definitely not to the Walt Whitman on a conquering steed of poetry. In his essay on Whitman, *Inquisiciones*, 1925, and in his *charlas* (chats) in *Borges at Eighty*, 1982, we see him identify not with the mythical person Walt that Whitman created in the poems, not with the healthy comrade and invincible optimist but with the failed poor man who couldn't hold down a job, with Walter Whitman, an outsider who traveled little, who had a modest self-created success, with the journalist, printer, and stubbornly eccentric poet from Brooklyn, with an old, sick writer aware of myths and his wasted glories. The ordinary hero is his figure of the old man in "Camden, 1892." The title of this sonnet records the place and date of the poet's death:

> The smell of coffee and of newspapers.
> Sunday and its monotony. The morning,
> Some allegoric verses are adorning
> The glimpsed at page, the vain pentameters
> Of a contented colleague. The old man lies
> Stretched out and white in his respectable
> Poor man's room. Then lazily he fills
> The weary mirror with his gaze. His eyes
> See a face. Unsurprised he thinks: That face
> Is me. With fumbling hand he reaches out
> To touch the tangled beard and ravaged mouth.
> The end is not far off. His voice declares:
> I'm almost gone, and yet my verses scan
> Life and its splendor. I was Walt Whitman.

The voyage of a few months lasted five years in Switzerland. The family then decided to go to Spain for a year, and this time the stay stretched out to only two years, spent in Mallorca, Sevilla, and Madrid. By the time Borges was in Spain, he was committed to writing poetry. And it was there he met his first worldly man of letters, Rafael Cansinos-Asséns, his early model and master. It is curious that Borges began as an avant-garde writer in Spain, although such loyalties were never realized in important early publications. He had already moved away from the rampant "isms" of the twenties. Then as he developed his own idiolect, neither modern nor old but born of Borges, then his impact on other writers was distinctly vanguard, and Julio Cortázar or García Márquez in their "magic realism" derive directly from a Borges who later could never be classified or confined to a movement or group. The vague category of "fantastic literature" he might have accepted for some pages of his writing; in the mid-thirties, with Adolfo Bioy Casares, he did an anthology of fantastic writing in which the editors include short works by themselves.

Buenos Aires and the basement municipal library where he cooked his fictions

Now learned in tongues, with a profession of letters, at the end of March 1921, Borges returned to Buenos Aires and discovered it like a foreign land, with a "peculiar shock and glow," he said, which had he not gone abroad, he might not have experienced. *Fervor of Buenos Aires* was born of his return. In those years, putting out a first book was an easy matter. It took five days after he delivered the manuscript to the printer. His sister did a woodcut for the cover and three hundred copies were made. Then he went to the offices of the literary magazine *Nosotros*, and with the amazed editor's permission, left copies of his book in the pockets of the coats hanging there. It resulted in good things, some favorable book reviews and his small reputation as a poet. Eventually, he began to say that all the themes he was to write about were already found and developed in that first volume. But for a while afterward, he was embarrassed about his first writing, and when he saw copies in a store, if he could afford it, he would buy them up and "lose" them.

Replacing Rafael Cansinos-Asséns was Macedonio Fernández, another great conversationalist, equally eccentric as was his Spanish master, and worldly as he was provincial. In the end he imitated virtually nothing in Macedonio as in the instance of the earlier Spanish master. The impact was nothing compared to Dante, Milton, Whitman, Melville, Hawthorne, Stevenson, Quevedo, and Cervantes, his abiding saints. For a moment, however, with all his humor and ironies, Macedonio was necessary for Borges:

> Before Macedonio, I had always been a credulous reader. His chief gift to me was to make me read skeptically. At the outset, I plagiarized him devotedly, picking up certain stylistic mannerisms of his that I later came to regret. I look back on him now, however, as an Adam bewildered by the Garden of Eden. His genius survives in but a few of his pages; his influence was of a Socratic nature. I truly loved the man, on this side of idolatry, as much as any. (*Essay* 320)

Borges set to work as reader and writer of poems, essays, and book reviews, co-inventor of short-lived periodicals, translator of Whitman and Kafka. His collaboration with Victoria Ocampo in *Sur*, a most important world periodical, and his friendship with Silvina Ocampo and her husband Adolfo Bioy Casares, in the early 1930s, were significant not only because eventually Borges and Bioy

Jorge Luis Borges

Casares got together to write a number of fiction books under the pseudonym Honorio Bustos Domecq, the *Chronicles of Bustos Domecq*, but because the friendships and collaborations represented a whole literary ambience, an era, and a dynamic spirit, not unlike the spirit of invention and camaraderie of that band of poet-friends in Spain who formed the Generation of '27. The literary acquaintances included the senior writer Leopoldo Lugones, the novelist Eduardo Mallea, and the Mexican essayist Alfonso Reyes for whom Borges had a special reverence in regard to both his classical prose style and his literary kindnesses to the younger Argentine author.

The limited income from free-lance editing jobs and contributions to *Sur*, *El Hogar*, and other journals, still left the poet dependent on his father's pension, which inflation had eroded. So in 1937 Borges took his first regular full-time job. He became first assistant in the Miguel Cané branch of the municipal library. There was very little official work to do, and there was resentment from the employees when on the first day, he classified and catalogued four hundred books instead of about a hundred. They said he would put them out of a job if he kept it up. For nine years he stuck it out, working in the basement, where he had time to read and to write stories and essays that were beginning to make him well-known— except in the Cané library. He recalls, "I remember a fellow employee's once noting in an encyclopedia the name of a certain Jorge Luis Borges—a fact that set him wondering at the coincidence of our identical names and birth dates" (*Essay* 242).

The despair and boredom in the infinite library in his story "The Library of Babel" were in part from Kafka, who more than anyone else was to turn him fully during these years to the writing of short fiction. But the focus and specific object that inspired his real misery was the branch of the municipal library where he reported for work. There was even a touch of tears and sentimentality, of rare self-pity, as Borges recounted, "Now and then during these years, we municipal workers were rewarded with gifts of a two-pound package of maté to take home. Sometimes in the evening, as I walked the ten blocks to the tramline, my eyes would be filled with tears. These small gifts from above always underlined my menial and dismal existence" (*Essay* 242).

A year after taking the position, he had a severe accident that changed his life. His father had just died. Soon after, on Christmas Eve 1938 to be exact, when he was running up a stairway, he suddenly felt something brush his scalp. He had knocked his head against a casement window. Pieces of glass got stuck in his head. For him, stairs are always an excuse to speak of Dante and dropping into the Inferno. When he fell to the floor on that historic afternoon, he wasn't sure where he was. One supper in Chicago, he showed me and had me feel the deep dent in his forehead at the hairline where he had bumped his head. The blow was more than a neglected infection.

"What did you do when you came to?"

"Why I took out my gold watch, looked at it and seeing that it was working, I said to myself, I must be alive."

It was not long before the wound became septic, and for a week or so, Borges lay sleepless every night, with hallucinations and high fever. Then he was taken to a hospital where the wound was not properly disinfected before being sutured. The septicemia was serious and for a month he hovered between life and death in the hospital. Unconscious for days, he was operated on in the middle of one night, and he said when he woke, he got the idea, for the first time, of writing fiction. Before that, it was poetry and essays but no *ficciones*. He decided to write stories, the first of which was "Pierre Menard, Author of *Don Quijote*," still "a halfway house between the essay and the true tale," to use his words. Coming directly out of that hospital experience is the story, "The South," with its dream levels of a medical operation and cutting scalpel, its Juan Dahlmann, ranch owner of Argentine military and Germanic ancestry and his uncertain knife fight, and Borges, the ubiquitous narrator. The very first action of "The South" is Dahlmann acquiring a copy of *The Thousand and One Nights* (not an unlikely book for a Borges double), then rushing up the stairs and brushing his head in the darkness perhaps against a bird or a bat, which causes a ghastly wound. In this case, a door (not a window as in Borges's real experience) had been left open onto the stairway. Dahlmann is taken forceably away to a sanitarium where a surgeon saves him from fatal septicemia. Then the details of the train ride south through the pampas, the meal in the general store, the challenge from the gaucho with hints of Chinese blood, and the naked dagger in his hand as he goes out the door to escape, to dream his double encounter with gaucho or surgeon, to fight and die liberated on the plain under the open sky. In that early story of the pampas—or was it in the sanitarium?— the precious elements of Borges thought and style are there: the book, the knife, the sumptuous joy of story and of action, the choice of knowledge through letters or military action, terminating with the unknown message of impending death.

In some ways Borges's dismal job at the library was perfect for the emerging fiction writer. In those years what could be better than a job that was grim, requiring escape, which he could and did do on the job through his pen:

> I kept up my writing at the library. Though my colleagues thought of me as a traitor for not sharing their boisterous fun,

Jorge Luis Borges

I went on with work of my own in the basement, or, when the weather was warm, up on the flat roof. My Kafkian story "The Library of Babel" was meant as a nightmare version of magnification of that municipal library, and certain details in the text have no particular meaning. The numbers of books and shelves that I recorded in the story were literally what I had at my elbow. Clever critics have worried over those ciphers, and generously endowed them with mystic significance. "The Lottery in Babylon," "Death and the Compass," and "The Circular Ruins" were also written, in whole or part, while I played truant. These tales and others were to become *The Garden of Branching Paths*, a book expanded and retitled *Ficciones* in 1944. *Ficciones* and *El Aleph* (1949 and 1952), my second story collection, are, I suppose, my two major books. (Essay 243–44)

In 1946 Borges was fired from the Miguel Cané Municipal Library, or rather, he was promoted to a higher position, that of inspector of poultry and rabbits, an attempt by the new leadership to humiliate the dissident intellectual. Borges considered Perón, the new president, a Nazi and didn't fail to say so openly. In his essay on his life, Borges explains how he received the distinction of his new position: "I went to the City Hall to find out what it was all about. 'Look here, I said. It's rather strange that among so many others in the library I should be singled out as worthy of this new position.' 'Well,' the clerk answered, 'you were on the side of the Allies—what do you expect?' His statement was unanswerable; the next day, I sent in my resignation" (244).

Borges didn't know what to do, but following the suggestion of a friend, he decided at the age of forty-seven to give lectures up and down Argentina and in Uruguay on the American Renaissance writers and other favorite people and subjects: Swedenborg, Blake, Persian and Chinese mystics, Buddhism, Martin Buber, Kabbalah, the Arabian Nights, Icelandic sagas, Heine, Dante, expressionism, and Cervantes. He made more money, enjoyed the new profession, and felt justified. With Bioy he did anthologies of other preferred subjects: Argentine poetry, tales of the fantastic, and detective fiction. They wrote their books together, translated stories together, founded a magazine. They even wrote film scripts, which didn't make it.

Borges was thoroughly happy with his new role as teacher, on his way to becoming the itinerant sage whose words would find their way electronically to scribes. Meanwhile his eyes were losing the little light they had. Gradually he was becoming blind. During this period of demagogic politics, just after fascism's defeat in Central Europe, noisy dictatorship flourished in Buenos Aires, with proper shirts, political prisons, slogans, goose step, and all. It must be said that the first Perón government was without the deadly "athletic camps" and "Olympic hotels" for those destined to "disappear." These specialties were to characterize the second coming of Perón. And while there was beating and torture, there was no López Rega (*el Brujo*), yet neither was there a "dirty war" or the execution squads of the AAA.

Borges had been made president of the Argentine Society of Writers. As he describes his last lecture there before the *peronistas* shut it down, annoyed as he was at the regime, he makes us laugh:

> The audience, quite a small one, included a very puzzled policeman who did his clumsy best to set down a few of my remarks on Persian Sufism. During this drab and hopeless period, my mother—then in her seventies—was under house arrest. My sister and one of my nephews spent a month in jail. I myself had a detective on my heels, whom I first took on long, aimless walks and at last made friends with. He admitted he too hated Perón, but that he was obeying orders. (248)

When Perón fell in September 1955, Borges's public nightmare ended. For his resistence to Perón, he was offered the position of director of the National Library. Borges viewed this as a great honor and an ultimate irony, since by then, at the time he was made head of books, he was nearly blind. Emir Rodríguez Mongegal, Borges's friend, disciple, and intellectual biographer, masterfully and gracefully describes Borges's euphoria as he took him on a tour through his new symbol-become-real, his library labyrinth:

> Borges took me in hand and led me around, seeing only enough to know where each book he wanted was. He can open a book to the desired page and, without bothering to read—through a feat of memory comparable only to that of his fictional Irineo Funes—quote complete passages. He roams along corridors lined with books; he quickly turns corners and gets into passages which are truly invisible, mere cracks in the walls of books; he rushes down winding staircases which abruptly end in the dark. There is almost no light in the library's corridors and staircases. I try to follow him, tripping, blinder and more handicapped than Borges because my only guides are my eyes. In the dark of the library Borges finds his way with the precarious precision of a tightrope walker. Finally, I come to understand that the space in which we are momentarily inserted is not real: it is a space made of words, signs, symbols. It is another labyrinth. Borges drags me, makes me quickly descend the long, winding staircase, fall exhausted into the center of darkness. Suddenly, there is light at the end of another corridor. Prosaic reality awaits me there. Next to Borges, who smiles like a child

who has played a joke on a friend, I recover my eyesight, the real world of light and shadow, the conventions I am trained to recognize. But I come out of the experience like one who emerges from deep water or from a dream, shattered by the (other) reality of that labyrinth of paper. (Monegal 430–31)

Borges liked to talk about Paul Groussac, the former blind director of the National Library and the splendid irony of he, Borges, becoming chief inspector and guardian of 800,000 books at the time when he was similarly granted darkness. All this he recorded in a major poem, with its mischievous title of "Poema de los dones" (Poem of the gifts), dedicated to his close friend and collaborator, María Esther Vásquez. Here he describes his ancient paradise of gloom, coming apart like sleep and like oblivion.

> Slow in my darkness, I am exploring the
> Thread of twilight with my faltering cane,
> I who imagined Paradise was the domain
> Under the heading of a library.
>
> . . . now I look upon
> A dear world coming apart like smoldering trash,
> Formless, burning into a vague, pale ash
> That looks like sleep and like oblivion.
>
> (*Obra poética* 113–14)

Blindness coming like twilight, gradually

Before his own blindness, Borges had witnessed the blindman in his own home as his father gradually entered the dusk of vision. Guillermo Borges's later years were like his own: futile operations, changes in life necessitated by declining vision, and then the fading of the recognizable world. Borges accepted blindness as a stage in life, a familiar one, one in which the man of all the books and all the memory would combine those forces into the interior library.

As for his father, Borges was absolutely devoted to him. Curiously he spoke of his father's blindness only on rare occasions. But he did speak very often of his father, and in the eighteen years I knew Borges, I cannot recall him uttering a word about his father that was not an affirmation of his powers and goodness. He once told me his father's theory of memory. If you wish to keep a memory intact, it is essential not to call back the memory, for once it is called back, you have the original memory plus a second level of recollection, and the first is altered by the new experience. The theory has qualities of the notion of infinite regressions in Borges's essay "A New Refutation of Time." Monegal suggests that in reality the father was a dark shadow over the boy and that such a shadow fit into patterns Borges had to free himself of, as in other ways he tried, but not very hard, to leave his mother. This, by the way, was accomplished only with her death. Borges, Sr., died blind, in 1938, the year of his son's near fatal accident on the stairway.

Borges's father *was* the English language through his mother Fanny Haslam; he was Palermo, Switzerland, Majorca and Spain, and back again to Buenos Aires where his limited pension made it possible for his son to pursue a literary career. Borges has a splendid and tender sonnet about his father, on one who enters death modest, wholly skeptical, with no delusions. In "La lluvia" (Rain), it is childhood, the rain, and the Palermo neighborhood that dominate a poem in which he misses the father of his childhood:

> This shower, darkening blind the windowpane,
> Will brighten some lost neighborhoods with rain
> On black grapes and an arbor that divide
> A backyard that is gone forever. Moist
> Evening brings back the voice, the wanted voice:
> My father coming back, who hasn't died.

As Borges's eyes faded, his ways and his writing changed. Blindness did not come all at once but like twilight, gradually. The features on the faces of friends faded, the letters in his books were a blur, and a yellow mist replaced the darkness of night. His memory, always alarming to ordinary mortals, contained a multitude of books, which he retrieved as an activity of "rereading." He took a cane and friends to guide him around. He also adjusted to loneliness, which he had never before venerated, but which he began to value as a time to think and to work out things; and he would soom claim he did not feel the need, as in sighted days, to fill out time constantly with people, books, and events.

In his writing Borges had, after his first three books, composed sonnets. The proportion of sonnets increased as his eyes declined, as did poetry itself in comparison with prose. Surprisingly he continued writing and gathering meditative essays on Dante and on his favorite authors, but it was harder to do scholarly reading he had once done for pleasure and that had resulted in a kind of essay he now put aside.

> One salient consequence of my blindness was my gradual abandonment of free verse in favor of classical metrics. In fact, blindness made me take up the writing of poetry again. Since rough drafts were denied me, I had to fall back on memory. It is obviously easier to remember verse than prose, and to

remember regular verse forms rather than free ones. Regular verse is, so to speak, portable. One can walk down the street or be riding the subway while composing and polishing a sonnet, for rhyme and meter have mnemonic virtues. In these years, I wrote dozens of sonnets and longer poems consisting of eleven-syllable quatrains. (*Essay* 250)

While Borges speaks in the *Autobiographical Essay* of the gradual abandonment of free verse in favor of classical meters, in later years the free verse persisted, and he wrote in both modes. What is certain is that he was more dependent on dictation for his free verse than for, say, a sonnet, which he could work out by himself, if necessary. In the end, dictation became his mode, and the dictated-to were his close friends, his intimates, and one among them, a few days before he died, became his wife.

As for those poems that he dictated in his half-light, they, their composition, their expression, his link with the other by means of them, became his "habit" (one of his preferred words and notions). As the people, maps, encyclopedias, all the paraphernalia that occupied the Borges of "Borges and I" slip away, the verse remains his center, as he says in a poem, "On his blindness," which uses the famous title, in English, of another blind poet, Milton:

After these many years, still circling near
me is an obstinate and luminous haze
reducing things to just one thing: a maze
formless and colorless, almost a mere
idea. Vast elemental night and day
swarming with people are that blur of light,
dubious, faithful, never dropping away,
that lies in wait at dawn. I would like sight
to see a face at last. I can't know old
and unexplored encyclopedias, the prize
of books that just my hand can recognize,
birds in the firmament and moons of gold.
For others there remains the universe;
in my half-light, the habit of my verse.

In his mid-fifties, as he lost his vision, Borges turned to an unlikely habit, the study of Anglo-Saxon. He began to teach Old English at the university and wrote a book on Germanic literatures, two-thirds of which treats Old English and Scandinavian writings. He often recalled the first intoxication when he and his students discovered words that fascinated them, like Old English terms for *London* and *Rome*. "All at once, we fell in love with a sentence in which Rome (Romeburh) was mentioned. We got drunk on these

words and rushed down Peru Street shouting them at the top of our
voices" (*Essay* 252). As for why he undertook that study, he claimed
that Anglo-Saxon was as intimate an experience to him as looking
at a sunset or falling in love. Yet what interior reasons could there
be for learning the tongue of the harsh Saxons, for adding it to his
already "weary memory" which like time's history, is seen and no
sooner gone? In his sonnet "Composición escrita en un ejemplar de
la gesta de Beowulf" (Poem written in a copy of *Beowulf*), he con-
fesses to the tremendous sensual love he has for the language itself
and its elemental narrative verse, which is "a secret way" in which
his own confined solitude, enriched by more of those unknown
words, pushes his soul closer and closer to the imminent universe:

> At times I ask myself what are the reasons,
> During my wandering night, that now impel
> Me to begin (expecting no miracle
> Of skill) to learn the tongue of the harsh Saxons.
> Exhausted by the years my memory
> Allows the futilely repeated words
> To slip away, the way my life first girds
> And then ungirds its weary history.
> I tell myself it must be that the soul,
> In a sufficient and a secret way,
> Knows it is endless, that its vast and grave
> Circle takes in and can accomplish all.
> Beyond the longing and beyond this verse,
> Waiting for me, endless: the universe.

As Borges got older, the fame he merited and seemed to avoid
came with lectureships at American universities, including the
Charles Eliot Norton Chair of Poetry at Harvard in 1967, and with
many prizes: the International Publishers Prize, which he shared
with Samuel Beckett in 1961, the Jerusalem Prize in 1971, and in
1980, the Cervantes Prize, which was awarded to him by the king
of Spain. He was also knighted by order of the queen of England,
thereby making him a companion of his closest friend and most
esteemed knight, Alonso Quijano of the Dark Countenance. He
received the degree of Doctor of Letters, *honoris causa*, from Colum-
bia, Oxford, and the University of Paris. Yet despite these measures,
he liked to dismiss the worth of his own writings—perhaps a single
phrase might persist anonymously in the Spanish language, he
would say. His shyness and gestures of modesty took other forms
too, such as the unwillingness to own or keep any copies of his
printed books in his apartment. Alastair Reid, in a wonderful public
exchange at the American P.E.N. Club, asked him, accusingly, why

he wielded such a mighty club of modesty, and Borges, always ready to spoof, offered his apologies.

Fame and modesty were interesting masks, and Borges enjoyed aspects of wearing both, in all their Whitmanian contradiction. He was after all a man of many voices, who lived a long life. The voice that persists and deepens in his poetry and in his life is of the meditative dreamer. Dream and nightmare are his metaphysical strategies. With them he enters the mind of Cervantes who has dreamt up the poor hidalgo Alonso Quijano, who from all his fantastic books on chivalry and personal aspirations has accepted, like an actor, the dream of Don Quijote, the ultimate dreamer with eyes wide open, who in his heart knows he is the dream of a veteran of Lepanto now cashiered from heroics, a failed, impoverished author named Miguel de Cervantes. So Borges himself, in "Sueña Alonso Quinjano" (Alonso Quijano dreams) uses reverie to skip from being to being, from life to literature to life:

> The man awakens from a confusing bed
> Of dream of scimitars and coastal land.
> He scratches beard and forehead with his hand,
> Wondering if he is wounded or is dead.
> Will all those sorcerers who put a curse
> On him—under the moon—keep plaguing him?
> Nothing. Almost no cold. Only a dim
> Sorrow from recent years that were adverse.
> The knight was dreamt up by Cervantes or
> Else Don Quijote was the dreaming knight.
> The double dream bewilders them: the sight
> Of something happening from long before.
> Quijano sleeps and dreams. Dreaming a battle,
> Dreaming the seas, Lepanto, and the schrapnel.

Secular mysticism and Spinoza's dark cup of infinity

Dream, labyrinths that are its most frequent symbol, the "other" and the "double," the "algebra" that is his alchemy between beings are all aspects of Borges's secular ways of seeking answers to the engimas, keys to the universe, or simply the "word" that he knows perfectly well is his goal and that over and over again he tells us he will never decipher. His characters may come close— but they are only characters confined to print—and if they know, as Laprida may at the moment of his slaying, it is too late to tell; Laprida will take his secret with him, away from us, imprisoned yet unrevealed in the poem and the reader's eyes.

In Borges, in any elusive secular or religiously mystical text, the ineffable is there; it is presented obliquely, by parable or metaphor, but never in ordinary conceptual language. Its causes, its subject, its images are there, but by definition, when one has moved under or beyond words into the vision of oblivion, the verbal connections with ordinary time and mind are poor in such a state of otherness, and hence the babbling, shaking, quaking, whirling, rolling, dancing, but no clear speech. As for "truth," it is abstract, elusive, and like all absolutes may be only language and certainly has no conceptual presence in the expression of the ineffable. Borges looks for the word, for the approach to the word, but has no patience for the fallacies and illusions of "truth saying."

As a writer and thinker, Borges wavers between the rawness of his sleepless nights, his eloquent insomnias, and the vision that in some form he perceives but will not, cannot, completely reveal.

In *Borges at Eighty*, he speaks eloquently of two occasions when he had secular mystical experiences, when he was outside time. His confession of total otherness resulted from a conversation we had on San Juan de la Cruz. He states:

> In my life I only had two mystical experiences and I can't tell them because what happened is not to be put into words, since words, after all, stand for a shared experience. . . . Twice in my life I had a feeling. . . . It was astonishing, astounding. I was overwhelmed, taken aback. I had the feeling of living not in time but outside time. I don't know how long that feeling lasted, since I was outside time. (Barnstone, *Borges at Eighty* 11)

As stone and moon in Spinoza long to be stone and moon, Borges longed to explore the metaphysics of his dream or nightmare, or the secular ecstasy of otherness. He invented personages to be his dream. In *The Cipher*, a volume of poems published in 1981, he created an enigmatic René Descartes who indeed doubted his existence. Now the real Descartes of "je pense, donc je suis" was playing a circular syllogistic game, leading not only to proof of his existence but eventually to that of God, which Borges could never accept unless it was Spinoza's pantheistic all, holding everything together: the stones, the people, their temporal souls, the map of all stars, the God that the Portuguese Jew in Holland constructed out of nothingness, imposing the infinite on his blank manuscript. So we read in "Baruch Spinoza":

> A haze of gold, the Occident lights up
> The window. Now, the assiduous manuscript
> Is waiting, weighed down with the infinite.

Jorge Luis Borges

Someone is building God in a dark cup.
A man engenders God. He is a Jew
With saddened eyes and lemon-colored skin;
Time carries him the way a leaf, dropped in
A river, is borne off by waters to
Its end. No matter. The magician moved
Carves out his God with fine geometry;
From his disease, from nothing, he's begun
To construct God, using the word. No one
Is granted such prodigious love as he:
The love that has no hope of being loved.

While Borges was curious about eternity, about the names and
faces of God, and through his many masks looked for and brought
us tantalizingly close to revelation, in the end he left the unsayable
word in mystery. So the Chinese emperor's slave-poet, who is about
to utter the word containing the universe, must be executed, and
Borges's ancestor Francisco Laprida in "The Conjectural Poem" dies
as he "discovers the key to all his years." Borges's characters know
something and "glimpse the riddle" but will not reveal it to Borges
or to us. The word, which Borges cultivates, which is in his kabbalis-
tic frame, the universe, will bring us to the enigma but not reveal
itself. The notion of the silence of the sound that contains the sum
total of the universe is stated in the paradox of the Taoist maxim:
One who speaks does not know; one who knows does not speak.

For all his certainty of the impossibility of crucial knowledge,
in his late sonnet "Un ciego" (A blindman), a poem about the mirror
and the infinite darknesses, hopes, and disappointments it leaves
in the gaze of the blindman, Borges still aspires, on some afternoon,
to know who he is:

I do not know what face looks back at me
When I look at the mirrored face, nor know
What aged man conspires in the glow
Of the glass, silent and with tired fury.
Slow in my shadow, with my hand I explore
My invisible features. A sparkling ray
Reaches me. Glimmers of your hair are gray
Or some still gold. I say I've lost no more
Than just the useless surfaces of things.
This consolation is of great import,
A comfort had by Milton. I resort
To letters and the rose—my wonderings.
I think if I could see my face I'd soon
Know who I am on this rare afternoon.

Friends, women, and love

As blindness settled on the poet, he became increasingly dependent on readers and scribes. As fame took over his publishings, he also became a collaborator in the translations. While he was adamant about keeping his publications out of his own library—"Why occupy space with the works of a mere minor South American author?" were his caustic words—he worked carefully with his editor Carlos Frías on each new work; with his collaborators on books, Alicia Jurado, María Ester Vázquez, Adolfo Bioy Casares, Ester Zemborain de Torres, Silvina Ocampo, and Margarita Guerrero; and with his translators Alastair Reid and Norman Thomas di Giovanni. Di Giovanni spent much of three years in Buenos Aires in the late sixties and early seventies, translating, even collaborating on Borges's remarkable *Autobiographical Essay*, which came out as a long afterword to *The Aleph and Other Stories, 1933–1969*. Eventually, Borges felt trapped by all the help and collaboration of di Giovanni, and the working together ceased.

Most of the people who assisted Borges were women. These literary women were not only coauthors of books but travel companions, readers, and scribes for his work, sister figures including his own sister Norah, and the main figure, his mother Leonor, who was for much of his life his closest companion and with whom he lived for thirty years in their Maipú apartment until her death at age ninety-nine. Borges was on the brink of marriage with his much younger literary collaborator María Esther Vázquez, but this threat was halted by Leonor, to be followed by the brief, unreal "rebound" marriage to Elsa Astete Millán in 1967, forty years after their original short courtship in 1927. Monegal comments in *Jorge Luis Borges*: "Many years later, Borges broke his rule of silence and confided to María Esther Vázquez that one of the things he found strange in Elsa was that she did not dream. Being a dreamer himself, he must have discovered that Elsa's incapacity to dream kept them hopelessly apart" (472).

He was truly devoted to his mother, who in her ninety-ninth year was, she said to him, "sick and punished by God" by being forced to endure so long before her release. His mother, for three decades his surrogate wife and rival of his lawful but short-term spouse, died in 1975. It was a terrible death. Borges told Monegal that "she begged the maid to come and throw her into the garbage can. For the last two years her moaning and cries could be overheard even over the phone. When the end came, she was reduced almost to the bare bones, held together by only a film of parched skin, like a mummified image of herself" (Monegal 474). After her death,

Jorge Luis Borges

Borges was depressed for many months. He composed a poem of pathos and disappointment, "El remordimiento" (Remorse):

> I have committed the worst sin of all
> That a man can commit. I have not been
> Happy. Let the glaciers of oblivion
> Drag me and mercilessly let me fall.
> My parents bred and bore me for a higher
> Faith in the human game of nights and days;
> For earth, for air, for water, and for fire.
> I let them down. I wasn't happy. My ways
> Have not fulfilled their youthful hope. I gave
> My mind to the symmetric stubbornness
> Of art, and all its webs of pettiness.
> They willed me bravery. I wasn't brave.
> It never leaves my side, since I began:
> This shadow of having been a brooding man.

Borges's women, if Monegal and others are right, were not lovers, nor did he have, with the exception of María Esther Vázquez, any very deep or extended love relationships. The latter absences were to change, however, as Borges increasingly became another person as María Kodama entered his life and his work. His last published book, *Atlas*, was also his last collaboration, published in English before it appeared in Spanish. It contained Borges's writings and Maria Kodama's photographs and mapped their global wandering, including a voyage in a hot-air balloon over California's Napa Valley.

María Kodama was born in Argentina of a German mother and a Japanese father, a very austere chemist who never once let her weep since early childhood. Once when she was three or four years old, she did weep. Her father picked her up, shook her, and admonished her severely, saying no decent person sheds tears, and since then she had not and could not. It seems that she met Borges in her childhood, but the first real encounter was at the University of Buenos Aires, where she took her doctorate in Old English. In her first class on Anglo-Saxon literature, she discovered that Borges was the professor. She decided to drop it because one so unworthy as she had no right to study with one so great as Borges. Her friends persuaded her that it would be rude to leave the class without first speaking to Professor Borges. Of course when she did so, he would have none of it, the ploy worked, and for the next decades she was hooked.

After Leonor died, María recorded the new books for Borges. There were other readers and scribes, but gradually María was the single one.

Jorge Luis Borges

Since there was a stubborn mutual pride, silence, and stupidity about money for their work together, she earned her own living by waking each morning at 5:30 to give Spanish lessons to Japanese businessmen in order to spend the rest of her day and weekends with Borges, to accompany him on trips, to be his eyes. When Borges and María went together to a formal occasion, they were an extraordinary pair. Borges, caning into a room, a lobby, an auditorium, holding onto María's arm, dominating every environment. María serene and alert, severe in her care, Borges, often gazing out or up with his dead eyes to take in the new setting. He was always ready to return any remark that any of the unknown figures in the ever-twilight of his vision would throw at him. In Buenos Aires when we were walking someone stopped him and said, "Borges, you are immortal."

"Don't be such a pessimist," he replied.

After a lecture or chat, Borges was mobbed. María would stand by, patient and high-minded, with no apparent distress while the chaos continued. At those mob scenes in the city of his birth, he signed books, shook hands, and exchanged wise pleasantries. For María these happenings were sometimes pleasant, more often tedious, yet she always acted with astute intuition and grace. But I should repeat and amplify her difficulties. Among the crowd of Borges admirers were inevitably some who behaved in hysterical, unpredictably painful ways and not without overt hostility toward her. María, as an insider with the master, was a person to flatter as a way to Borges. Yet who was this contemptuous shadow blocking their way to Borges? Few acted normally in her presence. She was Borges's extremely sensitive, genial, and enigmatic Lazarillo. But in the fuss over Borges, her fate was to be an instrument and be seen as nothing, or very little, in herself.

It was María Kodama who gave Borges life for more than twenty years. As with no other friend in his life, their friendship grew like seeds thrown into earth of an astonishing fertility. María was the one friend on whom Borges became truly reliant, but in those decades of dependence, she never encaged him. She read to him, took dictation for his poems, fictions, and essays, made travel arrangements, accompanied him, ate with him, unobtrusively ordered his food and cut up his meat and vegetables, all while carrying on an interested conversation. She was at every lecture and interview. She did everything but think and speak for him—as sometimes others had attempted to do. In every act there was an equipoise of authority and discretion, of skill and good feelings. It was she, on the contrary, who in full devotion during some periods felt enclosed. Yet that was not essential, and in the last few years something transcended and compensated for any limitations that devotion elicits. Eventually, their working arrangement, their professionalism, their duties helped their personal friendship; their closeness, their very intimacy began to assume an unusual tenderness.

In the last years Borges addressed love poems and dedicated publications to María. They traveled constantly. One day at daybreak they sailed together in a balloon over the Napa Valley. Of this voyage Borges spoke of his indescribable "felicity." He spoke to me now not of the error of that earlier marriage but of his love for María. Borges wrote, "María and I have shared the joy and surprise of finding sounds, languages, twilights, cities, gardens and people, all of them distinctly different and unique" (*Atlas* 8). He read everything into the moon, what the Persians called the mirror of eternity. In his new lyrics, she was the moon. When they were married at the end, it was only the world that might interpret this act as a Borgesian deed of paradox, as a gesture or something extraordinary. It bore no surprise. It was of course of legal importance, but in every other way by then nothing happened out of the ordinary. Their marriage, to use a phrase that Borges's Swinburne would have accepted, was already conceived and consummated in heaven.

When Borges entered the real labyrinth and was lost

When Borges entered the real labyrinth, the original stone one at Knossos, which has not departed from the earth or time, he entered together with María Kodama and became lost. In a labyrinth one is lost. That is its purpose. But now he entered in the morning with María and was not lost alone. María took a photo of Borges sitting with his cane on the steps of the maze. Four fingers of his hand show a useless compass, pointing nowhere. But his blind eyes are wide open, looking to María and her lens. Borges then recorded being so lost with her and in time: "This is the labyrinth of Crete whose center was the Minotaur that Dante imagined as a bull with a man's head in whose stone net so many generations were as lost as María Kodama and I were lost that morning, and remain lost in time, that other labyrinth" (*Atlas* 31).

Later, from my friend Anthony Kerrigan, the first (and the last) translator and editor of Borges's poems and fictions, I heard a few details about the months before his death. Tony was with him and María the last summer in Milano and the last December in Rome, just before they went to Switzerland.

In Milano Borges and María went to the season opening at La Scala, a serious social event, made possible by hard-to-find tickets given them by a wealthy princess whom Tony described as a Catholic Jew from northern Italy. When the couple entered the theater, Borges was recognized by the audience. There was spontaneous

Jorge Luis Borges

applause for him. Then the former president of Italy came and embraced Borges, followed by the incumbent president. It was a natural thing to do in Italy. As Tony related the event my own eyes became misty, but he sobered up sentimental me quickly by saying that Borges was bored stiff with *Aida*.

In later days in Rome, although Borges was sick with liver cancer, he gave no hint of the gravity of his disease. The teasing nobility, the outrageous behavior was as ever and perhaps enhanced by his knowledge of the impending last act. His old claim of physical cowardice was exposed for what it was, a humorous mask behind which was the stoicism he praised in the Socrates of the hemlock. To Tony he recited at odd moments, for no apparent reason, Dante Gabriel Rossetti's lines,

> Look in my face; my name is Might-have-been;
> I am also called No-more, Too-late, Farewell;

Only later, Kerrigan told me, did he catch the obvious message of goodbye, which as a gentleman, as a man of letters, Borges would only let be overheard, though insistently:

> I am called No-More, Too-late, Farewell.

As in a story where the clue lay in the writing on the leopard's hide, he had to disguise his intent for the sake of later decipherment and so spoke his farewell through the mirror of Dante Gabriel Rossetti.

After Rome, in the summer of 1986, Borges and María went to Geneva. They would roam no more. Earlier, Borges had written stories whose setting was in Geneva, often of the double, a theme common to his work. A year before he died he wrote of death and his return to Geneva, "I know I will always return to Geneva, perhaps after the death of my body" (*Atlas* 368). As it happened, the last dramas of his life were to be enacted in this Swiss city.

By this time it was known that Borges was planning to wed María Kodama. Borges was near death. Then untoward events took place. His sister Norah and her two sons objected to the marriage. Borges was always fond of Norah, whom he esteemed as an artist, and also fond of his nephews. But now the family raised an ugly campaign against María, privately and in the Argentine newspapers.

Marcos Ricardo Barnatán, the Argentine poet and author of several volumes on Borges, told me in Madrid the following information. I repeat the facts, if they are so, without change or comment.

215

Jorge Luis Borges

The final offense to Borges came when he discovered that his own bank account, to which his family had access, had, in anticipation of the marriage, been emptied of most of its contents. At this, Borges altered his will, leaving his entire estate to María. To the others he left "amplio lugar en la tumba en la Recoleta" (ample space in the tomb at la Recoleta cemetery).

Borges and María were married in Geneva

An Argentine friend of his and professor from Oberlin College, Ana Cara-Walker, spent some days with the couple in early June. Cara-Walker had, with the American poet and scholar David Young, been translating Borges's six *milongas*. These ballads were an accomplishment very dear to the poet, but as for their translation, they were devilishly elusive. Cara-Walker was consulting Borges about his low-life heroic songs. Borges, she observed, was as usual dressed in a fine suit yet because of his frailty, wore slippers rather than shoes. His humor and cunning erudition were as always. María had found an attractive apartment in the Vieille Ville, the section that Borges had always loved in that preferred, measured city of Geneva. Cara-Walker helped them move, and Borges was delighted with his new home with María, its quiet seclusion, and its rooftop view of the pastel buildings. Ana again saw Borges, but by now he could not leave his bed. That afternoon María was describing the walls of the bedroom with its beautiful wood paneling, the color of sand, and Borges was taking in his newfound riches. Cara-Walker offers us a picture of María and the poet resting peacefullly, memorizing the room as his chosen companion gave him eyes: "She guided Borges' hand over the panel molding. . . . Satisfied with María's description, he lay back and fell into silence. 'Are you all right, Borges?' María asked. 'Yes,' he answered. 'This is the happiest day of my life' " (Cara-Walker 8).

Cara-Walker left and by the time her plane reached New York, June 16, 1986, Borges was dead. She later wrote that Borges "entered death like a feast, with courage, lucidity, and happiness" (9).

Released from habit, the weight of waking again to the obligation of being Borges, the poet was free. Wisdom, if not divinity, served him till the border of darkness. For many of us the planet is indescribably lighter because of his physical departure. There is an emptiness of living anecdote, lightning wit, and compassionate presence. Yet his favorite pastime, memory, also conspires in others to return not only the person but the letter, his letter and word that give us permanently his own conjectural truth, his "final South American destiny" on a ruinous afternoon where in the missing letter, in the mirror of the night, he finds, "the unexpected mien of eternity." Although in his "Conjectural Poem" as elsewhere, Borges will never tell us all, and even when he observes the thunder and the rainbow, his own example is enough. If at that border Socrates knew something or nothing, Borges knew the same. But on the way, Borges mingled wisdom with laughter, added the genius and elegance of his unique word to the alchemy, and enhanced the mystery.

The deathbed marriage and Borges's own death soon thereafter left María doubly devastated: the loss of Borges and the calumny against her, which continued in the Argentine press for many months, only to be followed by unsuccessful court suits to break the will. She stayed on in Geneva, then went to Paris and later to New York for business; she was initially unwilling to go back to Argentina. Eventually, she did return to Buenos Aires, temporarily.

The romance of Borges and María was the last creation in Borges's life. The old *antiperonista*, the anti-Fascist Argentine during the war, the Spinoza of Maipú Street had died without a Nobel Prize, yet some fundamental aspect of this most metaphysical author was satisfied. The isolation of his being, the ignorance inherent in public language and in any ultimate word, in the second that would bring in the ordinary non-time after death—all these unknowns, along with his days and nights, he was now sharing, in a formal pact of love, with his other voice, María.

In the last decade of his life, Borges became an itinerant sage. *Kim* had always been one of his favorite books, one of his "habits," as he would say. He knew Kipling's words by heart as he did the Old English texts. Now he had a kinship with the itinerant Kipling hero. In all this wandering and chatting, in his *charlas*, Borges developed a special oral literature. Because of his blindness, his memory, his sagacity, his humor and nimble tongue, his love for repartee, his magical presence, Borges inevitably grew into a modern Socratic figure.

There is a well-known tradition of the sage whose work is spoken, the Buddha, Jesus, Lao-tzu, Socrates, those figures who, it is said, not only did not care to limit their thoughts by fixing them on a page but desired to avoid the risk and great possible danger of having their words turn into doctrine. So our record of these sages is largely from others who recorded with the instruments of the time: memory and the hands of the scribes.

The Chinese Taoist, Lao-tzu, who may actually have been three people or simply a tradition of quietism, is said to have ridden off one day on a water buffalo into the desert, beyond the realm of civilization, where he dictated his poems and parables. Borges continued to dictate poems, parables, essays, and stories until the end, but increasingly his new medium was the *charla*, the modern dialectic. In those dialogues between himself and his questioning colleagues and audiences, he created a public testament for our time, not different in quality, intensity, and range from personal dialogues with friends, which during most of his adult years had been his Chinese Tao, his way of sharing the unwritten word. In the walks, the shared meals, and talks, there is the voice of the blindman. Resonant, laughing, surprising. Opposing, intimate, profound. Equating the universe with a word, deciphering the alphabet of time. Despairing, spoofing. The voice that embraces the other. The voice of the blindman is the essential Borges. Those who have heard him or read him (the voice is the same) remain affected for life.

Un ciego

No sé cuál es la cara que me mira
Cuando miro la cara del espejo;
No sé qué anciano acecha en su reflejo
Con silenciosa y ya cansada ira.
Lento en mi sombra, con la mano exploro
Mis invisibles rasgos. Un destello
Me alcanza. He vislumbrado tu cabello
Que es de ceniza o es aún de oro.
Repito que he perdido solamente
La vana superficie de las cosas.
El consuelo es de Milton y es valiente,
Pero pienso en las letras y en las rosas.
Pienso que si pudiera ver mi cara
Sabría quién soy en esta tarde rara.

A mi padre

Tú quisiste morir enteramente,
La carne y la gran alma. Tú quisiste
Entrar en la otra sombra sin la triste
Plegaria del medroso y del doliente.
Te hemos visto morir con el tranquilo
Ánimo de tu padre ante las balas.
La guerra no te dio su ímpetu de alas,
La torpe parca fue cortando el hilo.
Te hemos visto morir sonriente y ciego.
Nada esperabas ver del otro lado,
Pero tu sombra acaso ha divisado
Los arquetipos últimos que el griego
Soñó y que me explicabas. Nadie sabe
De qué mañana el mármol es la llave.

A Blindman

I do not know what face looks back at me
When I look at the mirrored face, nor know
What aged man conspires in the glow
Of the glass, silent and with tired fury.
Slow in my shadow, with my hand I explore
My invisible features. A sparkling ray
Reaches me. Glimmers of your hair are gray
Or some still gold. I say I've lost no more
Than just the useless surfaces of things.
This consolation is of great import,
A comfort had by Milton. I resort
To letters and the rose—my wonderings.
I think if I could see my face I'd soon
Know who I am on this rare afternoon.

To My Father

You wished to die entirely and for good,
Your flesh and its great soul. You wished to go
Into that other shade with no sad flood
Of pleas from one whose pain and terror show.
We saw you die with that serenely calm
Spirit your father had before the lead
Of bullets. War gave you no wings, no psalm
Or shouts. The dreary Parc was cutting thread.
We saw you die smiling and also blind,
Expecting nothing on the other side.
But your shade saw or maybe barely spied
Those final archetypes you shared with me
That the Greek dreamt. No one will know or find
That day for which your marble is the key.

221

El remordimiento

He cometido el peor de los pecados
Que un hombre puede cometer. No he sido
Feliz. Que los glaciares del olvido
Me arrastren y me pierdan, despiadados.
Mis padres me engendraron para el juego
Arriesgado y hermoso de la vida,
Para la tierra, el agua, el aire, el fuego.
Los defraudé. No fui feliz. Cumplida
No fue su joven voluntad. Mi mente
Se aplicó a las simétricas porfías
Del arte, que entreteje naderías.
Me legaron valor. No fui valiente.
No me abandona. Siempre está a mi lado
La sombra de haber sido un desdichado.

La pesadilla

Sueño con un antiguo rey. De hierro
Es la corona y muerta la mirada.
Ya no hay caras así. La firme espada
Lo acatará, leal como su perro.
No sé si es de Nortumbria o de Noruega.
Sé que es del Norte. La cerrada y roja
Barba le cubre el pecho. No me arroja
Una mirada su mirada ciega.
¿De qué apagado espejo, de qué nave
De los mares que fueron su aventura,
Habrá surgido el hombre gris y grave
Que me impone su antaño y su amargura?
Sé que me sueña y que me juzga, erguido.
El día entra en la noche. No se ha ido.

Remorse

I have committed the worst sin of all
That a man can commit. I have not been
Happy. Let the glaciers of oblivion
Drag me and mercilessly let me fall.
My parents bred and bore me for a higher
Faith in the human game of nights and days;
For earth, for air, for water, and for fire.
I let them down. I wasn't happy. My ways
Have not fulfilled their youthful hope. I gave
My mind to the symmetric stubbornness
Of art, and all its webs of pettiness.
They willed me bravery. I wasn't brave.
It never leaves my side, since I began:
This shadow of having been a brooding man.

Nightmare

I'm dreaming of an ancient king. His crown
Is iron and his gaze is dead. There are
No faces like that now. And never far
His firm sword guards him, loyal like his hound.
I do not know if he is from Norway
Or Northumberland. But from the north, I know.
His tight red beard covers his chest. And no,
His blind gaze doesn't hurl a gaze my way.
From what extinguished mirror, from what ship
On seas that were his gambling wilderness
Could this man, gray and grave, venture a trip
Forcing on me his past and bitterness?
I know he dreams and judges me, is drawn
Erect. Day breaks up night. He hasn't gone.

Efiáltes

En el fondo del sueño están los sueños. Cada
Noche quiero perderme en las aguas obscuras
Que me lavan del día, pero bajo esas puras
Aguas que nos conceden la penúltima Nada
Late en la hora gris la obscena maravilla.
Puede ser un espejo con mi rostro distinto,
Puede ser la creciente cárcel de un laberinto,
Puede ser un jardín. Siempre es la pesadilla.
Su horror no es de este mundo. Algo que no se nombra
Me alcanza desde ayeres de mito y de neblina;
La imagen detestada perdura en la retina
E infama la vigilia como infamó la sombra.
¿Por qué brota de mi cuando el cuerpo reposa
Y el alma queda sola, esta insensata rosa?

De que nada se sabe

La luna ignora que es tranquila y clara
Y ni siquiera sabe que es la luna;
La arena, que es la arena. No habrá una
Cosa que sepa que su forma es rara.
Las piezas de marfil son tan ajenas
Al abstracto ajedrez como la mano
Que las rige. Quizá el destino humano
De breves dichas y de largas penas
Es instrumento de Otro. Lo ignoramos;
Darle nombre de Dios no nos ayuda.
Vanos también son el temor, la duda
Y la trunca plegaria que iniciamos.
¿Qué arco habrá arrojado esta saeta
que soy? ¿Qué cumbre puede ser la meta?

The Demon of Nightmare

At bottom of a dream are dreams. Each night
I want to lose myself in the dark water
Washing me from the day, yet throbbing under
Pure waters is an obscene wondrous light
With its gray hour of the coming Void.
Maybe it is a mirror with my strange face
Or great jail in a labyrinth. The space
May be a garden—always one destroyed.
A nightmare. An unworldly horror. Something
Unnamed stabs me from yesterdays of myth
And mist; the hated image burns the pith
Of the eye cursing darkness, wakening.
Why when my soul's alone and limbs repose
Is there—bursting in me—this insane rose?

That Nothing Is Known

The moon can't know it is serene and clear,
Nor can it even know it is the moon,
Nor sand that it is sand. No thing may soon
Or ever know it has a strange form here.
The ivory pieces profess no more care
For abstract chess than does the hand, the key,
That guides them. Maybe human destiny
Of hasty joy and lingering despair
Is the instrument of the Other. We don't know.
Nor will evoking God's name do much good.
While terror, doubt, incessant pleading would
Not help. Such things are futile bluff. What bow
Must have released the arrow that I am?
What peak will be the target of that hand?

Nubes (I)

No habrá una sola cosa que no sea
una nube. Lo son las catedrales
de vasta piedra y bíblicos cristales
que el tiempo allanará. Lo es la Odisea,
que cambia como el mar. Algo hay distinto
cada vez que la abrimos. El reflejo
de tu cara ya es otro en el espejo
y el día es un dudoso laberinto.
Somos los que se van. La numerosa
nube que se deshace en el poniente
es nuestra imagen. Incesantemente
la rosa se convierte en otra rosa.
Eres nube, eres mar, eres olvido.
Eres también aquello que has perdido.

Nubes (II)

Por el aire andan plácidas montañas
o cordilleras trágicas de sombra
que oscurecen el día. Se las nombra
nubes. Las formas suelen ser extrañas.
Shakespeare observó una. Parecía
un dragón. Esa nube de una tarde
en su palabra resplandece y arde
y la seguimos viendo todavía.
¿Qué son las nubes? ¿Una arquitectura
del azar? Quizá Dios las necesita
para la ejecución de Su infinita
obra y son hilos de la trama oscura.
Quizá la nube sea no menos vana
que el hombre que la mira en la mañana.

Clouds (I)

There cannot be a single thing which is
not cloud. Cathedrals have it in that tree
of boulders and stained glass with Bible myths
that time will soon erase. The Odyssey
contains it, changing like the sea, distinct
each time we open it. Your mirrored face
already is another face that blinked
in day, our dubious labyrinth of space.
We are the ones who leave. The multiple
cloudbank dissolving in the dropping sun
draws images of us. Ceaselessly will
the rose become another rose. You are
the cloud, the sea, you are oblivion,
and you are whom you've lost—now very far.

Clouds (II)

High in the air these placid mountains or
the cordilleras tragic in their shade
wander, darkening day. The name in store
for them is *clouds*. The forms tend to be strange.
Shakespeare observed one, and to him it was
a dragon. A stray cloud of afternoon
glitters, burns in his word, and we transpose
it into vision we still follow. Soon
we ask: What are clouds? An architecture
of chance? Maybe God needs them as a warning
to carry out His plan of infinite
creation, and they're threads of plots obscure
and vague. Maybe a cloud is no less fixed
than someone looking at it in the morning.

La cierva blanca

¡De qué agreste balada de la verde Inglaterra,
De qué lámina persa, de qué región arcana
De las noches y días que nuestro ayer encierra,
Vino la cierva blanca que soñé esta mañana?
Duraría un segundo. La vi cruzar el prado
Y perderse en el oro de una tarde ilusoria,
Leve criatura hecha de un poco de memoria
Y de un poco de olvido, cierva de un solo lado.
Los númenes que rigen este curioso mundo
Me dejaron soñarte pero no ser tu dueño;
Tal vez en un recodo del porvenir profundo
Te encontraré de nuevo, cierva blanca de un sueño
Yo también soy un sueño fugitivo que dura
Unos días más que el sueño del prado y la blancura.

La pantera

Tras los fuertes barrotes la pantera
Repetirá el monótono camino
Que es (pero no lo sabe) su destino
De negra joya, aciaga y prisionera.
Son miles las que pasan y son miles
Las que vuelven, pero es una y eterna
La pantera fatal que en su caverna
Traza la recta que un eterno Aquiles
Traza en el sueño que ha soñado el griego.
No sabe que hay praderas y montañas
De ciervos cuyas trémulas entrañas
Deleitarian su apetito ciego.
En vano es vario el orbe. La jornada
Que cumple cada cual ya fue fijada.

228

The White Deer

From what old border ballad out of green
England, what Persian print and what arcane
Region of days and nights that still contain
Our past emerged the white deer through the scene
I dreamt this morning? In a flash I saw
It cross the meadow, lose itself in gold
Of an illusory day: lithe creature mold-
ed from a bit of memory and the draw
Of oblivion—a deer on one side only then.
The gods who guard this strange world let me dream
Of you but not control you. Maybe in a seam
Of the deep future I'll find you again.
White deer of dream, I too am dream in flight,
Lasting a few days more than dream, fields, light.

The Panther

Behind the massive iron bars the panther
Will plod its boring road incessantly,
Which is (unknown to it) its destiny
As a black jewel and fated prisoner.
There are a thousand panthers padding back
And forth. The fatal panther in its cave
Is one, eternal, fixed to the straight track
Of an unbound Achilles when he gave
Himself into the dream of the Greek's dreams.
It doesn't know of mountains, a rich field
With deer whose shivering tripe would smell and yield
Savor to its blind appetite. All seems
A waste—this varied world. By now the day,
That each of us fulfills, has its fixed way.

El bisonte

Montañoso, abrumado, indescifrable,
Rojo como la brasa que se apaga,
Anda fornido y lento por la vaga
Soledad de su páramo incansable.
El armado testuz levanta. En este
Antiguo toro de durmiente ira,
Veo a los hombres rojos del Oeste
Y a los perdidos hombres de Altamira.
Luego pienso que ignora el tiempo humano,
Cuyo espejo espectral es la memoria.
El tiempo no lo toca ni la historia
De su decurso, tan variable y vano.
Intemporal, innumerable, cero,
Es el postrer bisonte y el primero.

Adam Cast Forth

¿Hubo un Jardín o fue el Jardín un sueño?
Lento en la vaga luz, me he preguntado,
Casi como un consuelo, si el pasado
De que este Adán, hoy mísero, era dueño,
No fue sino una mágica impostura
De aquel Dios que soñé. Ya es impreciso
En la memoria el claro Paraíso,
Pero yo sé que existe y que perdura,
Aunque no para mi. La terca tierra
Es mi castigo y la incestuosa guerra
De Caínes y Abeles y su cría.
Y, sin embargo, es mucho haber amado,
Haber sido feliz, haber tocado
El viviente Jardín, siquiera un día.

The Bison

Mountainous, crushing, indescribable,
Red like the hot coals that begin to fade,
It ambles slow and ponderous over blade
And wasteland in its vaguely lonely stroll,
Untiring. It lifts its nape of armor. Beast,
An ancient bull of slumbering rage, I watch
It roaming plains of red men of the West,
In caves of Altamira's crew, a batch
Of lost ones. I think it shuns human time
Whose ghostly mirror lingers in a memory.
Time doesn't touch it now, nor does its history
Of years from many down to zero cursed.
Intemporal, innumerable, and prime,
It is the final bison and the first.

Adam Cast Forth

Was there a Garden or was the Garden dream?
Slowly in my vague light, today I've asked,
Almost as consolation, if the past,
Of which this Adam is today a seam
Of misery, was ever master. Was
It magic fraud of the God I dreamt? My eyes
Have no clear memory now of Paradise,
And yet I know that it exists and does
Persist, though not for me. The stubborn clock
Of earth's my punishment, incestuous fray
And war of Cains and Abels and their flock.
Yet, notwithstanding, to have loved is much,
To have been happy, long ago to touch
The living Garden, even for a day.

231

Proteo

Antes que los remeros de Odiseo
Fatigaran el mar color de vino
Las inasibles formas adivino
De aquel dios cuyo nombre fue Proteo.
Pastor de los rebaños de los mares
Y poseedor del don de profecía,
Prefería ocultar lo que sabía
Y entretejer oráculos dispares.
Urgido por las gentes asumía
La forma de un león o de una hoguera
O de árbol que da sombra a la ribera
O de agua que en el agua se perdía.
De Proteo el egipcio no te asombres,
Tú, que eres uno y eres muchos hombres.

Juan, 1, 14

Refieren las historias orientales
La de aquel rey del tiempo, que sujeto
A tedio y esplendor, sale en secreto
Y solo, a recorrer los arrabales
Y a perderse en la turba de las gentes
De rudas manos y de oscuros nombres;
Hoy, como aquel Emir de los Creyentes,
Harún, Dios quiere andar entre los hombres
Y nace de una madre, como nacen
Los linajes que en polvo se deshacen,
Y le será entregado el orbe entero,
Aire, agua, pan, mañanas, piedra y lirio,
Pero después la sangre del martirio,
El escarnio, los clavos y el madero.

232

Proteus

Before the oarsmen of Odysseus came
Wearying the waves with coloring of wine,
There are some forms that no one can define:
An ocean god, and Proteus is his name.
A pastor of the flocks floating the sea,
Possessor of a wild prophetic gift,
He likes to ravish his profundity,
Gather in oracles banished to drift
Away. Then roused by humans, he becomes
The figures of a lion or a bonfire
Or a tree casting shade on the shore's briar
Or water vanishing in water. From
Egypt, don't let him flaunt his magic pen.
You, who are one man, are many men.

John 1:14

The oriental histories tell a tale
Of a bored king in ancient times who, fraught
With tedium and splendor, went uncaught
And secretly about the town to sail
Amid the crowds and lose himself in their
Peasant rough hands, their humble obscure names;
Today, like that Muslim Harum, Emeer
Of the true faithful, God decides to claim
His place on earth, born of a mother in
A lineage that will dissolve in bones,
And the whole world will have its origin
With him: air, water, bread, mornings, stones,
Lily. But soon the blood of martydom,
The curse, the heavy spikes, the beams. Then numb.

Ewigkeit

Torne en mi boca el verso castellano
A decir lo que siempre está diciendo
Desde el latín de Séneca: el horrendo
Dictamen de que todo es del gusano.
Torne a cantar la pálida ceniza,
Los fastos de la muerte y la victoria
De esa reina retórica que pisa
Los estandartes de la vanagloria.
No así. Lo que mi barro ha bendecido
No lo voy a negar como un cobarde.
Sé que una cosa no hay. Es el olvido;
Sé que en la eternidad perdura y arde
Lo mucho y lo precioso que he perdido:
Esa fragua, esa luna y esa tarde.

Sueña Alonso Quijano

El hombre se despierta de un incierto
Sueño de alfanjes y de campo llano
Y se toca la barba con la mano
Y se pregunta si está herido o muerto.
¿No lo perseguirán los hechiceros
Que han jurado su mal bajo la luna?
Nada. Apenas el frío. Apenas una
Dolencia de sus años postrimeros.
El hidalgo fue un sueño de Cervantes
Y don Quijote un sueño del hidalgo.
El doble sueño los confunde y algo
Está pasando que pasó mucho antes.
Quijano duerme y sueña. Una batalla:
Los mares de Lepanto y la metralla.

Ewigkeit

Let me turn over in my mouth a verse
In Spanish to confirm what Seneca
In Latin always says: his horrid curse
Declaring that the world's a formula
For worms. Let me sing out his pallid ash,
The calendars of death and victory
Of that bombastic queen who tries to smash
And stomp the banners of our vanity.
Enough of that. What may have blessed my dust
I'm not a fool and coward to deny,
And know there is one thing that can't exist:
Forgetting. Yet the precious things I've lost
Endure, burn in eternity: that sky
And moon, that blacksmith forge, that evening mist.

Alonso Quijano Dreams*

The man awakens from a confusing bed
Of dream of scimitars and coastal land.
He scratches beard and forehead with his hand,
Wondering if he is wounded or is dead.
Will all those sorcerers who put a curse
On him—under the moon—keep plaguing him?
Nothing. Almost no cold. Only a dim
Sorrow from recent years that were adverse.
The knight was dreamt up by Cervantes or
Else Don Quijote was the dreaming knight.
The double dream bewilders them: the sight
Of something happening from long before.
Quijano sleeps and dreams. Dreaming a battle,
Dreaming the seas, Lepanto, and the schrapnel.

*Alonso Quijano is the impoverished hidalgo in Miguel de Cervantes' *Don Quijote* whom Cervantes causes to believe he is a knight called Don Quijote. Cervantes himself was severely wounded in a sea battle off the coastal city of Lepanto (Nafpaktos), Greece.

El conquistador

Cabrera y Carbajal fueron mis nombres.
He apurado la copa hasta las heces.
He muerto y he vivido muchas veces.
Yo soy el Arquetipo. Ellos, los hombres.
De la Cruz y de España fui el errante
Soldado. Por las nunca holladas tierras
De un continente infiel encendí guerras.
En el duro Brasil fui el bandeirante.
Ni Cristo ni mi Rey ni el oro rojo
Fueron el acicate del arrojo
Que puso miedo en la pagana gente.
De mis trabajos fue razón la hermosa
Espada y la contienda procelosa.
No importa lo demás. Yo fui valiente.

Spinoza

Las traslúcidas manos del judío
Labran en la penumbra los cristales
Y la tarde que muere es miedo y frío.
(Las tardes a las tardes son iguales.)
Las manos y el espacio de jacinto
Que palidece en el confín del Ghetto
Casi no existen para el hombre quieto
Que está soñando un claro laberinto.
No lo turba la fama, ese reflejo
De sueños en el sueño de otro espejo,
Ni el temeroso amor de las doncellas.
Libre de la metáfora y del mito
Labra un arduo cristal: el infinito
Mapa de Aquél que es todas Sus estrellas.

Conquistador

Cabrera and Carbajal, these were my names.
I've drained the wineglass down to the last dram.
I've died and many times I've lived. I am
The Archetype. The others men. My claim:
For Spain and for the Cross I was the wan-
dering soldier. On unwalked lands and shores
Of an infidel continent I stirred up wars.
In fierce Brazil I carried the banner on.
Neither my king, nor Christ, nor the red gold
Were the instigating spur of all my bold-
ness that unleashed a terror in the wave
Of pagans. Yes, my justice was the sword
Handsome in bloody battle and its lord.
The rest? It doesn't matter. I was brave.

Spinoza

Here in the twilight the translucent hands
Of the Jew polishing the crystal glass.
The dying afternoon is cold with bands
Of fear. Each day the afternoons all pass
The same. The hands and space of hyacinth
Paling in the confines of the ghetto walls
Barely exists for the quiet man who stalls
There, dreaming up a brilliant labyrinth.
Fame doesn't trouble him (that reflection of
Dreams in the dream of another mirror), nor love,
The timid love women. Gone the bars,
He's free, from metaphor and myth, to sit
Polishing a stubborn lens: the infinite
Map of the One who now is all His stars.

Baruch Spinoza

Bruma de oro, el Occidente alumbra
La ventana. El asiduo manuscrito
Aguarda, ya cargado de infinito.
Alguien construye a Dios en la penumbra.
Un hombre engendra a Dios. Es un judío
De tristes ojos y de piel cetrina;
Lo lleva el tiempo como lleva el río
Una hoja en el agua que declina.
No importa. El hechicero insiste y labra
A Dios con geometría delicada;
Desde su enfermedad, desde su nada,
Sigue erigiendo a Dios con la palabra.
El más pródigo amor le fue otorgado,
El amor que no espera ser amado.

El ciego

Lo han despojado del diverso mundo,
De los rostros, que son lo que eran antes,
De las cercanas calles, hoy distantes,
Y del cóncavo azul, ayer profundo.
De los libros le queda lo que deja
La memoria, esa forma del olvido
Que retiene el formato, no el sentido,
Y que los meros títulos refleja.
El desnivel acecha. Cada paso
Puede ser la caída. Soy el lento
Prisionero de un tiempo soñoliento
Que no marca su aurora ni su ocaso.
Es de noche. No hay otros. Con el verso
Debo labrar mi insípido universo.

Baruch Spinoza

A haze of gold, the Occident lights up
The window. Now, the assiduous manuscript
Is waiting, weighed down with the infinite.
Someone is building God in a dark cup.
A man engenders God. He is a Jew
With saddened eyes and lemon-colored skin;
Time carries him the way a leaf, dropped in
A river, is borne off by waters to
Its end. No matter. The magician moved
Carves out his God with fine geometry;
From his disease, from nothing, he's begun
To construct God, using the word. No one
Is granted such prodigious love as he:
The love that has no hope of being loved.

The Blindman

The varied world is plundered. Gone the sweep
Of faces (that are what they were before),
The nearby streets, today remote. And more,
The hollow blue that yesterday was deep.
Left in the books is only what remains
In memory—forms of forgetfulness
Which keep the format yet undo the sense,
Flashing mere titles. But the street contains
Ambushing breaks and holes. And each step won
May be a fall. I am the very slow
Prisoner of a dreamlike time, with no
Way left to mark his dawn or fading sun.
It's night. No one is here. And with my verse
I must work out my insipid universe.

On his blindness

Al cabo de los años me rodea
una terca neblina luminosa
que reduce las cosas a una cosa
sin forma ni color. Casi a una idea.
La vasta noche elemental y el día
lleno de gente son esa neblina
de luz dudosa y fiel que no declina
y que acecha en el alba. Yo querría
ver una cara alguna vez. Ignoro
la inexplorada enciclopedia, el goce
de libros que mi mano reconoce,
las altas aves y las lunas de oro.
A los otros les queda el universo;
a mi penumbra, el hábito del verso.

Una rosa y Milton

De las generaciones de las rosas
Que en el fondo del tiempo se han perdido
Quiero que una se salve del olvido,
Una sin marca o signo entre las cosas
Que fueron. El destino me depara
Este don de nombrar por vez primera
Esa flor silenciosa, la postrera
Rosa que Milton acercó a su cara,
Sin verla. Oh tú bermeja o amarilla
O blanca rosa de un jardin borrado,
Deja mágicamente tu pasado
Inmemorial y en este verso brilla,
Oro, sangre o marfil o tenebrosa
Como en sus manos, invisible rosa.

On his blindness

After these many years, still circling near
me is an obstinate and luminous haze
reducing things to just one thing: a maze
formless and colorless, almost a mere
idea. Vast elemental night and day
swarming with people are that blur of light,
dubious, faithful, never dropping away,
that lies in wait at dawn. I would like sight
to see a face at last. I can't know old
and unexplored encyclopedias, the prize
of books that just my hand can recognize,
birds in the firmament and moons of gold.
For others there remains the universe;
in my half-light, the habit of my verse.

A Rose and Milton

Among the generations of the rose
That have been lost in time's old manuscripts,
I want to salvage one of them from its
Oblivion, one unmarked, unseen from those
Earlier things. Now destiny provides
Me with the gift of naming for the first
Time that one soundless flower, the rose, the last
One Milton chose and lifted to his eyes,
Not seeing it. O you, vermillion, white
Or yellow rose now in a garden blurred,
You leave your past and magically depose
All memory, yet in lines you persist bright
With gold or blood or ivory, as conferred
To darkness in his hands, invisible rose.

241

Emanuel Swedenborg

Más alto que los otros, caminaba
Aquel hombre lejano entre los hombres;
Apenas si llamaba por sus nombres
Secretos a los ángeles. Miraba
Lo que no ven los ojos terrenales:
La ardiente geometría, el cristalino
Edificio de Dios y el remolino
Sórdido de los goces infernales.
Sabía que la Gloria y el Averno
En tu alma están y sus mitologías;
Sabía, como el griego, que los días
Del tiempo son espejos del Eterno,
En árido latín fue registrando
Últimas cosas sin por qué ni cuando.

A John Keats
(1795–1821)

Desde el principio hasta la joven muerte
La terrible belleza te acechaba
Como a los otros la propicia suerte
O la adversa. En las albas te esperaba
De Londres, en las páginas casuales
De un diccionario de mitología,
En las comunes dádivas del día,
En un rostro, una voz, y en los mortales
Labios de Fanny Brawne. Oh sucesivo
Y arrebatado Keats, que el tiempo ciega,
El alto ruiseñor y la urna griega
Serán tu eternidad, oh fugitivo.
Fuiste el fuego. En la pánica memoria
No eres hoy la ceniza. Eres la gloria.

Emanuel Swedenborg

He loomed above the others when he walked,
That man who was remote among good men,
By secret names he called them when he talked
To angels. When he gazed beyond his pen,
He saw what earthly eyes can never look upon:
Burning geometry, the crystal dome
Of God, and the disgusting whirlwind home
Of those infernal joys nourished each dawn.
He knew that Glory and the gate of Hell
And their mythologies live in your soul.
He knew, like Heraclitus, that one day
Of time's a mirror of eternity,
And in dry Latin found the final role
Of things whose why or when he wouldn't tell.

To John Keats
(1795–1821)

From the beginning to his youthful death
A terrible beauty lay in wait for him
As proper fate for others bared its teeth
Or the reverse. It waited for you grim
In London's dawns, and in the casual pages
Of a dictionary of mythology,
In ordinary presents of the day,
And in a face, a voice, the mortally
Born lips of Fanny Brawne. O intuitive,
Enraptured Keats, whom time has now made blind,
The lofty nightingale and the Greek urn
Are your eternity, O fugitive.
You were a fire. In the frenzy of memory
You are not ash today. You are the glory.

243

Edgar Allan Poe

Pompas del mármol, negra anatomía
Que ultrajan los gusanos sepulcrales,
Del triunfo de la muerte los glaciales
Símbolos congregó. No los temía.
Temía la otra sombra, la amorosa,
Las comunes venturas de la gente;
No lo cegó el metal resplandeciente
Ni el mármol sepulcral sino la rosa
Como del otro lado del espejo
Se entregó solitario a su complejo
Destino de inventor de pesadillas.
Quizá, del otro lado de la muerte,
Siga erigiendo solitario y fuerte
Espléndidas y atroces maravillas.

Emerson

Ese alto caballero americano
Cierra el volumen de Montaigne y sale
En busca de otro goce que no vale
Menos, la tarde que ya exalta el llano.
Hacia el hondo poniente y su declive,
Hacia el confín que ese poniente dora,
Camina por los campos como ahora
Por la memoria de quien esto escribe.
Piensa: Leí los libros esenciales
Y otros compuse que el oscuro olvido
No ha de borrar. Un dios me ha concedido
Lo que es dado saber a los mortales.
Por todo el continente anda mi nombre;
No he vivido. Quisiera ser otro hombre.

244

Edgar Allan Poe

Pomp of marble, a black anatomy
That coffin worms in murkiness outrage
And victimize for death's pure triumph, he
Gathered those glacial symbols. But that page
Was nil. The other shadow, yes. He froze:
The fear of love, the common ways of people.
He wasn't blinded by a fulgent metal,
Nor the sepulchral marble, but the rose.
As passing through the tunnel of the mirror,
He gave himself alone to his complex
Mission of being the inventor of the nightmare.
Perhaps the other side of death and under
His will he goes on raising lonely decks
Of visionary and atrocious wonders.

Emerson

Closing the volume of Montaigne this tall
New England gentleman gets up, goes out
To find another joy that's not at all
Worth less than books, and so he strolls about
As afternoon exalts the fields; he walks
Into the deep and dropping sun's gold gown,
And through the meadows (now as someone locks
All this in memory and writes it down).
He thinks: The great essential books I've read
And written others. Dark oblivion
Will not efface them. Yes, a god gave me
What's given mortal men to know. I see
My name across a continent has spread.
I haven't lived. I'd be another man.

Camden, 1892

El olor del café y de los periódicos.
El domingo y su tedio. La mañana
Y en la entrevista página esa vana
Publicación de versos alegóricos
De un colega feliz. El hombre viejo
Está postrado y blanco en su decente
Habitación de pobre. Ociosamente
Mira su cara en el cansado espejo.
Piensa, ya sin asombro, que esa cara
Es él. La distraída mano toca
La turbia barba y la saqueada boca.
No está lejos el fin. Su voz declara:
Casi no soy, pero mis versos ritman
La vida y su esplendor. Yo fui Walt Whitman.

París, 1856

La larga postración lo ha acostumbrado
A anticipar la muerte. Le daría
Miedo salir al clamoroso día
Y andar entre los hombres. Derrribado,
Enrique Heine piensa en aquel río,
El tiempo, que lo aleja lentamente
De esa larga penumbra y del doliente
Destino de ser hombre y ser judío.
Piensa en las delicadas melodías
Cuyo instrumento fue, pero bien sabe
Que el trino no es del árbol ni del ave
Sino del tiempo y de sus vagos días.
No han de salvarte, no, tus ruiseñores,
Tus noches de oro y tus cantados flores.

Camden, 1892

The smell of coffee and of newspapers.
Sunday and its monotony. The morning,
Some allegoric verses are adorning
The glimpsed at page, the vain pentameters
Of a contented colleague. The old man lies
Stretched out and white in his respectable
Poor man's room. Then lazily he fills
The weary mirror with his gaze. His eyes
See a face. Unsurprised he thinks: That face
Is me. With fumbling hand he reaches out
To touch the tangled beard and ravaged mouth.
The end is not far off. His voice declares:
I'm almost gone and yet my verses scan
Life and its splendor. I was Walt Whitman.

Paris, 1856

The long prostration has accustomed him
To anticipate his death. His concrete dread
Is going out of doors into the whim
Of day to walk about with friends. Ravaged,
Heinrich Heine thinks about that river
Of time that slowly moves away into
That lingering penumbra and the bitter
Hurt destiny of being a man and Jew.
He thinks about exquisite melodies
Whose instrument he was, and yet he knows
The trilling doesn't come from trees or birds
But time and from the days' slim vagaries.
And yet your nightingales won't save you, no,
Nor golden nights and flowers sung in your words.

New England, 1967

Han cambiado las formas de mi sueño;
ahora son oblicuas casas rojas
y el delicado bronce de las hojas
y el casto invierno y el piadoso leño.
Como en el día séptimo, la tierra
es buena. En los crepúsculos persiste
algo que casi no es, osado y triste,
un antiguo rumor de Biblia y guerra.
Pronto (nos dicen) llegará la nieve
y América me espera en cada esquina,
pero siento en la tarde que declina
el hoy tan lento y el ayer tan breve.
Buenos Aires, yo sigo caminando
por tus esquinas, sin por qué ni cuándo.

                                   Cambridge, 1967

Una llave en Salónica

Abarbanel, Farías o Pinedo,
Arrojados de España por impía
Persecución, conservan todavía
La llave de una casa de Toledo.
Libres ahora de esperanza y miedo,
Miran la llave al declinar el día;
En el bronce hay ayeres, lejanía,
Cansado brillo y sufrimiento quedo.
Hoy que su puerta es polvo, el instrumento
Es cifra de la diáspora y del viento,
Afín a esa otra llave del santuario
Que alguien lanzó al azul cuando el romano
Acometió con fuego temerario,
Y que en el cielo recibió una mano.

New England, 1967

It is the forms in dream that seem to change;
Everywhere I see a slanting red house,
A full flora with leaves of slender bronze,
The winter chaste, fire logs piously strange.
As on the seventh day, the earth is good.
In twilight there is something that persists,
Something that almost isn't: daring, sad,
An ancient ring of Bible and the mists
Of war. Soon (we are told) will come the snow.
America at every corner waits
For me, but in the sinking afternoon
I feel the past so brief, the now so slow.
Buenos Aires, I'm walking through your streets.
I go on without why or when, but soon.

                                    Cambridge, 1967

A Key in Salonika

Abarbanel, Farías or Pinedo,
Hurled out of Spain in an unholy sweep-
ing persecution, even now they keep
The doorkey of an old house in Toledo.
At last, from hope and terror they are free
And watch the key as afternoon disbands.
Cast in its bronze are other days, far lands,
A weary brilliance, a calm agony,
Now that its door is dust, the instrument
Is a cipher of diaspora and wind
Like the other temple key someone flung high
Into the blue (when Roman soldiers bent
And charged with dreadful flames and discipline)
And which a hand received into the sky.

249

Una llave en East Lansing
                    A Judith Machado

Soy una pieza de limado acero.
Mi borde irregular no es arbitrario.
Duermo mi vago sueño en un armario
Que no veo, sujeta a mi llavero.
Hay una cerradura que me espera,
Una sola. La puerta es de forjado
Hierro y firme cristal. Del otro lado
Está la casa, oculta y verdadera.
Altos en la penumbra los desiertos
Espejos ven las noches y los días
Y las fotografías de los muertos
Y el tenue ayer de las fotografías.
Alguna vez empujaré la dura
Puerta y haré girar la cerradura.

La lluvia

Bruscamente la tarde se ha aclarado
Porque ya cae la lluvia minuciosa.
Cae y cayó. La lluvia es una cosa
Que sin duda sucede en el pasado.
Quien la oye caer ha recombrado
El tiempo en que la suerte venturosa
Le reveló una flor llamada *rosa*
Y el curioso color del colorado.
Esta lluvia que ciega los cristales
Alegrará en perdidos arrabales
Las negras uvas de una parra en cierto
Patio que ya no existe. La mojada
Tarde me trae la voz, la voz deseada,
De mi padre que vuelve y que no ha muerto.

A Key in East Lansing
To Judith Machado

I am a key whose steel has been filed out.
My crooked edge was not cut aimlessly.
I sleep vague sleep in channels I don't see
In which I am a captive held throughout
By chains. A sure lock waits for me within.
It is unique, its door made of forged steel
And tight glass. Inside, ready to reveal
Itself, is the hidden true house. Deep in
The scanty twilight, uninhabited
Mirrors are glaring into nights and days
And glare upon the photos of the dead,
The tenuous past of photos. In this maze,
One day I will push up against the rock-
Hard door and slip inside to turn the lock.

Rain

Suddenly the afternoon is clear and wan
with light, for now a minute rain is falling.
Falling and fell. The drizzle is a thing
That takes place surely in a past that's gone.
Whoever hears it falling is refed
With time in which mere chance begins to feel
A flower whose name is *rose,* and to reveal
The curious pigment of the color red.
This shower, darkening blind the windowpane,
Will brighten some lost neighborhoods with rain
On black grapes and an arbor that divide
A backyard that is gone forever. Moist
Evening brings back the voice, the wanted voice:
My father coming back, who hasn't died.

251

On His Blindness

Indigno de los astros y del ave
Que surca el hondo azul, ahora secreto,
De esas líneas que son el alfabeto
Que ordenan otros y del mármol grave
Cuyo dintel mis ya gastados ojos
Pierden en su penumbra, de las rosas
Invisibles y de las silenciosas
Multitudes de oros y de rojos
Soy, pero no de las Mil Noches y Una
Que abren mares y auroras en mi sombra
Ni de Walt Whitman, ese Adán que nombra
Las criaturas que son bajo la luna,
Ni de los blancos dones del olvido
Ni del amor que espero y que no pido.

Al espejo

¿Por qué persistes, incesante espejo?
¿Por qué duplicas, misterioso hermano.
El menor movimiento de mi mano?
¿Por qué en la sombra el súbito reflejo?
Eres el otro yo de que habla el griego
Y acechas desde siempre. En la tersura
Del agua incierta o del cristal que dura
Me buscas y es inútil estar ciego.
El hecho de no verte y de saberte
Te agrega horror, cosa de magia que osas
Multiplicar la cifra de las cosas
Que somos y que abarcan nuestra suerte.
Cuando esté muerto, copiarás a otro
Y luego a otro, a otro, a otro . . .

On His Blindness

I am unworthy of the stars and bird
Furrowing the deep blue, now a secret;
Of those warped lines that are the alphabet
That others use; of marble gravely blurred
And lost in shadow and whose lintel holds
More shadow for my wasted eyes; of the
Invisible still rose or quietly
Imposing multitudes of reds and golds.
But I'm not of A Thousand and One Nights
That open seas and daybreaks in my dark;
Nor of Walt Whitman—Adam whose names mark
The creatures under the moon; nor of the white
Gifts of oblivion. I am not cast
For love—for which I hope and do not ask.

To the Mirror

Incessant mirror, why do you persist?
And why, mysterious brother, duplicate
The slightest motion that my hands create?
And why reflect me startled in dark mist?
You are the other I of whom the Greek
Was speaking, always lurking. In the gloss
Of fickle waters and enduring glass,
Though I am blind you manage still to seek
Me out. The fact that I don't see or know
You adds more horror. You're a magic thing
And multiply what goes into our being,
Imprisoning our fate inside your glow.
When I am dead you'll copy out another,
Another, then another, and another . . .

Yo

La calavera, el corazón secreto,
Los caminos de sangre que no veo,
Los túneles del sueño, ese Proteo,
Las vísceras, la nuca, el esqueleto.
Soy esas cosas. Increíblemente
Soy también la memoria de una espada
Y la de un solitario sol poniente
Que se dispersa en oro, en sombra, en nada.
Soy el que ve las proas desde el puerto;
Soy las contados libros, los contados
Grabados por el tiempo fatigados;
Soy el que envidia a los que ya se han muerto.
Más raro es ser el hombre que entrelaza
Palabras en un cuarto de una casa.

Composición escrita en un ejemplar de la gesta de Beowulf

A veces me pregunto qué razones
Me mueven a estudiar sin esperanza
De precisión, mientras mi noche avanza,
La lengua de los ásperos sajones.
Gastada por los años la memoria
Deja caer la en vano repetida
Palabra y es así como mi vida
Teje y desteje su cansada historia.
Será (me digo entonces) que de un modo
Secreto y suficiente el alma sabe
Que es inmortal y que su vasto y grave
Círculo abarca todo y puede todo.
Más allá de este afán y de este verso
Me aguarda inagotable el universo.

The skull, the secret heart, the roads
Of blood I cannot see, tunnels of dream,
That Proteus, and skeleton with loads
Of viscera, the nape, the lungs, the steam,
I am those things. And I am even more
Incredibly the memory of a sword
And of a solitary sun before
It drops, ripping in gold, shadow, and void.
I am a man who sees the prows from port;
I am a precious book, a rare engraving
Time has worn out. I am a soul who's saving
Envy for those already dead. My sort
Is even stranger. I am one who chose
To spin some words in one room of a house.

Poem Written in a Copy of Beowulf

At times I ask myself what are the reasons,
During my wandering night, that now impel
Me to begin (expecting no miracle
Of skill) to learn the tongue of the harsh Saxons.
Exhausted by the years my memory
Allows the futiley repeated words
To slip away, the way my life first girds
And then ungirds its weary history.
I tell myself it must be that the soul,
In a sufficient and a secret way,
Knows it is endless, that its vast and grave
Circle takes in and can accomplish all.
Beyond the longing and beyond this verse,
Waiting for me, endless: the universe.

Miguel Hernández

(1910–1942)

Spain

Miguel Hernández

A self-taught goatherd from Alicante writes surreal sonnets

The appearance and disappearance of Miguel Hernández in the renaissance of Spanish poetry of our century marks its last illumination and its sudden darkness when in 1942, Hernández, not yet thirty-two and ill with tuberculosis, was moved from his cell in Alicante to the prison hospital, where he died soon thereafter. Because he was born in 1910, about a decade after most of the poets of 1927, and began publishing in the 1930s, Hernández, with Luis Rosales and Germán Bleiberg, has been placed chronologically in the Generation of 1936, which in his case coincides with the year of publication in Madrid by Manuel Altolaguirre of *El rayo que no cesa* (The unending lightning), his first major collection of poems; the year 1936 also marks the beginning of the Civil War, a disaster that was to put an end effectively to that rebirth of poetry in Spain.

Death and exile dissipated Spanish poetry. Lorca died in the first weeks of the war, Machado in the last months of the war, Hernández died three years after the conflict. Alberti went to Italy and Argentina; Juan Ramón Jiménez stayed in Florida and Puerto Rico (Jiménez, who won the Nobel Prize in exile, had been in America earlier but with the Civil War, his absence became permanent); Guillén and Salinas were at Wellesley College and Johns Hopkins, respectively; and Luis Cernuda went to Mexico. Only Vicente Aleixandre remained, and he became the champion of poets in Spain for the next forty-five years. When he was awarded the Nobel Prize, it was significant that he had remained, always in the opposition, always helping.

With the ending of the Civil War, moreover, Aleixandre did not end his innovative career in midstream. His *Poemas de la consumación* (Poems of consummation), written in his seventies, is one of his finest volumes. Guillén finished *Cántico* in 1950 (his best work) in Massachusetts, Salinas wrote on the East Coast and in Puerto Rico, and Alberti wrote in Rome and Buenos Aires.

Death and diaspora have withered the tree of Spanish poetry.

Miguel Hernández

The spirit, that extraordinary unity of poets and their mutual sympathy and common stimulation, are a unique phenomenon of the first half of the century. Many good poets have since appeared in Spain—Blas de Otero, Claudio Rodríguez, Gloria Fuertes, Francisco Brines, Angel González, to name a few. But with the huge international resonance of the Latin American boom novel and the canonization of poetry by the Peruvian César Vallejo, Chileans Pablo Neruda and Nicanor Parra, Argentine Jorge Luis Borges, and Mexican Octavio Paz, the fulcrum has changed to the New World.

Right or wrong the Spanish poetic rebirth now lies in the common museum of European and American modernism. Joyce, Eliot, Beckett, Lorca, Mann, Neruda, Seferis, Borges, Montale are dead. Only some novelists from Latin America do not understand that the age of giants is supposed to be over, and they keep emerging, and we add figures like Gabriel García Márquez and the late Julio Cortázar to our list of major authors, calling them magic realists, postmodernists, whatever.

By his birthdate in 1910, Miguel Hernández came after the famous Generation of '27. His own early achievement and premature death, however, fixed him in their company, linked him forever with them, as at the same time, it deprived him (and us) of the possibility of knowing a full developing career as poet, which after the 1940s, his two closest friends in poetry, Vicente Aleixandre and Pablo Neruda, were able to and did enjoy.

Miguel Hernández

> Miguel Hernández, whistling to me like a nightingale from the trees in the Calle Princesa until the garrison ensnared my nightingale.
>
> —Pablo Neruda

Miguel Hernández Gilabert was born on October 30, 1910, in the small city of Orihuela in the province of Alicante. It is southeastern Spain, just above Andalusia, bordering on Catalán-speaking Valencia, a region of estates, poor peasants, and migrant farmhands. The towns with ancient stone buildings and cobbled plazas, its landscapes lush with mud and beauty come right out of Eden, if we think of Eden as a garden of pomegranates, lemon groves, fig, palm, and almond trees, and of course the olive groves with their umbrellas of silver and black leaves. The Moors were expelled in 1264 by Jaime I the Conqueror, and since then this section has been a more traditionally Catholic region than others, with strong dissenters; silk and sugar have been the agricultural and industrial staples, and the meadows and fields are peopled by ox and mule drovers, pastors, and goatherds. Miguel Hernández was for most of his short life a pastor and goatherd. .

In that tradition of the pastoral, going back in the West to the Song of Songs in Hebrew, Theokritos, Moschos, and Bion in Greek, Virgil's *Eclogues*; Sannazaro's and Sidney's Acadias, and Garcilaso de la Vega's Renaissance tableaux, we have in Miguel Hernández Gilabert probably the only fully refined master of his tongue who was in reality—not in an idealized mask and gown—an experienced pastor. Hernández was not only a pastor in regard to the peasant figures and agricultural settings of his poems but remained a shepherd-poet even when creating surreally baroque sonnets, with tour de force verbal feats. He always longed nostalgically for the feel, touch, smell, and warmth of his goats in pasture.

Hernández's family was poor, and the houses of his childhood were, to use the feudal word in Spanish, *humilde* (humble). The small city home on the Calle de Arriba had a backyard and corral, with some fruit trees, sheep, goats, and manure piles. It seems that Hernández, from a very early age, had a passion for water, doused himself each day with buckets of well water, loved to walk shirtless in the rain. One day in Madrid, years after his death, Vicente Aleixandre told me that he had given Miguel a new wristwatch when the poet got married. It was proudly the first one he had owned. A few weeks later Aleixandre asked him where was the watch, and he said he "broke" it, swimming in a stream.

Miguel was out in the fields, tending and whistling at his flocks for years before he entered the Colegio de Santo Domingo, a religious school established by Dominicans and run by the Jesuits. There he learned to read and write very quickly and wrote his first poetry, religious poetry; though he was an exceptionally smart student, he was not comfortable among the wealthier, well-dressed children. At home he received terrible beatings from his authoritarian father for, among other things, neglecting the flock. These beatings, especially to his head, left him with severe recurrent headaches, which he was never able to cure. In 1925, at fourteen, he left school to return to the pasture. Thereafter his education continued vigorously as an autodidact.

He read in the fields and then worked late in his room at night, reading the classics and any important books he could find. He filled notebooks with his poems and play fragments. Juan Cano Ballesta describes these early moments:

> Enriched by the knowledge of such immense reading, he begins to get into the literary circles of Orihuela. The first in which he takes part is at the bakery of Efrén Fenoll on Arriba 5 street. There he spends long hours in a pleasant *tertulia* with the new

Miguel Hernández

friends: Carlos and Efrén Fenoll Felices, sons of a local poet who is owner of the bakery; the brothers Ramón and Gabriel Sijé. . . . Josefina Fenoll, sister of Carlos and Efrén and Ramón's fiancee to whom Miguel directs his elegy to the bakery. In the heat of the oven and under the aroma of fresh bread the literary discussions go on. The pastor recites his verses and receives wise advice from Ramón Sijé, a young man of rare intelligence and extraordinary culture. (Cano 19)

Miguel's first publications were in local Catholic and other small periodicals. Soon he was in the literary circle in Orihuela. Miguel was the talented pastor-poet. And an ambitious one. By December 1931 he was ready to go to Madrid, made contact with literary and other figures, including Concha Albornoz, and set off for the capital. Albornoz (who in later years taught at Mount Holyoke College, as did Luis Cernuda for a year) befriended the young poet and attempted to find him a job but nothing worked out. In the winter he was cold, hungry, and destitute. Juan Cano believes that he held out until May. Besides deprivation, Madrid was his first real entry into the nation's literary world with its new awareness of Garcilaso de la Vega (especially in the work of Pedro Salinas) and its rage for Góngora; and he himself became immersed in the spirit of the poets and scholars conjuring up Góngora's resurrection. But in the end, for lack of money, he had to return to Orihuela.

Back in Orihuela he continued his readings. Now it was San Juan de la Cruz (whose sensual-mystical darknesses and lights would be the ultimate source of his prison poems), the clarity and affirmations of Jorge Guillén, the bright austerities of Valéry, and the dazzle of Góngora. Miguel Hernández has been assigned to the Generation of '36 (and without him it would hardly be worth inventing such a generation), yet his strongest affinities were with the generation of '27, and not only with its poets, but with Góngora. The Cordoban poet died in 1627, his tricentenary was celebrated in 1927, and a generation of poets took its title from that significant year in which he was resurrected by a series of national conferences, lectures, and publications of and concerning his work. In reality, Góngora imposed himself on Miguel Hernández perhaps more powerfully than on any poet of that famous group of '27, including Alberti and Lorca. The mixture of formalism and extravagantly fantastic imagery that is Góngora is found almost uniquely in Hernández's rigorously formal sonnets with their fantastic and surreal images. By contrast Aleixandre, Neruda, Lorca, in keeping with Paris rather than Góngora, wrote their surreal poems in free verse rather than in traditional forms.

Miguel Hernández's closest friend in literature was Ramón

Miguel Hernández

Sijé, a conservative, Catholic youth, who encouraged and chastised Miguel in all his literary and intellectual ventures, and who instigated and arranged the publication of his early poems and first book in 1933, *Perito en lunas* (Expert in moons). Miguel admired him for his general learning and intellect and his attentive sensibility. Though a year his junior, Ramón was his first real literary master. Sijé was not happy with Miguel's avant-garde tendencies, however, and was insistent that Miguel pursue religious themes, which culminated in the poet's first dramatic work, an *auto sacramental* (an equivalent to the English miracle or mystery play), *Quién te ha visto y quién te ve y sombra de lo que eras* (Who has seen you and who sees you and shadow of what you were). Strongly influenced by the *autos* of the seventeenth-century playwright Calderón de la Barca, the author of the great *autos* in the Spanish language, including *El gran teatro del mundo* (The great theater of the world), Hernández did something that no Golden Age author was likely to do. He prepared for his religious piece by living out the drama and its theological symbols in the fields, and specifically by spending fifteen days with local pastors of the earthly meadows. Consequently, his play brings in the pastors' voices, their ventures, the caves they sleep in, and even their ordinary daily rations of grapes and bread.

After the 1933 publication in Murcia, by the Editorial La Verdad, of *Expert in Moons*, Miguel sent a letter and a copy of his book to Federico García Lorca—whom he had met briefly a year earlier in Orihuela. Lorca replied with a strong letter of encouragement for the younger poet. He urges him to "STRUGGLE!" and also to calm down and be patient. He goes on,

> Today in Spain the finest poetry in Europe is being written. But on the other hand it is unjust. *Perito en lunas* doesn't deserve this stupid silence, no. It deserves the attention and encouragement and love from good people. Those qualities you have yourself and you will go on having them, because you have the blood of a poet and even when you protest in your letter you reveal, in the midst of brutal things (that I like), the gentleness of your luminous and tormented heart. (Lorca, *Obras completas*, 15th ed. 1682)

In 1934 Miguel met Josefina Manresa, daughter of a *guardia civil*, an attractive woman who worked as a seamstress in a sewing shop. Miguel fell in love with her. His early major volume of poems, *El silbo vulnerado* (The wounded whistle), records the fire, confusion, and passion in explosive images; this extraordinary collection is in sonnet form. The title immediately recalls his sixteenth-cen-

Miguel Hernández

tury mentor, Juan de la Cruz, and his *Cántico espiritual* (Spiritual canticle). In San Juan's version of the Song of Songs, he speaks of the *ciervo vulnerado* (the wounded deer), who is of course the crucified rabbi Jeshua (Jesus). The whistle in the title also is reflective of many aspects of Hernández's life. The most obvious source of whistling relates to his early years as a goatherd when he learned to use his fingers to whistle a whole language of commands to his flock. He transferred his coded whistle signs to his meetings with Josefina and whistled his message of arrival outside the *Guardia Civil* compound where his love lived with her family. But a parrot learned the whistle speech and imitated it when it felt like it, completely confusing Josefina by the intrusion of its own zoosemiotic calls. Parrot or not, Josefina and Miguel became *novios* (fiancés). Miguel was exuberantly overwhelmed by his encounter with Josefina, and in the sonnets she provoked in him his zany imagination, humor, torment, and passion all mixed together, as in his sonnet which begins with the notion—a very ancient one also found on the island of Lesbos—that Josefina tossed a sphere at him:

You threw a lemon at me so austere
and bitter, with your hand of warmth so pure,
it hardly shattered its architecture
as I explored its bitterness so near.
Stunned with a yellow blow of lethargy
and softly slipping into anguished heat,
my blood experienced the sudden bite
of a hard breast, a nipple large and free.
And as I looked at you and saw your smile
that gave you meadows of a lemon nest,
my blood fell dead asleep under my shirt,
paralyzed far from my voracious bile.
Then entering my pocked and golden chest
came pain, a pointed glow beyond all hurt.

("Me tiraste un limón" [You threw a lemon at me])

The pastor-poet in Madrid

It was time again to go again to Madrid, and by then Miguel Hernández had mature poetic credentials—his *auto*, *Expert in Moons*, and a revision and expansion of *The Wounded Whistle*, which would soon be his *El rayo que no cesa* (The lightning that never ends)—as well as more supportive friends. He was in Madrid in March 1934. José Bergamín immediately published his entire three-act *auto* in *Cruz y Raya*, and he obtained an editorial position with José María de Cossío who was publishing a tauromachian encyclopedia. Miguel wrote to Josefina, complaining about his lot, although surely in part to show her that life with her in Orihuela was better. His true response to the city was certainly ambiguous, for while he had little money and missed the purity of the country-side and Josefina, he was also glad to be gone from its stifling provincialism and was experiencing his glory years of recognition and friendship with Aleixandre, Neruda, and Altolaguirre (his publisher and a poet). Neruda was especially important in dampening Hernández's religious side and drawing him more politically to the socialist left. At the time there was a side to his visceral reaction to Madrid which recalls aspects of Lorca, who was always at home in Madrid but who in New York found himself in a desolate, urban nightmare, which he also found fascinating and liberating. Hernández wrote Josefina Manresa:

> I go about like a sleepwalker, sadly, in and out of these streets filled with smoke and streetcars, so different from those hushed and happy streets of our happy land. What I most regret is not to see the processions with you, not to give you candies with my lips and kisses with my imagination. . . . Maybe I should move to another place. Where I am is very expensive. I pay ten *reales* a day just for bed, laundry and breakfast. . . . Besides, the apartment under mine is an academy of dancers and cabaret singers and they don't let me get anything done with their piano racket, songs and stamping. (Zardoya 20)

When Vicente Aleixandre published *La destrucción o el amor* (Destruction or love), Miguel wrote Aleixandre a letter saying that he had seen his book in a bookstore but didn't have money to buy it and could the poet send him a copy. He signed the letter, "M. H., pastor of Orihuela." Aleixandre replied by inviting him to his house and giving him a copy of *Destruction or Love*. So began their remarkable, immediate friendship. Soon he met Neruda and a second great friendship began. Neruda wrote a magnificent portrait of Hernández in his *Memoirs*:

> The young poet Miguel Hernández was one of Federico's and Alberti's friends. I met him when he came up, in espadrilles and the typical corduroy trousers peasants wear, from his native Orihuela, where he had been a goatherd. I published his poems in my review *Caballo Verde* (Green Horse), and I was enthusias-tic about the radiance and vigor of his exuberant poetry.
> Miguel was a peasant with an aura of earthiness about him. He had a face like a clod of earth or a potato that has just been pulled up from among the roots and still has its subterranean freshness. He was living and writing in my house. My American

poetry, with other horizons and plains, had its impact and gradually made changes in him.

He told me earthy stories about animals and birds. He was the kind of writer who emerges from nature like an uncut stone, with the freshness of the forest and an irresistible vitality. He would tell me how exciting it was to put your ear against the belly of a sleeping she-goat. You could hear the milk coursing down to the udders, a secret sound no one but that poet of goats has been able to listen to. (Neruda 117)

Zardoya's words coincide with Neruda's: "Miguel has conquered everyone with his natural innocence and because he brings to those in the big city, through his own person, a reverberation of the earth—his brotherly smile with the trees and with the unstained bubbling of cascades" (Zardoya 21). Miguel was also conquered by others, and Neruda, with his negative, volcanic yet urban passion that tears through his *residencia* poems he was then writing, made him Miguel's primary idol. In his voice, which was not given to understatement, Hernández reviewed Neruda's *Residence on Earth* for *El Sol*. The review reveals as much about Miguel Hernández as it does about Neruda:

Pablo Neruda's voice is an oceanic clamor that cannot be limited, it is an overly primitive and great lament which has no rhetorical bounds. We are listening to the virgin voice of a man who hauls his lion's instincts over the earth; it's a roar, a roar no one can hold back. Seek in others the subjugation of what is officially called form. In him things are created as in the Bible and in the sea: free and grandiosely. (Folletones de *El Sol*, 1935)

Hernández's own triumph in the literary circles continued. He was exactly what he was, the shepherd-poet, meaning a vital person from the countryside, without middle-class or aristocratic wealth and sophistication, and a very young writer already perceived to be a master of prosody and a diversely talented major poet. At least three distinct stages of his poetry would follow: the social poems of great pathos written during the war; the mysterious, elliptical songs and fragments of "absence", and the prison poems where he moves into final Dantesque light and death music, which relates him, in a secular way, to that special poetry of prison and wisdom, which includes the Spanish mystical poets as well as Quevedo, who even before his four years in prison lived in the metaphysical dungeons of the soul.

Miguel's love life prospered less. He became detached for a year or so from Josefina, did not return to Orihuela on his vacation, and suggested to her in his letters that it might be best for her to find

Miguel Hernández

another *novio* who would be better for her than he could be; he wanted her to forget him a bit and not suffer over him. He now had friends in Madrid who understood him perfectly and, he wrote, he could never again live in Orihuela. Meanwhile he sought the company of other city women of Madrid. He was also beginning to distance himself from his Orihuela literary circle and particularly from Ramón Sijé and his militant Catholicism and strident Falange attachments. Between Hernández and Sijé was his new life and also Neruda's anticlericalism and politics. Sijé was editing a magazine in Orihuela, *El Gallo Crisis*, which Hernández tried to help by adding his own work and by asking others for poems. Neruda wrote Miguel, saying the magazine smelled of the Church. After Miguel published his poem "Vecino de la muerte" (A neighbor of death) in the first issue of Neruda's magazine *El Caballo Verde*, Miguel received a scathingly reproachful letter from Ramón Sijé, condemning him for taking up Neruda's corrupting ideas and for having lost his purity and Catholic faith. Then in December 1935, came word of Sijé's death. It shook Hernández. Despite their ideological differences, Sijé, only twenty-two when he died, had been his *compañero del alma* (soul companion), and Miguel wrote a moving elegiac poem on the death of his first literary friend.

In January of 1936 two events happened, each decisively significant. Early in the month, on an outing to San Fernando del Jarama, a village near Madrid, Hernández was stopped by the *Guardia Civil*, and since he didn't have his identity card with him he was taken to the *cuartel*, the police headquarter barracks, where he was cursed, threatened, and roughed up. After he was allowed to call Pablo Neruda, then Chilean consul in Madrid, he was released without further explanation. Miguel was embittered. A few weeks later Manuel Altolaguirre and Concha Méndez published his *Lightning that Never Ends*. Here it required no call to the Chilean counsul to bring him good news. Concha Zardoya describes the moment:

> The book is, in reality, Miguel Hernández's consecration as a poet, and he feels happy with his work, including the typographical aspect, and he banks on its success. The book has a good sale and reaches all or virtually all the known poets of the moment, including the critic psychologist Gregorio Marañón among others. Yet despite all this, the book did not receive the startling rave reviews it deserved. (26)

Miguel was disappointed and even resentful against members of the literary community. Although he was accepted as a country phenomenon, as a Cinderella author discovered among the families of the country poor, he still had enough insight to understand that this role of "the natural man" had its penalties, and he felt slighted and scorned as a peasant outsider. He may have envied or felt personal injustice when he considered an idol like Lorca who seemed to have a fabulous publishing career—his books effortlessly famous even before they were in print as was the case with *Gypsy Ballads*. Miguel's enthusiasm for his own work was thoroughly justified, his impatience understandable, his genius not to be misconstrued because he disguised and guarded it in espadrilles in a society of *señoritos* (fashionable young men). In reality Lorca had fearful enemies, who did more than ignore or belittle him. His political and puritanical enemies, speaking through literary organs, attacked him viciously and repeatedly. During those exciting prewar years in Madrid, Hernández was the youngest of the Generation of '27 icons; and later during the apocalypse, he *was* consecrated as the poet of the Spanish Civil War. In reality he had a recognition that few poets enjoy in their life experience.

Even during his discontent, José Ortega y Gasset wrote him requesting poems for *La Revista de Occidente*, the most esteemed literary periodical in Spain, equivalent to Victoria Ocampo's *Sur* in Buenos Aires. *Occidente* published six sonnets by Hernández and his elegy to Ramón Sijé. After the poems appeared, Juan Ramón Jiménez, whose caustic pen was constantly at work, punishing the work of Guillén, Lorca, and others, wrote a piece of amazing praise for the young Hernández, whom he refers to as "the extraordinary boy [*el muchacho*] from Orihuela": "All friends of *pure poetry* should look for and read these lively poems. They have a Quevedesque appearance, which is their pure, Old Spain inheritance. But the harsh tremendous beauty of his deep-rooted heart breaks through appearances and floods out in all its naked elemental nature" (qtd. in Guerrero Zamora 266).

And along with public praise, he also had his close and unfailingly loyal and supporting friends, Aleixandre and Neruda. Hernández's work was printed by the most prestigious printer and poet of the generation, Manuel Altolaguirre. Indeed, the pastor-poet, the natural prodigy from Orihuela, was felicitously and tragically at the center of Spain's literary and political history during its most dynamic and critical years. The decade of his mature writing corresponded to the poetry of Spain's three pivotal moments of decisive change: prewar, war, and postwar.

In a sonnet in *The Wounded Whistle*, he speaks of "loneliness stripping me naked, and going like a wretch from pole to pole." The poem ends with simply: "I am nothing at all when I'm alone." Essentially lonely for a woman, Hernández turned back to the woman who was, he claimed, the one he addressed in each of the love poems in *The Lightning*. He wrote letters to Josefina Manresa at first hoping tentatively that she might be interested in those poems. He wrote to her, attempting to restore their pact. The poems are his best love epistle to Josefina:

Your heart, a frozen orange, and inside
an unlit darkness of sweet turpentine;
a porous vision stained with gold outside,
offering danger to a gazing tide.
My heart, a feverish pomegranate full
of blushing scarlet and a candid wax,
offering a tender necklace and climax
of loving stubbornness and gentle wool.
Oh what a happening of breaking down
to journey to your heart and find an ice
of irreducible and shocking snow!
At outer borders where I want to drown
a parching handkerchief in sacrifice
flies off in hope that waters soon will flow.

("Tu corazón, una naranja helada" [Your heart, a frozen
orange, and inside])

Miguel wrote letter after letter, declaring his love, and asked Josefina to marry him. He said, "Know that your shepherd—and I hope it might be for all through our lives—loves you." In another letter he tells her he will come "revolutionizing skies and lands." Of course the revolution was only a few months away, a political one, and not very glorious.

Perhaps one small incident reveals that storm of emotion in Miguel Hernández, a storm of noon sun and night depression, which in his poetry he had the genious to enclose austerely in regulated verse. Zardoya quotes a story told her by Enrique Azcoaga. On a trip to Salamanca, Hernández went to the University of Salamanca where Luis de León had taught Latin, Greek, and Hebrew in the sixteenth century. During the Inquisition, León survived nearly five years' incarceration in the prison at Valladolid where the Augustinian monk of *converso* origin wrote many of his humane, angry, and mystical poems. When Miguel visited the mystical poet's lecture room, "he wildly kissed the steps which the poet had once walked on" (Zardoya 27).

July 18, 1936: Guerra

We have witnessed the Spanish Civil War and the death of two poets: Antonio Machado, driven out of Spain, dying of exhaustion and unspecified causes a few weeks after his arrival in Collioure; Federico García Lorca executed on the roadside before dawn outside his Granada. Our third poet will experience the war in another way, as soldier and prison victim. His prison poems, mostly written on toilet paper and smuggled out, are his poems with maximum darkness and light.

When war broke out, Hernández went back to Orihuela to see Josefina; then in Madrid, he enlisted in the Fifth Regiment of the Republican army. Less than a month later, Josefina's father, Manuel Manresa, a *guardia civil*, was killed at the front. Hernández had not yet married the Manresa daughter, but poor as he was, he took over the responsibility as head of her family and sent them any funds he could. His religious concern was transferred to "the people" and social justice. He became the "poet-soldier," in the trenches and in his poems of the war. On March 9, 1937, he married Josefina Manresa in a civil ceremony in Orihuela.

The subject of Miguel's poetry is not love now, but the war, which we read in *Viento del pueblo* (Wind from the people), 1937, and *El hombre acecha* (Man hunts), 1939. A terrible originality has come back to his poems, in the few very powerful ones from the corpus of war poems. In contrast to the sonnets of *The Lightning that Never Ends*, his subsequent Neruda period is interesting but secondary, for his free-verse surrealism has not quite the earned spontaneity of Neruda's or Aleixandre's or Lorca's (in *Poet in New York*). It has the imitative quality of the enthusiastic apprentice, and one feels even in extraordinary lines from "A Neighbor of Death" that the "eyeglasses," for example, are borrowed merchandise (from Neruda's poem "Walking Around"):

> pintadas con recuerdos y leche las paredes
> a mi ventana emiten silencios y anteojos.

> the walls, painted with memories and milk,
> emit silences and eyeglasses to my window

> (*Antología* 67)

In the war poems, however (and war hasn't left the world to make war poetry obsolete), the images are trains of the wounded, sweat, jails, trenches, and blood; an incessant deluge of blood and death. His poems are another Goya's *Disasters of the War*. From "The Wounded Man" we have a few lines:

> Blood smells of the sea, tastes of sea and wine cellar.
> The wine cellar of the sea, with bold wine, cracks open
> where the convulsing, wounded man drowns
> and flowers and finds out where he is.

> (Baland and St. Martin 45)

Miguel Hernández

The cumulative deaths of two years of war take him from the specifically symbolic images of the previous stanza, and in "18 de Julio 1936" (July 18, 1936), he writes with an ageless, sorrowful, general resignation learned from the nature of war:

> It's blood. It isn't hail whipping my skull.
> It is two years of blood, a monstrous flood.
> Blood, hungry like the sun, you come to annul,
> eat, drown balconies, turn people into mud.
> Blood is the best of all our human gains,
> Blood gathers all its gifts for love. Its irons—
> look at them stirring seas, surprising trains,
> breaking bulls' spirits as it heartens lions.
> And time is blood. In my veins time is breath
> circling, and before clocks and dawn I'm more
> than wounded. I hear blood of every size
> and shape colliding. Blood where even death
> can hardly bathe; a brilliance that will soar
> because its thousand years hide in my eyes.

Hernández was a delegate at the Second International Congress of Anti-Fascist Writers in Madrid, which was addressed by André Malraux among others; Nicolás Guillén, Octavio Paz, Alberti, and Bergamín were there. A dominant theme was the protest against the nonintervention of the European democracies to save Spain from fascism.

Miguel was writing, fighting, and sent from city to city to read his war poems in his role as the poet of the Spanish Civil War. Between the trenches and feverish literary activity, he was sick, suffering from cerebral anemia and blistering headaches, but most of the time the enthusiasm that was his was evident, now directed to saving the Republic. In late August he left with a small delegation for Russia to see their "war theater," and stopped in Paris on the way. These two months were his only time outside of Spain except for one fateful day in Portugal at the end of the war. In Cox for a few days of leave, where Josefina and their newborn son Miguelín were now living, he finished a four-act play, *The Pastor of Death*. He was, Cano says, drunk with happiness over his first son, and "Miguelín inspired the poem triptych 'Son of the Light and of the Shadow,' perhaps the best of all his poetry" (49). Death came soon after for the infant. His son, not quite a year old, died in October 1938.

> The cemetery lies near
> where you and I are sleeping,
> among blue prickly-pear,
> blue century plants and children
> who scream their heads off
> if a dead body clouds the road.

Miguel Hernández

From here to the cemetery
all is blue, gold, limpid.
Four steps and the dead.
Four steps and the living.

Limpid, blue and gold,
there my son becomes remote.

(Antología 121)

The war was lost. On the March 28, 1939, Madrid fell. Miguel
was in Andalusia. He went to Sevilla, looking for help and safety
with a friend but couldn't find him. Then he crossed the Portuguese
border, intending to take refuge in the Chilean embassy. Having no
money to get to Lisbon, he sold his blue suit to someone who turned
him over to the Portuguese police, who in turn took him back to
the Spanish border, despite protests of being a political refugee.
There at Rosal de la Frontera, the *Guardia Civil* beat him constantly
until "he pissed blood." Then he was sent to prison in Madrid.

The poet writes and dies in prison

On May 18 Hernández was taken to the Prisión Celular de
Torrijos. He was, despite everything, not in bad spirits, and was
visited by José María de Cossío whom Miguel thought would soon
get him out. In a letter to his wife, he tells her he has learned not
to despair as others around him have, that he spends his days sewing
his clothes, washing so he won't have bugs on his body, and he
draws and cuts out paper birds. "I am almost in a first-class hotel,
no elevator, but with a great hope of seeing you" (Zardoya 38). He
takes showers from the sky, he reads, writes, and thinks of Josefina,
and nothing hurts.

Josefina wrote him about her hunger and his child's hunger.
His newborn son Manolillo must suck onions for their juice instead
of sucking milk. For Manolillo Miguel wrote "Lullaby of the On-
ion." The letters written by Hernández from prison constitute a
popular literature. They are the novels, the prose fiction of the
postwar period, but they are not fiction:

September 12, 1939

These days I have been thinking about your situation, each day
more difficult. The smell of the onion you are eating reaches
me here and my child must feel indignant about having to suck
and draw out onion juice instead of milk. To console you I send
some verses that I have done, since I have no other task but to
write you or despair. I prefer the former, so I do only that,
besides washing and sewing with extreme seriousness and agil-

ity, as if I had done nothing else in my life. Also I spend time purging myself of a tiny family which I'm never free of, and at times I breed it robust and big like a chickpea. It will all be over with by means of fighting and patience—or they, the lice, will finish me off. But they are too small a thing for me, brave as always, and even if these bugs that want to carry off my blood were elephants, I would wipe them from the map of my body. Poor body! Between scabies, lice, bedbugs and every kind of animal vermin, without freedom, without you, Josefina, and without you, Manolillo of my soul, I don't know at times what attitude to take, and finally, I decide on hope, which I never lose. (Zardoya 39)

In the prisons Hernández became, in my opinion, the consummate poet of light, darkness, soul, time, death. There is gravity, there is illumination. We see these poles of spirit in the sonnet "Sigo en la sombra" (I live in shadow):

> I live in shadow, filled with light. Does day
> exist? Is this a grave or mother's womb?
> Against my skin a throbbing makes its way
> like frozen stone sprouting red, tender, warm.
> Maybe I'm waiting to be born or see
> that I've been always dead. These shadows rule
> me, and if living's this, what can death be?
> Intensely groping and the eternal fool,
> chained to my clothes, it looks like I go on
> stripping and getting rid of everything,
> leaving me gone, my eyes in far distress.
> But the remote black clothing that I don
> plods with me: shadows, shadows, shadows fling
> me through bare life blooming from nothingness.
>
> Torrijos prison

In Torrijos he wrote much of his *Cancionero y romancero de ausencias* (Songbook and ballad book of absences). These are the plainest of Hernández's poems and as the title suggests, infused with the *popular* (folkloric) rather than the neogongorist tradition of earlier poems. Often they contain clearly discernable resonances of early Lorca *popular* poems and songs, with their familiar *estribillos* (refrains). They are the most insistently metaphysical, biographical sequence we have in Hernández's work. One of the poems has for some twenty years been a popular song in the Americas, Spanish- and English-speaking, *Llegó con tres heridas* (He came with three wounds). Joan Baez includes it as a haunting cut in her disk of Spanish recordings.

273

Llegó con tres heridas:
la del amor,
la de la muerte,
la de la vida.

Con tres heridas viene:
la de la vida,
la del amor,
la de la muerte.

Con tres heridas yo:
la de la vida,
la de la muerte,
la del amor.

He came with three wounds:
one of love,
one of death,
one of life.

He comes with three wounds:
one of life,
one of love,
one of death.

I am here with three wounds:
one of life,
one of death,
one of love.

(Antología 113)

In his cell Hernández also wrote what have been entitled simply
Ultimos poemas (Last Poems). The most desolate of these poems
is "Eterna sombra" (Eternal shadow). Unable to despair without
resorting to light, here the gravity persists into the last lines of light
and salvation:

I who believed that light was mine now see
myself thrown headlong into shadow. Fire
of solar coal, stellar felicity
burning with sea foam, light, and with desire.

Nimble round blood and pomegranate: bite
of longing. No penumbra. Only mud.
Outside, the light lies down entombed in light.
I feel that only shadow lights my blood.

Shadow alone. No star. No firmament.
Beings. Volumes. Tangible bodies still
inside the air that has no wings, and bent
inside the tree of the impossible.

Miguel Hernández

Passion in mourning, livid frowns. And teeth
thirsting to turn into the red of hell.
Darkness of total rancor, and the seeth-
ing bodies equal to a blinded well.

Not enough space. Laughter has shipwrecked. Now
it is too late to hurtle into flight.
The heart wants to beat quicker to allow
a force to open up constricting night.

Flesh without north, drifting on a great wave
to an infertile evil night. The way?
Who is the outside ray of sun? I rave.
I look around. But find no trace of day.

Only the glowing of the frozen fists,
splendor of teeth ambushing to attack.
On every side, the teeth and straining wrists.
More than the hands, the mountains now contract.

I am an open window and it hears
where life is moving darkly in retreat,
but in the fight a ray of sun appears
that always leaves the shadow in defeat.

(*Antología* 145–46)

While Hernández was in Madrid, he had friends working for
his release. Pablo Neruda in Paris had a copy of his Catholic *auto*
read to Cardinal Baudrillart, who was blind, and a friend of Franco.
According to Neruda, Baudrillart then petitioned Franco for his
freedom, and he was accordingly released. Others suggest that the
release came as a result of a decree including certain kinds of politi-
cal prisoners. In any case, unexpectedly, Hernández was released in
mid-September in "provisional liberty." Neruda states, though it
has not been confirmed, that "M. H." went to the Chilean embassy
to seek refuge there but was denied it by Carlos Morla Lynch for
having written poems insulting to General Franco. Whatever the
truth, what is certain is that Miguel Hernández, like Federico García
Lorca, decided fatally, in a moment of freedom, to return to his
native city.

His friends counseled him not to return to Orihuela where his
wife and son were again living. But he took the train to Alicante
where his relatives came to plead with him not to go back to
Orihuela. Even the mayor came to warn him. He was no criminal,
he insisted, and he took the train to Orihuela. On arrival he greeted
his wife and family, went to eat with Gabriel Sijé, and on leaving
the house on September 29, his Saint's Day, he was arrested. There
in a convent converted into a jail, he remained until December,

under starvation conditions. As a result of Neruda's intervention, Germán Vergara Donoso in the Chilean embassy in Madrid began to send his wife and Miguel money, which alleviated some of their economic problems. In December he was sent back to Madrid. He wrote little in the prisons from now on, or if he did so, we do not have what he wrote. One poem he did write in Madrid in the Conde de Toreno jail is "Sepultura de la imaginación" (Tomb of the imagination), one of his most important and compelling poems. Its quatrains end:

A mason loved . . . But the stone pays for all
its grim and brutal density at once.
That man was carving out his prison, and
into his work, he and the wind were hurled.

(*Antología* 142)

While much of his poetry has not survived, his letters, as a testament to his spirit, have. They reflect a mixture of stoicism, humor, grief. Hernández wrote that his cell was his university and he spent his days studying languages—he learned to say "all right" in English—and reading other books. He did wish to leave his university, he confessed, for his house. Many of the letters have cartoon drawings of clowns thumbing their nose with all ten fingers, pictures of doves and shy foxes. Even when the bugs seemed near victory he saw the allusive humor in it all:

May 6, 1940

For some days now the rats have taken up wandering across my body while I sleep. The other night I woke up and had one next to my mouth. This morning I pulled one out of my sweater sleeve, and every day I have to pick their dung out of my hair. Seeing my head shit on by the rats I say to myself: How little one is worth now! Even the rats ascend to dirty the roof of our thoughts. That's what's new in my life: rats. Now I've got rats, lice, fleas, bedbugs, mange. This corner I use for a home will very soon turn into a zoological park, or more likely, a wild animal cage. (Zardoya 42)

In Madrid some time in January 1940, Hernández was condemned to death. For months his life hung from a thread. José María de Cossío again intervened, finally reaching General Varela, minister of the army, who ordered a revison of the order, and so Hernández was condemned to thirty years. After a year in Madrid, Palencia, and Ocaña jails—he called these changes his "tourism" days—he was sent to the Reformatory for Adults in Alicante, not far from Orihuela, where it was possible to be visited by his wife and son.

Miguel thought up all kinds of plans, including making toys for extra money and insisted that the funds from the Chilean embassy be spent on food for Josefina and Manolillo. Thoughtfully, he encouraged Josefina in all ways and told her how well he was. By November 1941, he had contracted turberculosis. He was operated on by Dr. Antonio Barbero but the disease, with its complications, took a rapid course. Miguel wanted to get out of the prison hospital and go to a clinic, and one of the doctors was ready to arrange it, but he was too sick to be moved. His last letter is terrible:

Early spring 1942

Josefina, the hemorrhaging has stopped. But you must tell Barbero that the pus is not draining through the tube he put in, for the opening has enlarged, the pus is building up and spills on the bed with any coughing fit. This is a bother and an obstacle to my rate of recovery from the disease. I want to get out of here as soon as possible. They are curing me by stops and starts through their bright ideas, sloppiness, ignorance, negligence. Well, love, I feel better, and as soon as I get out, my recovery will be like lightning. Kisses for my son. I love you, Josefina, MIGUEL. (Zardoya 48)

His words—and a last macabre drawing of him by a cellmate belies the truth of the elements of optimism that still persist in the letter— are not different from the earlier prison song:

I am here with three wounds:
one of life,
one of death,
one of love.

On the March 28, 1942, at 5:30 in the morning, Miguel Hernández died. Over his cot were written on the hospital wall his last verses:

Adiós, hermanos, camaradas, amigos:
despedidme del sol y de los trigos!

Goodbye, brothers, comrades, friends:
say my farewell to the sun and wheat!

Miguel Hernández was not yet thirty-two. It is reported that they could not close his eyes.

Lorca and Hernández were not lucky. War caught them both

when others, with more luck, survived. Of the poets of their generations, they were almost primordially fixed on life and on death. Lorca lived longer. At least Hernández was able to reach his apogee as a poet while in his cells. And if context prevails at all in our reading of his poems, then, unfortunately, the death in prison framed the poems with authenticity. I always think of Miguel Hernández in the same frame as the religious writers, although during his mature life his religion revealed itself not in theology but in other matters: friendship, love, war, the people, suffering, prisons. But his vision, and it was a compassionate one, had one central imagery in common with the Buddha, the Gnostics, the Spanish mystics—and some secular friends—which was *la sombra y la luz*, the shadow and the light.

Como el toro

Como el toro he nacido para el luto
y el dolor, como el toro estoy marcado
por un hierro infernal en el costado
y por varón en la ingle con un fruto.
Como el toro lo encuentra diminuto
todo mi corazón desmesurado,
y del rostro del beso enamorado,
como el toro a tu amor se lo disputo.
Como el toro me crezco en el castigo,
la lengua en corazón tengo bañada
y llevo al cuello un vendaval sonoro.
Como el toro te sigo y te persigo,
y dejas mi deseo en una espada,
como el toro burlado, como el toro.

El toro sabe al fin de la corrida

El toro sabe al fin de la corrida,
donde prueba su chorro repentino,
que el sabor de la muerte es el de un vino
que el equilibrio impide de la vida.
Respira corazones por la herida
desde un gigante corazón vecino,
y su vasto poder de piedra y pino
cesa debilitado en la caída.
Y como el toro tú, mi sangre astada,
que el cotidiano cáliz de la muerte,
edificado con un turbio acero,
vierte sobre mi lengua un gusto a espada
diluída en un vino espeso y fuerte
desde mi corazón donde me muero.

Like the Bull

Like the bull I was born for doom and pain,
like the bull I parade the burning mark,
the infernal wound under my ribs. The stark
fruit of a man stabs in my groin insane.
Like the bull no arena can contain
my heart that finds all others small. The flow
of loving kisses floors me in its tow.
Like the bull I argue for your love in vain.
Like the bull I thrive on punishment,
My tongue is washed in my own heart. I hoard
a thundering seawind in my leather skull.
Like the bull I seek you and cannot relent,
but my desire you welded to a sword,
like the bull become a fool, like the bull.

The Bull Knows at the End of Rushing Strife

The bull knows at the end of rushing strife,
where he confronts a sudden spurting whine
of blood, he knows the taste of death's a wine
whose balance maims and overcomes his life.
He breathes in hearts inhabiting the wound
from a gigantic heart of strange design,
and his enormous strength of stone and pine
comes to a weakened end where he falls stunned.
And like the bull are you, my punctured blood,
who in the daily chalice where I lie
in death, constructed out of obscure steel,
pours on my tongue a special taste of sword
diluted in a wine, heavy with bile,
fermented in my heart in which I die.

No me conformo, no: me desespero

No me conformo, no: me desespero
como si fuera un huracán de lava
en el presidio de una almendra esclava
o en el penal colgante de un jilguero.
Besarte fue besar un avispero
que me clava al tormento y me desclava
y cava un hovo fúnebra y lo cava
dentro del corazón donde me muero.
No me conformo, no: ya es tanto y tanto
idolatrar la imagen de tu beso
y perseguir el curso de tu aroma.
Un enterrado vivo por el llanto,
una revolución dentro de un hueso,
un rayo soy sujeto a una redoma.

Guiando un tribunal de tiburones

Guiando un tribunal de tiburones,
como con dos guadañas eclipsadas,
con dos cejas tiznadas y cortadas
de tiznar y cortar los corazones,
en el mío has entrado, y en él pones
una red de raíces irritadas,
que avariciosamente acaparadas
tiene en su territorio sus pasiones.
Sal de mi corazón del que me has hecho
un girasol sumiso y amarillo
al dictamen solar que tu ojo envía:
un terrón para siempre insatisfecho,
un pez embotellado y un martillo
harto de golpear en la herrería.

282

No. I Will Not Conform. But I Despair

No. I will not conform. But I despair
as if I were a hurricane of lava
locked in the fortress of an enslaved guava,
a hummingbird clawing to a hanging hair.
To kiss you was to kiss a hornet nest
that nails me to this torment and unnails
me; digging out a funeral pit, it sails
into my heart where in my death I rest.
No. I will not conform. I've tried so long
to worship the illusion of your kiss
and trail behind the curse of your rich smell.
And now my body buried live and wrong,
rebelling in its bones, I boil and hiss,
a lightning flash—but dead in glassy hell.

While You Were Guiding Home a School of Sharks

While you were guiding home a school of sharks
as if you held two eclipsed scythes in hand,
as if you held two eyebrows cut with sand
from cutting and from sanding hearts on land,
you entered in my cave, and in it place
a net of irritated slicing roots
that keep their passions as forbidden fruits
in total greed in this unentered space.
Now leave my heart from which you made for me
a yellow sunflower, a submissive plant,
your eye sent out by your sunhot command:
a plot of land always in misery,
a bottled fish, a hammer in a hand
weary of pounding iron until it can't.

Me tiraste un limón, y tan amargo

Me tiraste un limón, y tan amargo,
con una mano cálida, y tan pura,
que no menoscabó su arquitectura
y probé su amargura sin embargo.
Con el golpe amarillo, de un letargo
dulce pasó a una ansiosa calentura
mi sangre, que sintió la mordedura
de una punta de seno duro y largo.
Pero al mirarte y verte la sonrisa
que te produjo el limonado hecho,
a mi voraz malicia tan ajena,
se me durmió la sangre en la camisa,
y se volvió el poroso y áureo pecho
una picuda y deslumbrante pena.

Tu corazón, una naranja helada

To corazón, una naranja helada
con un dentro sin luz de dulce miera
y una porosa vista de oro: un fuera
venturas prometiendo a la mirada.
Mi corazón, una febril granada
de agrupado rubor y abierta cera,
que sus tiernos collares te ofreciera
con una obstinación enamorada.
¡Ay, qué acontecimiento de quebranto
ir a tu corazón y hallar un hielo
de irreducible y pavorosa nieve!
Por los alrededores de mi llanto
un pañuelo sediento va de vuelo
con la esperanza de que en él lo abreve.

You Threw a Lemon at Me So Austere

You threw a lemon at me so austere
and bitter, with your hand of warmth so pure,
it hardly shattered its architecture
as I explored its bitterness so near.
Stunned with a yellow blow of lethargy
and softly slipping into anguished heat,
my blood experienced the sudden bite
of a hard breast, a nipple large and free.
And as I looked at you and saw your smile
that gave you meadows of a lemon nest,
my blood fell dead asleep under my shirt,
paralyzed far from my voracious bile.
Then entering my pocked and golden chest
came pain, a pointed glow beyond all hurt.

Your Heart, a Frozen Orange, and Inside

Your heart, a frozen orange, and inside
an unlit darkness of sweet turpentine;
a porous vision stained with gold outside,
offering danger to a gazing tide.
My heart, a feverish pomegranate full
of blushing scarlet and a candid wax,
offering a tender necklace and climax
of loving stubbornness and gentle wool.
Oh what a happening of breaking down
to journey to your heart and find an ice
of irreducible and shocking snow!
At outer borders where I want to drown
a parching handkerchief in sacrifice
flies off in hope that waters soon will flow.

Después de haber cavado este barbecho

Después de haber cavado este barbecho,
me tomaré un descanso por la grama
y beberé del agua que en la rama
su esclava nieve aumenta en mi provecho.
Todo el cuerpo me huele a reciénhecho
por el jugoso fuego que lo inflama,
y la creación que adoro se derrama
a mi mucha fatiga, como un lecho.
Se tomará un descanso el hortelano
y entretendrá sus penas combatido
por el salubre sol y el tiempo manso.
Y otra vez, inclinando cuerpo y mano,
seguirá ante la tierra perseguido
por la sombra del último descanso.

Por tu pie, la blancura más bailable

Por tu pie, la blancura más bailable,
donde cesa en diez partes tu hermosura,
una paloma sube a tu cintura,
baja a la tierra un nardo interminable.
Con tu pie vas poniendo lo admirable
del nácar en ridícula estrechura
y a donde va tu pie va la blancura,
perro sembrado de jazmín calzable.
A tu pie, tan espuma como playa,
arena y mar me arrimo y desarrimo
y al redil de su planta entrar procuro.
Entro y dejo que el alma se me vaya
por la voz amorosa del racimo:
pisa mi corazón que ya es maduro.

After Having Dug Up This Fallow Site

After having dug up this fallow site
I'll lie down on the ordinary grass
and drink some water which in branches pass
and grow from slave snow to my appetite.
And my whole body smells of someone born
today with juicy fire inflaming lead,
and the creation I adore is borne
flowing to my fatigue as to a bed.
This plain farmhand will also take his rest,
and though oppressed will entertain his grief
with healing sun and weather mildly tame.
Then up again, bending his hands and chest,
he'll journey on the earth with no relief
before the shadow of the final frame.

Along Your Foot, the Whiteness That Is Most Danceable

Along your foot, the whiteness that is most
danceable, where your beauty ends in ten
components, a dove rises to your waist,
and to the earth unending nard descends.
Using your foot you situate the best
mother-of-pearl in tight intimacy,
and where your foot goes goes the whiteness first,
a dog sown from a jasmine shoeably.
And by your foot, as foam as it is beach,
sand and the sea, I come near and return,
try entering the sheepfold of your sole.
I go inside and let my soul leave me
through a grape cluster's loving voice. Please learn
to stamp upon my heart. It's ripe and whole.

¿Recuerdas aquel cuello, haces memoria?

¿Recuerdas aquel cuello, haces memoria
del privilegio aquel, de aquel aquello
que era, almenadamente blanco y bello,
una almena de nata giratoria?
Recuerdo y no recuerdo aquella historia
de marfil expirado en un cabello,
donde aprendió a ceñir el cisne cuello
y a vocear la nieve transitoria.
Recuerdo y no recuerdo aquel cogollo
de extrangulable hielo femenino
como una lacteada y breve vía.
Y recuerdo aquel beso sin apoyo
que quedó entre mi boca y el camino
de aquel cuello, aquel beso y aquel día.

Por una senda van los hortelanos

Por una senda van los hortelanos,
que es la sagrada hora del regreso,
con la sangre injuriada por el peso
de inviernos, primaveras y veranos.
Vienen de los esfuerzos sobrehumanos
y van a la canción, y van al beso,
y van dejando por el aire impreso
un olor de herramientas y de manos.
Por otra senda yo, por otra senda
que no conduce al beso aunque es la hora,
sino que merodea sin destino.
Bajo su frente trágica y tremenda,
un toro solo en la ribera llora
olvidando que es toro y masculino.

Do You Recall That Neck, a Memory Ago?

Do you recall that neck, a memory ago
of privilege, and other times so full
it was almondly white and beautiful,
an almond of girating cream and flow?
I do recall and don't recall that glow
of ivory expiring in a hair
where the swan neck learned how to rope its glare
and scream about the transitory snow.
I do recall and don't recall that head
of strangulatable and female ice
like a congealing, brief, and milky way,
And I recall that unprotected kiss
that stuck inside my mouth, and then the road
into that neck, that kiss, that sudden day.

The Peasants Ramble Down a Single Path

The peasants ramble down a single path
and at the holy hour of the return
their blood's insulted by the cold and burn
of winters, springs, and summers' wrath.
They come from superhuman aches and toil,
meander to a song and to a kiss,
and go on signing air with genesis
of hands, of iron tools, and reeking oil.
I walk another path, another now
not leading to a kiss, although it's time,
but to an unfixed, vagrant origin.
Under its tragic and tremendous brow
a bull alone weeps on a bed of slime,
forgetting it is bull and masculine.

289

18 de Julio 1936–18 de Julio 1938

Es sangre, no granizo, lo que azota mis sienes.
Son dos años de sangre: son dos inundaciones.
Sangre de acción solar, devoradora vienes,
hasta dejar sin nadie y ahogados los balcones.
Sangre que es el mejor de los mejores bienes.
Sangre que atesoraba para el amor sus dones.
Velda enturbiando mares, sobrecogiendo trenes,
desalentando toros donde alentó leones.
El tiempo es sangre. El tiempo circula por mis venas.
Y ante el reloj y el alba me siento más que herido,
y oigo un chocar de sangres de todos los tamaños.
Sangre donde se puede bañar la muerte apenas:
fulgor emocionante que no ha palidecido,
porque lo recogieron mis ojos de mil años.

Sonreír con la alegre tristeza del olivo

Sonreír con la alegre tristeza del olivo,
esperar, no cansarse de esperar la alegría.
Sonriamos, doremos la luz de cada día
en esta alegre y triste vanidad de ser vivo.
Me siento cada día más leve y más cautivo
en toda esta sonrisa tan clara y tan sombría.
Cruzan las tempestades sobre tu boca fría
como sobre la mía que aún es un soplo estivo.
Una sonrisa se alza sobre el abismo: crece
como un abismo trémulo, pero batiente en alas.
Una sonrisa eleva calientemente el vuelo.
Diurna, firme, arriba, no baja, no anochece.
Todo lo desafías, amor: todo lo escalas.
Con sonrisa te fuiste de la tierra y el cielo.

July 18, 1936—July 18, 1938

It's blood. It isn't hail whipping my skull.
It is two years of blood, a monstrous flood.
Blood, hungry like the sun, you come to annul,
eat, drown balconies, turn people into mud.
Blood is the best of all our human gains,
Blood gathers all its gifts for love. Its irons—
look at them stirring seas, surprising trains,
breaking bulls' spirits as it heartens lions.
And time is blood. In my veins time is breath
circling, and before clocks and dawn I'm more
than wounded. I hear blood of every size
and shape colliding. Blood where even death
can hardly bathe; a brilliance that will soar
because its thousand years hide in my eyes.

To Smile with Cheerful Grief of the Olive Tree

To smile with cheerful grief of the olive tree,
to hope for happiness, hope to survive
smiling, plating each day with gold, and be
this glad, sad vanity of being alive.
And every day I feel lighter and caught
up in that smile of brilliance and black shade.
Stormwinds punish your mouth freezing and taut
while mine is struck by summer winds that strayed
into my cell. A smile soars the abyss
and grows like a shocked pit—yet flapping wings.
A smile climbs hotly over caves, in flight,
diurnal, firm. It will not drop or miss
or darken. Love, you brave and climb all things,
and smiling fled the earth, the sky, the light.

Ascensión de la escoba

Coronada la escoba de laurel, mirto, rosa,
es el héroe entre aquellos que afrontan la basura.
Para librar del polvo sin vuelo cada cosa
bajó, porque era palma y azul, desde la altura
Su ardor de espada joven y alegre no reposa.
Delgada de ansiedad, pureza, sol, bravura,
azucena que barre sobre la misma fosa,
es cada vez más alta, más cálida, más pura.
¡Nunca! La escoba nunca será crucificada
porque la juventud propaga su esqueleto
que es una sola flauta, muda, pero sonora.
Es una sola lengua, sublime y acordada.
Y ante su aliento raudo se ausenta el polvo quieto,
y asciende una palmera, columna hacia la aurora.

                                       Torrijos, Septiembre de 1939

Sigo en la sombra, lleno de luz

Sigo en la sombra, lleno de luz; ¿existe el día?
¿Esto es mi tumba o es mi bóveda materna?
Pasa el latido contra mi piel como una fría
losa que germinará caliente, roja, tierna.
Es posible que no haya nacido todavía,
o que haya muerto siempre. La sombra me gobierna
Si esto es vivir, morir no sé yo qué sería,
ni sé lo que persigo con ansia tan eterna.
Encadenado a un traje, parece que persigo
desnudarme, librarme de aquello que no puede
ser yo y hace turbia y ausente la mirada.
Pero la tela negra, distante, va conmigo
sombra con sombra, contra la sombra hasta que ruede
a la desnuda vida creciente de la nada.

                                              Torrijos prison

Ascension of the Broom

The broom, costumed in myrtle, rose, and bay,
the hero among us who face the trash,
frees everything from dust that cannot fly,
since it was palm tree blue and dropped to earth.
Fiery and young, a constant cheerful sword,
slender with worry, pure, courageous, sun,
the lily sweeps the floors—our grave and ward—
moves higher, hotter, purer than a gun.
Never! The broom will not be crucified,
our youth is propagating a long bone,
a lonely flute of mountain notes, though mute,
a lonely tongue, sublime, perfect in tone.
Before its breath the quiet dust has died,
and a palm tree, a column climbs toward dawn.

                          Torrijos Prison, September 1939

I Live in Shadow, Filled with Light

I live in shadow, filled with light. Does day
exist? Is this a grave or mother's womb?
Against my skin a throbbing makes its way
like frozen stone sprouting red, tender, warm.
Maybe I'm waiting to be born or see
that I've been always dead. These shadows rule
me, and if living's this, what can death be?
Intensely groping and the eternal fool,
chained to my clothes, it looks like I go on
stripping and getting rid of everything,
leaving me gone, my eyes in far distress.
But the remote black clothing that I don
plods with me: shadows, shadows, shadows fling
me through bare life growing from nothingness.

                          Torrijos prison

References

Index

References

Introduction

Barnstone, Willis, ed. *Borges at Eighty: Conversations.* Bloomington: Indiana UP, 1982. Photographs by Barnstone.

——, ed. *Spanish Poetry from Its Beginnings Through the Nineteenth Century.* New York: Oxford UP, 1970.

García Lorca, Federico. *Diván del Tamarit. Obras completas.* Edited by Arturo del Hoyo. 22nd ed. Vol. 2. Madrid: Aguilar, 1972. 3 vols. Introduction by Jorge Guillén. Afterword by Vicente Aleixandre. 555–75.

——. "La imagen poética de Góngora." *Obras completas.* 15th ed. 1969. 62–85.

John of the Cross. *The Poems of St. John of the Cross.* Translated by Willis Barnstone. Bloomington: Indiana UP, 1968; rpt. New York: New Directions, 1972. Introduction by Barnstone.

Kelley, Emilia Navarro de. *La poesía metafísica de Quevedo.* Madrid: Guadarrama, 1973.

León, Luis de. *The Unknown Light: The Poems of Fray Luis de León.* Translated by Willis Barnstone. Albany: State U of New York P, 1979. Introduction by Barnstone.

Sappho. *Sappho and the Greek Lyric Poets.* Translated by Willis Barnstone. New York: Schocken, 1988. Introduction and annotations by Barnstone.

Francisco de Quevedo

Astrana Marín, Luis. *La vida turbulenta de Quevedo.* Madrid: Editorial "Gran Capitán," 1945.

Barnstone, Willis, ed. *Spanish Poetry from Its Beginnings Through the Nineteenth Century.* New York: Oxford UP, 1970.

Bartolomé Pons, Esther. *El autor y su obra.* Barcelona: Barcanova, 1984.

Borges, Jorge Luis. "Quevedo." *Otras inquisiciones.* Buenos Aires: Emecé, 1960. 36–42.

Crosby, James O. *En torno a la poesía de Quevedo.* Madrid: Castalia, 1967.

References

Durán, Manuel. *Francisco de Quevedo*. Madrid: EDAF, 1978.

Green, Otis H. *Courtly Love in Quevedo*. Boulder: U of Colorado P, 1952.

Kelley, Emilia Navarro de. *La poesía metafísica de Quevedo*. Madrid: Guadarrama, 1973.

Nelson, Lowry. *Baroque Lyric Poetry*. New Haven: Yale UP, 1961.

Quevedo, Francisco de. *Obras en verso*. Edited by Felicidad Buendía. Madrid: Aguilar, 1967. Vol. 2 of *Obras completas*. Introduction and notes by Buendía.

———. *Poesia varia*. Edited by James O. Crosby. Madrid: Ediciones Cátedra, 1981.

Theobaldus. *Physiologus Theobaldi Episcopi De Naturis Duodecim Animalium*. Translated by Willis Barnstone. Bloomington: Indiana UP, 1964. Lithographs by Rudy Pozzatti.

Walters, D. Gareth. *Francisco de Quevedo, Love Poet*. Washington, DC: Catholic U of America P; Cardiff: U of Wales P, 1985.

Sor Juana Inés de la Cruz

Allen, Woody. *God. Without Feathers*. New York: Random, 1975, 137.

Barnstone, Willis, ed. *The Other Bible: Jewish Pseudepigrapha, Christian Apocrypha, Gnostic Scriptures*. San Francisco: Harper & Row, 1984. Introduction by Barnstone.

Bradstreet, Anne. *The Complete Works of Anne Bradstreet*. New York: Twayne, 1981.

———. "The Prologue." *Norton Anthology of American Literature*. Edited by Ronald Gottesman et al. Vol. 1. New York: Norton, 1979, 42.

Juana Inés de la Cruz. *Fama, y obras posthumas del fenix de México, dezima musa, poetisa de America*. 1714. Facsimile ed. Mexico City: Frente de afirmación hispanista, 1989. Introduction by Fredo Arias de la Canal.

———. *Obras completas*. Edited by Alfonso Méndez Plancarte and Alberto G. Salceda. 4 vols. Mexico City: Fondo de Cultura Económica, 1951–57.

———. *Poesía: Teatro y prosa*. Edited by Antonio Castro Leal. Mexico City: Editorial Porrua, 1965. Introduction by Leal.

———. *Poesías completas*. Mexico City: Ediciones Botas, 1940. Introduction by Ermilio Abreu Gómez.

———. *Response to Sor Filotea*. Sor Juana Inés de la Cruz: Obras selectas. Barcelona: Editorial Noguer, 1976. Introduction, selection, and notes by Georgina Sabàt de Rivers and Elias L. Rivers.

———. *A Sor Juana Anthology*. Translated by Alan S. Trueblood. Cambridge: Harvard UP, 1988. Foreword by Octavio Paz.

———. *Sor Juana Inés de la Cruz, 1651–1691*. Translated by Margaret Sayers Peden. Binghamton, NY: Bilingual, 1985.

———. *A Woman of Genius: The Intellectual Autobiography of*

References

Sor Juana Inés de la Cruz. Translated by Margaret Sayers Peden. Salisbury, CT: Lime Rock, 1982. Introduction by Peden. Photographs by Gabriel Seymour North.

Paz, Octavio. *Sor Juana, or the Traps of Faith.* Translated by Margaret Sayers Peden. Cambridge: Harvard UP, 1988.

Sappho. *Sappho and the Greek Lyric Poets.* Translated by Willis Barnstone. New York: Schocken, 1988. Introduction and annotations by Barnstone.

Trueblood, Alan S. Introduction. *A Sor Juana Anthology.* By Sor Juana Inés de la Cruz. Cambridge: Harvard UP, 1988. Foreword by Octavio Paz. 2–5.

Antonio Machado

Azorín. *Clásicos y modernos.* Madrid: Archivos, 1919.

Barea, Arturo. *Lorca: The Poet and His People.* Translated by Ilsa Barea. New York: Grove, 1951.

Barnstone, Willis. "Antonio Machado and Rubén Darío: A Failure of Literary Assassination, or the Persistence of Modernism in the Poetry of Antonio Machado." *Hispanic Review* 57.3 (1989): 281–306.

Espina, Concha. *De Antonio Machado a su grande y secreto amor.* Madrid: Lifesa, 1950.

John of the Cross. *The Poems of St. John of the Cross.* Translated by Willis Barnstone. Bloomington: Indiana UP, 1968; rpt. New York: New Directions, 1972. Introduction by Barnstone.

Machado, Antonio. *Antonio Machado: Selected Poems.* Translated and edited by Alan S. Trueblood. Cambridge: Harvard UP, 1982.

———. *The Dream Below the Sun: Selected Poems of Antonio Machado.* Translated by Willis Barnstone. Trumansburg, NY: Crossing, 1981. Introduction by John Dos Passos. Reminiscence by Juan Ramón Jiménez. Drawings by William Bailey. Rev. ed. of *Eighty Poems of Antonio Machado.* New York: Las Américas, 1959.

———. *Nuevas canciones y de un cancionero apócrifo.* Edited by Jose María Valverde. Madrid: Clásicos Castalia. 1971.

———. *Obras: Poesía y prosa.* Edited by Aurora de Albornoz and Guillermo de Torre. Buenos Aires: Editorial Losada, 1964. Introduction by Torre. In the text, reference to poems from the *Obras* is abbreviated *OPP.*

Pradal-Rodríguez, Gabriel. *Antonio Machado.* New York: Hispanic Institute, 1951.

Salinas, Pedro. "Spanish Literature." *Columbia Dictionary of Modern European Literature.* Edited by Horatio Smith. New York: Columbia UP, 1947.

Federico García Lorca

Adams, Mildred. *García Lorca: Playwright and Poet.* New York: Braziller, 1977.

References

Alberti, Rafael. *La arboleda perdida. Libros I y II de memorias.* Buenos Aires: Fabril Editora, 1959. 264–66.

Alonso, Dámaso. "Federico García Lorca y la expresión de lo español." *Poetas españoles contemporáneos.* 3rd ed. Madrid: Gredos, 1978.

Bosquet, Alain. *Entretiens avec Salvador Dalí.* Paris: Belfond, 1966.

Cano, José Luis. *García Lorca: Biografía ilustrada.* Barcelona: Ediciones Destino, 1962.

Durán, Manuel Durán, ed. *Lorca: A Collection of Critical Essays.* Englewood Cliffs: Prentice, 1962.

García Lorca, Federico. *Obras completas.* Compiled by Arturo del Hoyo. 15th ed. Madrid: Aguilar, 1969. Introduction by Jorge Guillén. Afterword by Vicente Aleixandre. All references to Lorca's works are to this edition, except *El público* and *Sonetos del oscuro amor,* in which reference is to 22nd edition.

———. *Obras completas.* 22nd ed. 3 vols. Madrid: Aguilar, 1972.

Gibson, Ian. *The Assassination of Federico García Lorca.* Harmondsworth, Eng.: Penguin, 1983.

———. *Federico García Lorca: A Life.* New York: Pantheon, 1989.

Honig, Edwin. *García Lorca.* New York: Octagon, 1981.

John of the Cross. *The Poems of St. John of the Cross.* Translated by Willis Barnstone. Bloomington: Indiana UP, 1968; rpt. New York: New Directions, 1972. Introduction by Barnstone.

Machado, Antonio. *Obras: Poesía y prosa.* Edited by Aurora de Albornoz and Guillermo de Torre. Buenos Aires: Editorial Losada, 1964. Introduction by Torre.

Morla Lynch, Carlos. *En España con Federico García Lorca: Páginas de un diario íntimo, 1928–1936.* Madrid: Aguilar, 1958.

Neruda, Pablo. *Antología poética.* Madrid: Espasa-Calpe, 1985. Selections and introduction by Rafael Alberti.

———. *Memoirs.* Translated by Hardie St. Martin. New York: Farrar, 1977.

Quevedo, Antonio. *El poeta en la Habana: Federico García Lorca, 1898–1936.* Havana: Consejo Nacional de Cultura, Ministerio de Educación, 1961.

Río, Angel del. *Federico García Lorca (1898–1936). Vida y obra.* New York: Hispanic Institute in the United States, 1941.

———. "El poeta Federico García Lorca." *Revista Hispánica Moderna* [New York and Buenos Aires] 1 (1935): 174–84.

Salinas, Pedro. *Poesías completas.* Edited by Soledad Salinas de Marichal and Jaime Salinas. Barcelona: Barral Editores, 1971. Introduction by Jorge Guillén.

Jorge Luis Borges

Barnstone, Willis, ed. *Borges at Eighty: Conversations.* Bloomington: Indiana UP, 1982. Photographs by Barnstone.

Borges, Jorge Luis, with María Kodama. *Atlas.* Translated by Anthony Kerrigan. New York: Dutton, 1987.

References

———. *Autobiographical Essay* (Afterword). *The Aleph and Other Stories, 1933–1969*. Translated by Norman Thomas di Giovanni, with the author. New York: Dutton, 1968.

———. *Borges: A Reader, A Selection from the Writings of Jorge Luis Borges*. Edited by Emir Rodríguez Monegal and Alastair Reid. New York: Dutton, 1981.

———. *La cifra*. Madrid: Alianza, 1984.

———. *Los conjurados*. Madrid: Alianza, 1985.

———. *Obra poética 1923–1977*. Buenos Aires: Emecé, 1977.

Cara-Walker, Ana. "A Death in Geneva: Jorge Luis Borges, 1899–1986." *World Literature Today* (Winter 1988): 5–11.

Monegal, Emir Rodríguez. *Jorge Luis Borges: A Literary Biography*. New York: Dutton, 1978.

Miguel Hernández

Baland, Timothy, and Hardie St. Martin, eds. *Selected Poems: Miguel Hernández and Blas de Otero*. Boston: Beacon, 1972.

Cano Ballesta, Juan. *La poesía de Miguel Hernández*. Madrid: Editorial Gredos, 1962.

García Lorca, Federico. *Obras completas*. Compiled by Arturo del Hoyo. 15th ed. Madrid: Aguilar, 1969. Introduction by Jorge Guillén. Afterword by Vicente Aleixandre.

Guerrero Zamora, Juan. *Miguel Hernández, poeta*. Madrid: Colección "El Grifón," 1955.

Hernández, Miguel. *Antología*. Buenos Aires: Editorial Losada, 1960. Selections and introduction by María de Gracia Ifach.

———. *Obra escogida: Poesía-Teatro*. Madrid: Aguilar, 1952. Introduction by Antonio del Hoyo.

———. *Obras completas*. Edited by Elvio Romero and Andrés Ramón Vázquez. Buenos Aires: Losada, 1960. Introduction by María de Gracia Ifach.

Neruda, Pablo. *Memoirs*. Translated by Hardie St. Martin. New York: Farrar, Straus and Giroux, 1977.

———. "Residencia en la tierra: Poesía 1925–1935, Pablo Neruda." *Follentones de El Sol*. 1935.

Zardoya, Concha. *Miguel Hernández 1910–1942): Vida y obra*. New York: Hispanic Institute in the United States, 1955.

301

Index

Index

Index

Index

Index

Index

Madrid, 107, 115, 116, 120–22, 152, 153, 155, 158, 163, 164, 165, 166, 170, 174, 193, 198, 215, 259, 261, 262, 264, 265, 267, 270, 272, 275, 276
Mairena, Juan de, 118
Mallarmé, Stephane, 157
Mallea, Eduardo, 200
Malraux, André, 271
Mancha, Don Quijote de la. *See* Quijano, Alonso
Mandelstam, Osip, 271
Manresa, Josefina, xvii, 263–66, 268–72, 277
Manrique, Jorge, 103, 166
Marañón, Gregorio, 267
Marichal, Juan, xvii
Marinetti, Filippo Tommaso, 147
Martial, 28
Martín, Abel, 118–19
Martínez Nadal, Rafael, 170
Marvell, Andrew, 13–14
Mata, Juan de, 68
Mayakovsky, Vladimir, 161
Medinaceli, Duke of, 25
Melville, Herman, xvii, 191, 194, 199
Menard, Pierre, 194, 201
Méndez, Concha, 267
Mendoza, Esperanza de, 25
Middlebury College, xvi
Miguel Cané Library, 194, 200, 202
Milonga, 196
Milton, John, 77, 199, 206
Miranda, Juan de, 72
Miranda, Núñez de, 71, 83
Miró, Joan, 103
Modernisme, 102, 106, 109, 119, 147
Molina, Tirso de, 59, 68
Moreno Villa, José, 152
Moriscos, 2
Morla Lynch, Carlos, 156, 275

Moschos, 261
Mount Holyoke College, 262
Mozart, Wolfgang Amadeus, 154
Mussolini, Benito, 164

Navagero, Andrea, 3
Navarro de Kelley, Emilia, 12
Navarro Tomás, Tomás, xvi, 117, 122, 123
Nazis, 192
Nebrija, Antonio de, 2
Neoplatonism, 3, 10, 65, 82
Neruda, Pablo, xviii, 85, 148, 153, 155, 165, 166, 170, 174, 260, 262, 265–68, 270, 275–76
New York, 159–61, 162, 163, 166

Ocampo, Silvina, 199, 211
Ocampo, Victoria, 165, 199, 211, 268
Old English, 194, 206, 212, 217
Olivares, Count-Duke of, 23–26
Olivares, Countess of, 20
Onís, Federico de, 159
Orihuela, 260–68, 270, 275, 277
Ortega y Gasset, José, 103, 111, 147, 268
Otero, Blas de, 260

Pacheco de Narváez Luis, 22
Page, Denys, 67
Palatine Anthology, 14
Palermo, 194–95, 205
Parker, A. A., 13
Parra, Nicanor, 260
Paul, Saint, 26, 64
Paul V, 23
Paz, Octavio, 61–62, 64–65, 72, 75, 80, 81, 82, 85, 153, 154, 260, 271

Index

Index

Index

Whitman, Walt, xv, 7, 126, 159, 162, 191, 192, 197–99, 208
Wilbur, Richard, xviii
Wilde, Oscar, 108
Wojohn, David, xviii
Woolf, Virginia, 68
Wordsworth, William, xviii

Xirau, Joaquín, 122
Xirgu, Margarita, 163

Yeats, William Butler, xviii
Young, David, 216

Zamora, Guerrero, 268
Zardoya, Concha, 266–67, 269, 272–73
Zemborain de Torres, Ester, 211
Zorrilla y Moral, José, 158
Zurbarán, Francisco de, 7, 59

Willis Barnstone is professor of comparative literature and Spanish at Indiana University. Author of *The Poetics of Translation* and *The Other Bible*, he has translated books of six poets from the Spanish: Saint John of the Cross, Fray Luis de León, Antonio Machado, Pedro Salinas, Vicente Aleixandre, and Jorge Luis Borges. For his new book of poems, *Funny Ways of Staying Alive*, he did 113 dry-brush ink drawings.